THE PSYCHOLOGY OF MEDITATION

The
Psychology
of
Meditation

EDITED BY

Michael A. West

Research Fellow,
MRC/ESRC Social and Applied Psychology Unit
University of Sheffield

CLARENDON PRESS · OXFORD
1987

Oxford University Press, Walton Street, Oxford OX2 6DP

Oxford New York Toronto
Delhi Bombay Calcutta Madras Karachi
Petaling Jaya Singapore Hong Kong Tokyo
Nairobi Dar es Salaam Cape Town
Melbourne Auckland

and associated companies in
Beirut Berlin Ibadan Nicosia

Oxford is a trade mark of Oxford University Press

Published in the United States
by Oxford University Press, New York

British Library Cataloguing in Publication Data
The Psychology of meditation.
1. Meditation — Psychology
I. West, Michael A.
158'.12   BL627
ISBN 0-19-852169-3

Library of Congress Cataloging in Publication Data
The Psychology of meditation.
Bibliography: p.
Includes indexes.
1. Meditation.   I. West, Michael A. [DNLM:
1. Psychotherapy.   2. Relaxation Technics.   3. Thinking.
BF 637.M4 P974]
BF637.M4P78   1987   158'.12   87-11160
ISBN 0-19-852169-3

Typeset by
Dobbie Typesetting Service, Plymouth, Devon
Printed in Great Britain
at the University Printing House, Oxford
by David Stanford.
Printer to the University

For Kay and Thomas —
Principal dancers in my meditation

'*In a world of fugitives, the person*
taking the opposite direction will
appear to run away'

T. S. Eliot (1939)

PREFACE

In the last 20 years meditation has attracted considerable professional and popular interest and, with the growth of holistic medicine and wider concerns with fitness, health, and emotional well-being, it continues to be attractive to many as a means of natural and healthy development. In 1976, on the basis of a Gallup Poll, it was estimated that 6 million people in the United States were practising meditation and 5 million were practising yoga (in Graham 1986). The promise of a natural form of therapy and relaxation which enhances mental health and self-actualization has proved alluring. So much so that many psychologists are now using meditation in clinical settings throughout Europe and North America. But meditation has also attracted many because of its potential spiritual or 'existential' benefits—its promise to guide the person towards a unity with his or her existence or towards a clearer and more direct experience of reality.

After 15 years of sustained psychological research on meditation, a careful evaluation of the evidence of the effects and effectiveness of meditation techniques is needed. The contents of this book provide just such an evaluation—the contributors being drawn from among those most knowledgeable about meditation research. The book also describes the context of this research by presenting relevant theoretical bases in Eastern and Western psychology. Finally new research and theoretical directions are needed if our knowledge about the psychology of meditation is to be clearly articulated and developed, and the contributors signpost directions they think are most appropriate.

Part I presents an outline of what meditation is and how it has been viewed from the very different perspectives of the spiritual traditions of the East and the positivist orientations of Western psychology. The place and aims of meditation in Buddhist psychology are described along with contemporary Western theoretical approaches to understanding human behaviour. The purposes of this first section are to describe meditation very fully in mechanical terms, to provide the reader with a clear understanding of both how and why it has traditionally been practised, and to describe the perspectives that Western psychologists have adopted in viewing meditation.

Part II reviews research on the phenomenology of meditation, the physiological effects of meditation, and research on personality change associated with meditation practice. Phenomenological research is carefully appraised and new research methods are proposed. The review of research evidence on the physiological effects of meditation is divided into two areas. First is a review of effects on somatic arousal which describes the controversy over the extent of declines in arousal during meditation. Second is a review of research on the EEG and meditation which discusses the limits of inferences which can be drawn from such research. In the final chapter of this section, personality changes associated with meditation practice are described and the problems of determining causality are outlined.

Part III offers a new approach to understanding meditation as psychotherapy based on a skills analysis, along with a detailed description of how meditation can be used in clinical settings. The wider research field of evaluating psychotherapeutic outcomes is described and research on meditation is discussed in this context.

Part IV concludes with an overview of the research evidence presented in the book along with comments about the adequacy of the research questions posed. Suggestions are made about the theoretical bases from which meditation could be further explored, and radical new orientations towards the subject are proposed.

The book has a number of aims. The first aim is to present a balanced and comprehensive review of research in this area. Opinions within psychology about the value of meditation range from unbridled enthusiasm to cold cynicism, and students of psychology are apt to be mystified rather than informed by such a wide divergence of views. The second aim stems from the fact that, like all researchers, those exploring the psychology of meditation (whether through their own practice or through empirical research) need theoretical guidance for their endeavours. Both Eastern and Western psychology are rich in sources of such guidance and a variety of such sources are identified. The contributors to the book also propose new and improved methods of conducting research, while aiming to offer alternative orientations to meditation to spur researchers to break set from their habitual ways of investigating. But most importantly, it is hoped that the reader will achieve an enriched understanding of meditation and, at the same time, find valuable new perspectives for understanding human behaviour (both their own and others') more generally.

Sheffield   M. A. W.
1986

ACKNOWLEDGEMENTS

Thanks are due to all of the contributors to this book including those who are not named on the contents page. My colleagues at the MRC/ESRC Social and Applied Psychology Unit, University of Sheffield, gave time to read and comment most helpfully on drafts of all the chapters in the book. Much inspiration has come from a group of psychologists who share an interest in Buddhism and meditation—John Crook, Guy Claxton, Martin Skinner, Colette Ray, Sue Blackmore, Myra Thomas, and David Fontana. They have, by being sources of stimulation and warmth, provided the opportunity for uninhibited exploration of ideas. Kathryn Beadsley has given time, care, patience, and her special ability to create attractive order out of disorder. Kay West has enabled me to continue my work on meditation by being there, being loving, and encouraging me to meet challenges. I acknowledge with humility her contribution to this book. To all of those who have contributed to the book—*namas te*.

CONTENTS

CONTRIBUTORS

MICHAEL A. WEST has been involved in conducting research on meditation for 14 years and received his Ph.D. from the University of Wales for work on physiological and psychological correlates of meditation in 1977. He is currently Research Fellow at the MRC/ESRC Social and Applied Psychology Unit, University of Sheffield, UK. He is the author of numerous research articles and book chapters on meditation as well as of books and articles in other areas of psychology. He has spoken widely on the subject of meditation on radio and television in Europe and North America and has taught meditation in occupational, counselling, and clinical settings. His other research interests are stress and innovation among health care professionals.

GUY CLAXTON is currently Senior Lecturer in Psychology of Education at the Centre for Educational Studies, King's College London. He is the author of *Wholly human: Western and Eastern visions of the self and its perfection* (RKP 1981) and editor of *Beyond therapy: The impact of Eastern religions on psychological theory and practice* (Wisdom 1986). His publications concern personal learning and personality change as they occur in everyday, educational, therapeutic, and spiritual settings.

MICHAEL M. DELMONTE gained a BSc in Natural Sciences in Trinity College, Dublin—'majoring' first in genetics and later again in psychology. His M.Sc. and Ph.D. in psychology involved both research into, and clinical work with, meditation and relaxation procedures and related physiology. He has almost 40 publications in this area to date. Currently he works as a Senior Clinical Psychologist in the Health Care and Psychosomatic Unit in St James's Hospital, Dublin.

RONALD J. PEKALA, Ph.D. is Staff Psychologist and Biofeedback Clinic Co-Director at the Coatesville VA Medical Center in Coatesville, Pa. He is also in private practice specializing in biofeedback, hypnosis, and psychotherapy for stress disorders and is an Assistant Professor at Jefferson Medical College and an Adjunct Professor at Immaculata College. Dr Pekala's research interests include hypnosis, meditation, and biofeedback, psychotherapy and stress management, and psycho-phenomenological approaches to consciousness. He has recently developed a questionnaire for phenomenologically mapping consciousness and is using the questionnaire to research how altered state induction procedures affect the structures and patterns of subjective experience.

DAVID S. HOLMES received his Ph.D. degree from Northwestern University in 1965. He has been on the faculty at Northwestern University, the University of Texas, and the University of Kansas. Professor

Holmes devotes most of his research efforts to studying stress and stress reduction in humans. He has published over 100 articles in leading psychological and medical journals, and has won a variety of awards for his research and teaching. At the present time, Professor Holmes is studying the influence of physical fitness on the physiological response to acute and chronic stress.

DR PETER FENWICK is Consultant Neuropsychiatrist to the Maudsley Hospital and Consultant Neurophysiologist at St Thomas's Hospital, Senior Lecturer at The Institute of Psychiatry, and Honorary Research Consultant in Neurophysiology to Broadmoor Hospital. He took his Natural Science degree at Cambridge and did his medical training at St Thomas's Hospital. As a psychiatrist and neurophysiologist he is interested in the functioning of the brain and unusual mental states and has published widely on these subjects.

JONATHAN C. SMITH received his BA from Oberlin College and his Ph.D. in psychology from Michigan State University. He is currently Associate Professor of Psychology at Chicago's Roosevelt University and Director of the Roosevelt University Stress Institute. Dr Smith is a psychotherapist specializing in stress management. In addition he has conducted hundreds of workshops for universities, hospitals, government agencies, and businesses. His books *Meditation: A sensible guide to a timeless discipline* (Research Press 1986) and *Relaxation dynamics: Nine world approaches to relaxation* (Research Press 1985) present a unique approach to meditation and are internationally acclaimed.

PATRICIA CARRINGTON, Ph.D. is a clinical psychologist. Eleven years a member of the Psychology Faculty at Princeton University, she is presently Adjunct Associate Professor of Psychiatry at CMDNJ/Robert Ward Medical School, Rutgers University. The author of numerous articles in the sleep/dream field, her books *Freedom in meditation* (Doubleday 1977) on the clinical use of meditation techniques, and *Releasing* (William Morrow 1984), which presents a unique method of stress management, are internationally acclaimed. Dr Carrington serves as Administrative Consultant to the Health Maintenance Program at the New York Telephone Company, where she has assisted this company's medical department in training over 5000 employees to meditate.

DAVID A. SHAPIRO studied psychology and philosophy at Oxford University before clinical psychology training at the Institute of Psychiatry in London. Having published widely in clinical and social psychology, he now leads a clinical research team at the MRC/ESRC Social and Applied Psychology Unit, University of Sheffield. His central concern is with the mechanisms linking process and outcome in different psychological treatments. He was until recently editor of the *British Journal of Clinical Psychology* and is active in the Society for Psychotherapy Research. His personal and professional use of stress management techniques is lastingly influenced by having learned TM.

Part I:

Western and
Eastern perspectives

Introduction

The psychology of meditation has a history stretching back at least 2500 years, but it is not a psychology of the West, the history of which is barely a century old. Rather it is in Eastern psychology that meditation has played a central part, variously conceptualized as therapy, research tool and perceptual training device. Recognition of the sophistication of Eastern approaches to mind and self has been slow to dawn upon Western psychology and it would be remiss to present an account of the psychology of meditation which did not reflect in part that sophistication. At the same time, Western psychology has developed quickly in its short history and it too offers a variety of valuable perspectives which can aid our understanding of meditation.

The first part of the book introduces meditation and locates it within both its traditional spiritual/philosophical contexts and its theoretical psychological context. Chapter 1 describes meditation as an historical and cross-cultural phenomenon, demonstrating its ubiquity in secular and religious domains. Instructions for a simple and relatively permissive type of meditation are presented so that the reader with no previous experience of meditation can, to a limited extent, explore meditation in a practical way. The chapter goes on to discuss why people meditate, examining this question from a wide variety of viewpoints, before concluding that stress management is a peculiarly Western orientation and that meditation is more widely used for spiritual purposes. Psychological approaches to understanding meditation are presented via a history of psychological research in this area. The discussion explores the causes and consequences of the particular research orientations which have developed, arguing that there has been slow progress in understanding. The need to distinguish between different types of meditation is highlighted in a discussion of the different typologies of meditation developed by Western psychologists. Finally some of the problems of conducting meditation research are described.

In Chapter 2, Guy Claxton presents an account of Buddhist doctrines that is unusual in its accessibility to psychologists. He acts as a translator of Eastern concepts by using psychological terminology and theory. For example, he uses constructivist approaches to explain Buddhist theories of perception, and the doctrine of 'dependent origination' and the 'Four Noble Truths' are described in ways which make them understandable (if not acceptable) to Western psychologists. The role of meditation in Buddhist psychology is then explained in relation to the foregoing discussion; the value of meditation in psychotherapy is explored and suggestions for future research are offered. The outcome is a clear exposition of the challenge that Buddhism offers to notions central to Western psychology. Thus he explains that Buddhists view the self as an illusion and meditation as a practical way of revealing the illusion.

In Chapter 3, Michael Delmonte presents the views of the other hemisphere by describing and discussing the various theoretical approaches which have been taken by Western psychologists studying meditation. Attention is a central component in descriptions of the mechanics of meditation and Michael Delmonte places emphasis upon the potential value of studying meditation from an information-processing orientation. Interest in bilateral brain explanations of experience and abilities is reflected in the discussion of consciousness and meditation. The psychoanalytic orientations described by Delmonte suggest that meditation induces regression in the service of the ego to preverbal levels of experience and facilitates primary process mentation. Behavioural orientations, in contrast, see meditation as a form of systematic desensitization, involving reciprocal inhibition and counter-conditioning. Finally Delmonte, like Claxton, argues for the utility of constructivist approaches in describing the processes involved in meditation, though he cautions that constructivist and Buddhist approaches to meditation are ultimately mutually exclusive.

1 Traditional and psychological perspectives on meditation

Michael A. West

The Zen Buddhist monk sits in meditation in the clear silence of the meditation hall in order to gain insight and dispel the clouds of ignorance which prevent pure perception. The prison officer sits in meditation in her bedroom at the end of the day to feel a stillness, a calmness, and a release from the stress of her work. What is meditation? Struggles to define meditation always seem to end unsuccessfully, possibly because the problem lies within the fact that meditation means different things to the Zen Buddhist monk and the prison officer. And yet both may be practising precisely the same meditation, perhaps focusing on the sensation of breathing while sitting with eyes closed in a quiet place, watching the intrusion of thoughts and trains of sensations.

In order to answer the question 'What is meditation?', I shall describe a number of common meditation practices before giving some flavour of their historical and cultural ubiquity. Then I shall describe psychological approaches and the difficulties inherent in them. In this way the reader will be prepared with some understanding of meditation before moving on to examine the charts produced by psychological explorations, which are presented in subsequent chapters.

Traditionally meditation has been practised to achieve a direct experiential knowledge of an absolute such as God, Being, Oneness, Buddha nature—each of these labels being a product of a religious or personal belief system and representing the essence of existence. In the last 20 years large numbers of people in Europe and North America have learned and practised meditation, many of them with a quite different purpose in mind: to relieve distress or improve psychological well-being (West 1980a). By what methods do people seek these differing outcomes? One of the more common forms of meditation involves repeating a sound (sometimes called a 'mantra') either silently or aloud, and the meditator is taught to focus attention on the sound excluding other thoughts, external stimuli, and desires from consciousness. The sound or mantra may be chosen by the meditation teacher as being particularly suitable or powerful for the individual, it may be the name or attribute of a god, or it may be the name of a revered teacher (examples are 'rama', 'so-hum', 'om', 'she-am'). The degree of focus or concentration on the mantra varies according to teachers, schools, and systems. In some the meditator is urged to grit the teeth and push away thoughts and sensations which intrude during meditation. But most practitioners are taught to develop a more passive awareness, neither driving thoughts and sensations away nor holding on to them, but persistently and easily returning attention to the central focus (Hewitt 1978). For example, in Transcendental Meditation (TM), the initiate is instructed not to hold on to thoughts and not to push them away; the instruction is to watch them come and go and then when the practitioner becomes aware of having drifted away from the repetition of the mantra, very easily to go back to it.

Objects of meditation can also be visual such as a candle flame, a picture of a teacher or 'guru', or special visual symbols such as the Christian cross and the Judaic star. Even movement can be used as a focus of meditation; the repetitive touching of the tips of the four fingers with the thumb or the simple act of walking are both movements used as a focus for attention.

Less well known are 'mindfulness' techniques in which the meditator may attempt to let the attention dwell on 'all that is here and now' in her environment and consciousness.

Historical and transcultural perspectives

Meditation in various forms has been practised for at least 2500 years and probably for very much longer, yet we have no real understanding of why these practices have been sustained for so long and across so many different cultures. Curious too is how elaborate methods can quite strikingly resemble techniques in other cultures. American Indians practise a form of meditation remarkably similar to the *zazen* of Japan. In Africa, the people of the Kung Zhu/twasi practise a form of ritual dancing which they believe activates an energy (n/um) located at the base of the spine and which produces an ecstasy experience (Katz 1973). According to Hindu philosophy and yoga teachings there are subtle psychic sense organs and a particular force called the Kundalini. In Kundalini yoga, the meditator focuses attention on the energy source which is located at the base of the spine and, through concentration, arouses this energy. The energy is then believed to travel up the spine through six centres or *chakras*, evoking at each stage a higher state of consciousness. Eventually it reaches the seventh *chakra* (the crown *chakra*) and the meditator achieves a state of perfect enlightenment.

Many African peoples practise ritual dancing coupled with chanting to produce an altered state of consciousness. Shamanism is a form of mysticism in which a chant is intoned by a holy person (the Shaman) to achieve trances (Benson 1975); it is widely practised in North and South America, Indonesia, Siberia, and Japan. Freuchen in *The book of the eskimoes* (1959) describes how Eskimoes would sit facing a large soft stone and, using a small hard handstone, continuously carve a circle in the large stone for periods stretching to days, to produce a spiritual trance state (for further details of diverse meditation practices see Ornstein 1972; Benson *et al.* 1974a; White 1974; Goleman 1977; Hewitt 1978).

But meditation techniques are not confined to the religions of the East or to those of simpler societies; meditation has long been used throughout Christendom. St Augustine (AD 350–430) wrote of a method of contemplating which he used to:

pass even beyond this power of mine which is called memory; yea I will pass beyond it, that I might approach unto thee, O sweet light. (Butler 1922)

One of the best-known examples of Christian meditation comes from an anonymously written fourteenth-century work called *The cloud of unknowing* (Progoff 1969). The author writes that the way to attain union with God is to beat down thoughts through the repetition of a single-syllable word such as 'God' or 'love',

clasp this word tightly in your heart so that it never leaves it no matter what may happen. This word shall be your shield and your spear whether you ride in peace or in war. With this word you shall beat upon the cloud and the darkness, which are above you. With this word you shall strike down thoughts of every kind and drive them beneath the cloud of forgetting. After that, if any thoughts should press upon you . . . answer him with this word only and with no other words.'

Fray Francisco de Osuna, a tenth-century monk, writing in *The third spiritual alphabet*, describes an exercise very similar to Buddhist techniques,

keep (your eyes) fixed steadily on the ground, like men who are forgetful and, as it were, out of themselves, who stand immovable, wrapt in thought . . . it is better . . . to keep our gaze fixed on the ground, on some places where there is little to look at so there may be less to stir our fancy and our imagination. Thus, even in a crowd you may be deeply recollected by keeping your gaze bent, fixed on one place. The smaller and darker the place, the more limited your view will be and the less will your heart be distracted. (Osuna 1931)

The Desert Fathers, who were among the earliest Christians, used to silently repeat the '*kyrie eleison*' to help them achieve a state called '*quies*' — a state of rest where 'nowhereness and nomindness' purified the soul. They sustained this silent repetition throughout their daily lives 'until it became as spontaneous and instinctive as their breathing' (Merton 1960). In the fifth century AD, Hesychius gave instruction in the 'Prayer of the Heart', the practice of which was intended to provide a 'sure knowledge of God, the Incomprehensible' (French 1968). The instructions are indistinguishable in their mechanics from many practices we call meditation:

Sit down alone and in silence. Lower your head, shut your eyes, breathe out gently, and imagine yourself looking into your own heart. Carry your mind i.e. your thoughts, from your head to your heart. As you breathe out say 'Lord, Jesus

Christ, have mercy on me'. Say it moving your lips gently or say it in your mind. Try to put all other thoughts aside. Be calm, be patient and repeat the process very frequently. (French 1968)

In the Judaic religion, it is common to repeat a simple prayer accompanied by swaying movements in order to bring exaltation. There are practices involving mental focusing on body posture and techniques of concentration on magic seals. In the *Chandogya upanishad* of Hinduism, devotees are urged to 'reverence meditation'. In the *Sutra-kritanga sutra* Jains are taught that 'he whose soul is purified by meditating is compared to a ship in water. Like a ship reaching the shore, he gets beyond misery'. Meditation practices are widely used in Sikhism, Taoism, Zen Buddhism, and Islam.

Meditation by any other name

Is meditation, confined to its context, just another religious ritual and have we made the mistake of reifying an everyday experience which most of us do not bother to comment on or analyse excitedly? In a fascinating discussion of mysticism in English Literature, Spurgeon (1970) has focused on the writings of Brontë, Wordsworth, and Tennyson to illustrate her theme. Her evidence suggests that meditation experiences are not confined to religious contexts and have been seen as significant by many authors outside the religious and mystical traditions. Wordsworth believed a passive attitude, beyond the intellect and desires and above petty disputes, would enable one to reach a 'central peace subsisting for ever at the heart of endless agitation'. Such practice would lead to,

. . . that serene and blessed mood
In which . . . the breath of this corporeal frame
And even the motion of our human blood
Almost suspended, we are laid asleep
In body, and become a living soul;
While with an eye made quiet by the power
Of harmony, and the deep power of joy
We see into the life of things

Tennyson would repeat his name mentally over and over to encourage experience of the 'unity of all things, the reality of the unseen, and the persistence of life'. Lines from *The ancient sage* illustrate his experience:

More than once when I
Sat all alone, revolving in myself
The word that is the symbol of myself
the mortal limit of the Self was loosed
And passed into the nameless, as a cloud
Melts into heaven

No doubt we all experience something of such states, perhaps sitting on a hilltop with someone for whom we feel deep love, gazing down at the stillness of the hills and trees; or perhaps in moments of deep peace and relaxation. Indeed, meditation may, when practised regularly, be a way of achieving such feelings of equanimity, wholeness, and understanding.

Meditation has long been a part of Western culture but in the last 20 years it has come to be viewed as an Eastern technique transposed to the West. Hundreds of thousands of North Americans and Europeans have learned meditation, often seeing it as a safe and effective way of combating the stresses of their lives. The best-known of the modern meditation systems is TM, which has been adapted from ancient techniques for mass teaching. Secret mantras are assigned to initiates, usually on the basis of their ages. Zen meditation is also popular in the West, though Zen generally involves less concern with advanced states of consciousness than techniques such as TM, since the aim is to achieve an alert insightful attention (Crook 1980). Various metods are used in Zen Buddhism, including sitting meditation or *zazen*. This '. . . is simply a quiet awareness, without comment, of whatever happens to be here and now. This awareness is attended by the most vivid sensation of 'non-difference' between oneself and the external world, between the mind and its contents — the various sounds, sights, and other impressions of the surrounding environment' (Watts 1957). In the Rinzai Zen school, the meditator is asked to hold in his or her mind an illogical question ('*koan*') such as 'What is the sound of one hand clapping?'; or 'What did my face look like before I was born?'; or 'What am I?'. As a result of persistently gnawing away at the question, the individual is supposed to achieve a sudden and intuitive understanding — 'One seeks and seeks, but cannot find. One then gives up, and the answer comes by itself' (Watts 1957).

Questions, dances, candle flames, movements, sitting quietly, secret sounds, repetition — can all these be subsumed under the same heading of meditation techniques, or is there a danger of categorizing together quite dissimilar behaviours? This question is one that is addressed repeatedly in this book and one which psychologists must answer, if study is to be focused. Naranjo (1974) believes that all these practices have a common element,

Just as we do not see the stars in daylight, but only in the absence of the sun, we may never taste the subtle essence of meditation in the daylight of ordinary activity in all its complexity. That essence may be revealed when we have suspended everything else but US, our presence, our attitude, beyond any activity or the lack of it . . . Against the background of the simplicity required by the exercise, we may become aware of ourselves and all that we bring to the situation, and we may begin to grasp experientially the question of attitude (p. 19)

But perhaps this is not enough for most psychologists whose training demands empirical approaches to understanding behaviour. In a psychological analysis of meditation it is important first to define what we mean by the term and then to operationalize it. Thus, meditation may be defined as an exercise in which the individual turns attention or awareness to dwell upon a single object, concept, sound, image, or experience, with the intention of gaining greater spiritual or experiential and existential insight, or of achieving improved psychological well-being. How then might we operationalize it? Consider the following instructions, which were used in a 6-month study of the effects of the regular practice of a meditation-like exercise upon arousal (West 1979a). The reader may also wish to practise the exercise for about 10 minutes.

Instructions for meditation

(1) Sit quietly in an upright position in a room where you are not likely to be disturbed.
(2) Close your eyes and relax your body. Sit quietly like this for about half a minute.
(3) Begin to easily repeat the word 'one' silently to yourself.
(4) Don't try to concentrate on the sound too hard. Don't try to think the sound clearly at all times to the exclusion of everything else. The word need only be a faint idea at times—you don't have to keep repeating it clearly.
(5) Think the word easily. It may change by getting louder or softer, longer or shorter, or it may not change at all. In every case just take it as it comes.
(6) The word has no meaning or special significance. It is a simple device which helps in meditation.
(7) Continue the meditation in this way for a quarter of an hour. Don't worry about achieving a deep level of meditation or about whether you are concentrating enough on the sound.
(8) Don't try to control thoughts. If thoughts come during meditation, don't worry about it. They are part of the practice. When you become aware that you have slipped into a train of thought, just go very easily back to the sound. Don't make great efforts to exclude thoughts—just favour the sound. Remember to take it easily, quietly, and simply.
(9) There may be noises outside which are distracting—just do the same as you would with thoughts. When you become aware of the outside noises, go easily back to the word; don't fight to exclude those outside noises. Accept them but favour the sound.
(10) Above all you are meant to enjoy this meditation, so don't try too hard, just take it easily as it comes.

This gentle, passive approach to meditation (characteristic also of TM) is in some contrast to practices like *zazen*, which initially are quite demanding. Difficult too are 'opening-up' meditations, which practitioners are sometimes urged to sustain throughout their daily lives.

This involves being aware and mindful of whatever you do physically, verbally, and mentally during the course of the day,

Whether you walk, stand, sit, lie down, or sleep, whether you stretch or bend your limbs, whether you look around, whether you put on your clothes, whether you talk or keep silent, whether you eat or drink — even whether you answer the call of nature — in these and other activities you should be fully aware and mindful of the act performed at the moment. That is to say, that you should live in the present moment, in the present action. (Rahula 1959)

Why meditate?

Do people share fundamentally similar objectives in their persistence with meditation practice or do those from different traditions have unique aims? During the period of preparation of this book I have spent a number of weekends with a small group of British psychologists at Winterhead Hill Farm near Bristol, England. We meet to discuss common interests in Buddhism, meditation and altered states of consciousness and one of our discussions revolved around why each of us practised meditation. The reasons given were in many ways dissimilar and often rather vague, but there seemed to be one underlying theme — that each of us felt that through meditation we somehow had a clearer experience of our existence and that increasing clarity helped in some way in our daily lives. But perhaps we were simply seeking consensus. Consider then these explanations for meditation practice offered by long term meditators from a variety of different traditions whom I interviewed while preparing this book.

It's my central belief, the heart of me. I feel I should honour that part of me . . . all of it leads up to the purest expression of me.

I enjoy meditation because physically it feels good and it's interesting in terms of the insight that I get into myself and the more I can watch all this stuff going on and accept it, the more I can reveal myself to others.

It's the heart of life . . . It makes life whole . . . you can make it take in the whole day or everybody you know or everything you have to do. It has the sense of pulling everything together, so it's a real centre.

I meditate because it calms me down and I see it as the only real hope to get rid of suffering by gaining complete control over the mind so that eventually your thoughts, feelings and actions are totally positive.

It's a way of being in touch with the Universe.

Meditation provides me with space. It's a time of caring for myself, free from demands and needs and a time of being peacefully alone and still to allow my pure and perfect self to open more and more.

To what extent is there a consensus of objectives amongst the many traditions which encourage the practice of meditation? Goleman (1977) in a careful survey has argued that there is a common objective hidden by the differing folds of customs, language, and symbols. In the Hindu Bhakti tradition it is believed that love for the deity, which is expressed in regular meditation on the name of the god, changes to a transcendental love,

'the devotee loses all sense of decorum and moves about the world unattached . . . His heart melts through love as he habitually chants the name of his beloved lord . . .' (Srimad Bhagavata)

Eventually beyond this somewhat abandoned state, the devotee will arrive at a point where he perceives the divine in everything and everyone,

The devotee need no longer observe any special forms or symbols for worship. He worships in his heart, the world having become his altar. (Goleman 1977)

In the Jewish cabbala, it is believed that there are multiple levels of reality with corresponding levels of consciousness. Most of us are at the lowest levels and live very mechanical lives of habit and routine with little awareness of our existence. Through meditation, according to the cabbalist view, we first become disillusioned with the mechanical games of life, and then begin to break free from the bondage of our egos. The ultimate goal along the path of the cabbalist is '*devekut*', in which the seeker's soul becomes one with God. At this point, the cabbalist is now a supernatural saint who has equanimity, indifference to praise and blame, a sense of being alone with God, and the gift of prophesy. All of her behaviour is directed to serving God's purpose not the ego; there is a union between the individual and the essence of existence (Halevi 1976).

In Christian Hesychasm and other Christian mystic traditions, meditation was practised to enable 'the old superficial self to be purged away and (permit) the gradual emergence of the true, secret self in which the Believer and Christ were "one spirit"' (Merton 1960). St Isaac describes the enlightened Christian as one who,

has reached the summit of all virtues, and has become the abode of the Holy Spirit . . . when the Holy Spirit comes to live in a man, he never ceases to pray, for then the Holy Spirit constantly prays in him. (Kadloubovsky and Palmer 1969)

In the Sufi tradition of Islam, meditation is a central practice in the attempt to reach a state called *fana* or 'passing away in God'. According to Sufi doctrine, our lives are a thin illusion of habitual reactions, imprisonment by desires, and endless suffering. We are asleep but we do not know it. Through regular practice of meditation and remembrance of God we can achieve an increased absorption in God.

The goal of Sufi meditation or '*zikr*' is to overcome the mind's waywardness and random play, and to achieve one-pointedness on God, so that God pervades the mind's activity.

Perhaps there is an echo across these different paths of a merging or submerging of the self in some absolute. Certainly, a similar notion exists at the heart of the teaching of the TM organization. Through TM, according to Maharishi Mahesh Yogi, the meditator can achieve the experience of pure Being, devoid of content, thoughts, specific sensations, memories, reactions; one experiences simply what it is to be. With regular practice the meditator is supposed to achieve cosmic consciousness, in which state awareness of pure Being permeates all of her activities during waking, sleeping, and dreaming. In this state of permanent pure awareness, the individual is free from desire and needs for personal gain. She acts spontaneously, in accordance with a divine cosmic purpose as an instrument of God. Beyond this, at the highest states of consciousness, the meditator experiences all things without illusion and experiences a complete unity with God in all creation.

Krishnamurti (1973) held that all techniques are a further obstacle to the unfettered, unblemished experience of existing. Meditation systems with mantras, techniques, teachings, traditions, and stipulations simply lead us to exchange one form of illusion for another. He argued that we are in a constant state of mental conflict as a result of making comparisons between what is and what should be. Consequently, we hide away in a construction of daily habits, mechanical repetition, dreams of the future and memories; we do not live in the present moment. Krishnamurti urged the development of a kind of opening-up meditation — 'choiceless awareness' — a clear and direct perception of experience now, without imposing names, preconceptions, and habitual perceptions upon our experience. It is only through watching the contents of consciousness that we can perceive the ways of our minds and begin to understand experience directly and not through symbols created by our intellects (Krishnamurti 1973). Freed from conditioned habits of perception and cognition one can be free of the self and therefore free to love. This leads to a state of aloneness beyond loneliness and an ability to attend without motive; thus one can live in the world 'with clarity and reason' (Coleman 1971).

Daniel Goleman (1977) has surveyed the varieties of religious experience and concludes that there are commonalities both of method and of objectives across these disparate traditions and approaches. He sees the need to retrain attention during meditation as the 'single invariant ingredient in the recipe for altering consciousness of every meditation system. At their end the distinction between meditation avenues melts'. Although each path uses different names, Goleman believes that they, propose the same basic formula in an alchemy of the self: the diffusion of the effects of meditation into the meditator's waking, dreaming and sleep states . . . As the states produced by his meditation meld with his waking activity, the awakened state ripens. When it reaches full maturity, it lastingly changes his consciousness, transforming his experience of himself and of his universe. (p. 117–18)

But perhaps we should be wary of assuming too easily a commonality of objectives and require of researchers a more careful analysis of this question and the assumptions of previous research. This is an issue we shall return to in Chapter 11.

So far we have examined what meditation is, how it is practised, and what the objectives of meditation have been in the various traditions surveyed. How psychologists have explored these practices and what their conclusions have been will occupy much of this volume. The diversity of traditions and practice, the richness of their philosophical discussions, and the extraordinariness of experiential accounts from those within these traditions have presented exciting challenges to those psychologists who have focused their attention on meditation. How have they responded?

The history of psychological research into meditation

Scientific research on meditation represents a meeting of psychological methodologies from two quite distinct philosophical and theoretical backgrounds. Meditation may be described as the methodology of Eastern psychology in that it is a means to experiential knowledge of mind and self, whereas Western psychology has adopted the scientific approach to understanding, relying on procedures which are publicly verifiable and observable. Amongst the earliest studies on meditation were those carried out in the 1950s and 1960s by Das and Gastaut, Bagchi and Wenger, and Kasamatsu and his colleagues. Their interest was primarily in physiological changes occurring during the practice of meditation, and they chose as subjects expert practitioners — yogis and Zen Buddhist monks. Indeed Bagchi and Wenger transported sophisticated recording equipment around temples, monasteries, and even into remote mountain caves to contact these meditators. The research showed unusual patterns of brain wave activity during meditation, especially during periods of ecstasy (or '*samadhi*').

In 1970 Keith Wallace published the results of his research on physiological changes occurring during the practice of TM, creating a stir of interest among both psychologists and doctors. Wallace *et al*. (1971) claimed that they had evidence of a fourth major state of consciousness which was characterized by very low levels of physiological arousal (Chapters 5 and 6). Shortly after this psychologists began to examine the effects of meditation practice upon behaviour and personality (see Chapter 7). Early interest was also aroused by the possibility that meditation might be a useful treatment for drug addiction and irresponsible claims were made by researchers and meditators alike on the basis of inadequate research (see West 1979b for a review). The 1970s and 1980s have since seen much research work in this area with a recent bibliography (Jarrell 1985) listing nearly 1000 published articles on meditation. What is the status of this research?

When research into meditation first began in earnest in the early 1970s, it was regarded by many psychologists and doctors as a rather esoteric and fringe area. Consequently some of those who pursued this interest may have been motivated to make their studies more respectable by using well-established dependent variable measures such as heart rate, oxygen consumption, brain wave patterns, and even rectal temperature. To measure more complex changes in behaviour, standardized paper and pencil test instruments were used, such as the Eysenck Personality Questionnaire and Cattell's personality measure, the 16PF. Many of the researchers were themselves new meditators with an investment in discovering positive effects of meditation in their research. Conceptual analysis often sits uneasily with experiential knowledge and perhaps these researchers were eager to ease their own intellectual doubts about meditation. Hence much of the earlier research is on short-term easily demonstrated outcomes, such as physiological parameters and personality change.

The research also tended to follow a conventional 'medical model' approach. Those who participated as subjects in this research were viewed rather like patients with an illness for which meditation was the hypothesized cure. Thus, measures of personality were taken before they began meditation and again after a short period of practice; 'improvement' was then assessed in relation to these measures. Meditation came to be seen as a potential therapy for current maladies such as hypertension, headaches, drug abuse, and even as an aid to memory and scholastic performance. Such concerns seem far from the traditional objectives of Eastern philosophies outlined above. They may also be far from the objectives of some of those Westerners taking up meditation (see West 1986).

The emphasis on short rather than long-term effects of meditation is apparent when we look at the studies examining physiological and personality changes. Almost all physiological studies have examined changes during meditation rather than longer term changes outside of meditation, or changes during meditation but over a long period of regular practice. Personality is a term used to describe relatively stable and consistent patterns of behaviour yet researchers in this area were looking for change over periods as short as 3 or 4 weeks (see Chapter 7). Similar criticisms apply to studies of meditation in therapy (see Chapters 8 and 10).

Studies of meditation have relied almost exclusively upon the experience of relatively novice Western practitioners, yet in the East meditation is a path to be followed for years in pursuit of clarity, wisdom, and insight. This emphasis on novice practitioners is a pragmatic response to the perennial difficulty of finding sufficiently large numbers of volunteers for research studies. Thus, because TM meditators are the easiest sample to contact, we find so few studies of long-term practitioners of techniques such as *zazen*. The consequence of this bias has been a concern with short-term gross effects of meditation, compounded by the fact that many of those who take up TM (and other meditation practices) lapse in their practice in the first 3 to 6 months and meditate only very sporadically, if ever, thereafter. Estimates vary, but probably fewer than one-third continue meditation with any regularity, that is four or more sessions per week (West 1980a; Delmonte 1984b).

But not only has most of the research been conducted with short-term practitioners, the vast majority of studies have also examined TM as the method of meditation. This may be partially due to the astute marketing of TM as an antidote to stress 'which produces a more effectively functioning nervous system and relief from psychosomatic disorders'. Many scientists simply set out to evaluate these claims rather than generating their own hypotheses from the Western or Eastern psychological literatures. And yet as early as 1971 psychologists such as Naranjo and Ornstein were differentiating between meditation systems and generating typologies.

Typologies of meditation

Naranjo (in Naranjo and Ornstein 1971) distinguished between three types of meditation which he called respectively the Way of Forms, the Expressive Way and the Negative Way. The Way of Forms includes meditation upon external symbols and objects such as candle flames, mandalas, and mantras. He calls this the way of concentration, absorption, union, outer-directed, and Apollonian meditation. One example of concentrative meditation is Ramana Maharshi's method of meditating upon the question 'Who am I?'. There is a focusing of attention and a centredness on the question (which could be substituted by a mandala, flame, lotus flower, mantra, or focus on breathing). The Expressive Way includes those meditations which involve receptivity to the contents and processes of consciousness. In this type the meditator 'dwells upon the form that springs from his own spontaneity, until he may eventually find that in his own soul lies hidden the source of all traditions'. Naranjo describes the Expressive Way as the way of freedom, transparence, surrender, inner-directed, Dionysian. It involves letting go of control and being open to inner voices, feelings, and intuitions. Naranjo suggests the best illustration is to be found in shamanism — 'Not only is shamanism in general a mysticism of possession, but the shaman's trance is usually content-oriented . . . He is one who has attained communication with the supernatural and may act as a mediator between spirits or gods and man, making the desires of each known to each other' (p. 97).

Finally, there is the Negative Way — involving elimination, detachment, emptiness, centring — the middle way. The meditator in this type puts effort into moving away from all objects and not identifying with anything perceived, 'By departing from the known he thus allows for the unknown, by excluding the irrelevant he opens himself up to the relevant, and by disidentifying from his current self concept, he may go into the aconceptual awakening of his true nature' (p. 29). In this approach the aim is to withdraw attention from both external perceptions and internal experience 'to cultivate a detachment toward psychological acting in general' (Naranjo 1974, p. 29). Thus, a good example of the Negative Way is *vipassana* meditation, a Buddhist approach involving 'bare attention'. In this method the meditator merely registers sense impressions, feelings, and mental states without reacting to them by deed, speech, or mental comment,

By cultivating a receptive state of mind, which is the first stage in the process of perception, bare attention cleans the mind and prepares the mind for subsequent mental processes (in Naranjo and Ornstein 1971).

Ornstein (1972) describes two major types of meditation — concentrative and 'opening-up' meditations. The first type he sees as developing one-pointedness of mind and gives as an example the technique of Zen breath counting. This involves counting the breaths from one to ten and then repeating the process. When the count is lost the meditator returns to one and begins again. He sees the 'opening-up' exercises not as attempting to isolate the practitioner from ordinary life processes but rather as involving those processes in the training of consciousness. Thus the Zen practice of '*shikantaza*' or just sitting is an exemplar of this type of meditation. Watts (1957) describes it as:

not therefore, sitting with a blank mind which excludes all the impressions of the inner and outer senses. It is not 'concentration' in the usual sense of restricting the attention to a single sense object, such as a point of light or the tip of one's nose. It is simply a quiet awareness, without comment, of whatever happens to be here and now. This awareness is attended by the most vivid sensation of 'non-difference' between oneself and the external world, between the mind and its contents — the various sounds, sights and other impressions of the surrounding environment. Naturally this sensation does not arise by trying to acquire it. (p. 175)

D. H. Shapiro (1982) describes three major attentional strategies in his typology — a focus on a whole field (wide-angle lens attention), a focus on a specific object within a field (zoom-lens attention), and a shifting back and forth between the two. The first type would include mindfulness techniques such as 'just sitting'. Another example would be *vipassana*, which Baker (1981) describes as the central practice of Buddhism,

the continual effort to at first note and later to just be one with the immediacy of one's situation; to break the adhesive of one's constant train of conceptual thought about past, present and future; and to bring oneself with clarity to the touch and consciousness of the present. The practice of mindfulness greatly deepens the power of concentration and the ability to stay with one's life situation.

Zoom-lens attention is what both Ornstein and Naranjo call concentrative meditation but the third type, shifting back and forth, is a novel category quite different from Naranjo's, and includes passive concentrative techniques such as TM. It is argued that in TM there is both concentration and mindfulness and that with increasing adeptness, mindfulness becomes more dominant (Brown and Engler 1980; Welwood 1982).

Goleman (1977) distinguishes two types and paths of meditation, essentially the same as those seen by Ornstein; he calls them the paths of concentration and insight. Not only are the meditation types different, he argues, but the experiences along the paths of meditation practice will be quite distinct too. On the path of concentration the meditator will develop deeper and deeper absorption and one-pointedness, going through eight '*jhanas*' (full absorptions) to achieve a final state 'so subtle that it cannot be said whether it is or not (p. 19). The path of insight involves developing deeper mindfulness and insight through stages of pseudonirvana, realization, and effortless insight to nirvana, in which state the meditator 'will have utterly given up the potential for impure acts' (p. 32).

The extent to which these different typologies are useful for researchers or represent distinct and valid categories within the traditional contexts of meditation has not been critically examined in the literature. Both the suggestion that there are major types of meditation and the proposal that the experiences and responses of those practising these different types will differ over time have important implications for researchers in the design of their studies. The responses of researchers and writers to the crucial issues of distinctions between meditation types and the implications of these distinctions will be explored further in Chapter 11.

The problems of research on meditation

In describing psychological approaches to meditation we have looked at the history of research and described the typologies that have been developed to impose order upon the multiplicity of meditation techniques. Now we turn to examine the particular difficulties that face researchers trying to increase understanding of this area of human behaviour. It is true that some of these problems are created by researchers themselves, tied to particular methodological approaches or concerned with quick and easy outcome studies, and this will become apparent in the following chapters. The reader should note too that a number of the problems described here are characteristic of the research on psychotherapeutic outcome generally and are explained more fully in Chapter 10.

The meditator's motivations

The prospective meditator is motivated to achieve personal growth, to learn to relax, to achieve spiritual insight, or to gain whatever benefits she believes the practice of meditation may bring. This motivation may well be the agent for reductions in arousal levels, or pathology, or increases in psychological well-being, no matter what exercises or techniques are practised. The very decision to learn meditation may itself herald change just as the simple decision to consult a psychiatrist is often associated with some relief of symptoms (Frank 1961). There is also the danger (from the researcher's viewpoint) that the new meditator will be an enthusiastic convert, motivated to 'spread the word' about the beneficial effects of practice. Her motivation in the research may be to prove how beneficial meditation is (this may be particularly so among TM meditators persuaded by 'scientific research') and vested interests in research outcomes may well be high. After paying a sum of money to learn meditation, feeling subjective benefits, and exhorting friends to learn, the meditator would have to cope with uncomfortable dissonance were the research outcome to suggest that meditation was ineffective or even harmful.

The researcher's motivations

Despite the prescriptions of Popper (1959) to strive for falsification, researchers are subject to the same range of emotions, thoughts, hopes, disappointments, and fears as the rest of humanity and have hopes that their experiments will 'work' and that hypotheses will be supported. It is clearly frustrating and disappointing not to find significant or interesting results (though such failures are often due to researchers failing to base designs on theoretically driven questions). The researcher often therefore has biases and these are powerful in producing desired results (Rosenthal 1966). These problems are exacerbated by the fact that many researchers are themselves committed meditators; in some cases the researcher is also a TM teacher, and the research subjects are taught meditation by the researcher. Putting together the subjects' motivations, the researchers' motivations, and the demand character-istics of the research in this case, it would not be surprising to find very positive answers to the question 'What effect is meditation having?'

Demand characteristics of meditation research

Orne (1962) describes demand characteristics as the totality of cues in an experimental situation which convey an experimental hypothesis to the subject and which become significant determinants of the subject's behaviour. Orne has shown that subjects display a desire to 'perform well' in research and to bear out the researcher's hypotheses. The demand characteristics in meditation research are often strong and clear. The central question 'What effect is meditation having?' is usually obvious to even the most naive of subjects. Few studies have set out to determine whether meditation is having only negligible or no effects.

Methods of teaching meditation

Payment of large sums of money to learn meditation, elaborate and ritualized teaching methods and ceremonies, group pressures, scientific rationales, and charismatic teachers or leaders are all likely to influence the person in his or her response to taking up and regularly practising a technique of meditation. Controlling for the effects of such factors in traditional methodologies has only been possible in recent years as a result of the development of standardized forms of meditation by psychologists (e.g. Carrington 1978 and see Chapter 9). But this solution, while enabling research on the mechanics of meditation, may divert researchers from looking at meditation as a practice which may be inextricably bound up with belief systems and expectations. Conclusions may therefore be based on sterile and mechanical practices rather than on meditation as a central part of the belief system and day to day life of the meditator. Such issues require more exploration and examination.

The meditator's expectancies

The outcomes of meditation will be much influenced by the expectations the meditator brings to his or her practice. These expectations will differ markedly between traditions and schools and are seen as confounding effects in experimental designs. In order to exclude these effects from influencing outcomes, researchers develop elaborate control procedures which may involve people learning and regularly practising techniques designed to be ineffective. Aside from the ethical considerations of conducting such research, the attempts seem doomed to failure. Encouraging people to alter their routines and take time out to help themselves is likely to produce some beneficial effects. Surprisingly few researchers have decided to accept and make explicit the expectancies of meditators and to incorporate these in their designs by comparing reactions to meditation across different traditions or paths.

Regularity and length of practice

The focus on novice meditators in most research has created problems of ensuring that subjects practised meditation regularly. As we have already observed, attrition rates are high and many subjects practise only sporadically. Consequently it becomes difficult to say whether outcomes are a consequence of meditation practice or a lack of it. Furthermore the focus on short-term practitioners rather than long-term practitioners has led to a concern with short-term change and what often seem in the context of the meditative traditions, rather trivial questions. Part of the research problem here is that it is difficult to find large numbers of people who have been practising meditation regularly over a long period of time unless they are members of organizations like the TM movement, which tend to be evangelical and propound a 'party line'.

It may also be that the behaviour we observe in long-term meditators and which seems unique is not a consequence of their meditation practice. Rather it may be that the kind of people motivated in the first place to take up and sustain for a very long period their practice of meditation differ from others in relation to the specific characteristics under study (i.e. subject self-selection).

Choice of dependent and independent variables

Which meditation practice to study is a decision few researchers appear to take consciously, preferring instead to ask for volunteer subjects from those practising or about to be trained in TM. Others simply use the techniques devised to satisfy the needs of experimenters. Similarly choice of independent variables is often pragmatic with measures being used because they are well validated or because the researcher has used them before in other contexts. Indeed, the hallmark of meditation research over the last 20 years has been its atheoretical orientation. Despite the many different meditation practices, the many different religious and philosophical traditions from which they spring, the many different areas of pertinent theory in psychology, and the large bodies of useful theory in Eastern philosophy, researchers have followed similar patterns using only traditional methodologies and with few deriving hypotheses from theory. Consequently designs have sought to answer those questions which are least interestingly theoretically and process issues have been all but ignored in the concerns with outcome and physiological indices.

Summary

Meditation has been practised in widely differing cultures for thousands of years. Meditation practices can be found in traditional cultures throughout the world and are principally practised in spiritual contexts.

The reasons given by people for their meditation practice seem to differ according to the belief system of those concerned but some authors believe there is a fundamental commonality of objectives. It has been argued that the meditator is seeking to alter the way he or she perceives and experiences existence. The intent is often to achieve a spiritual unity with all existence.

In recent years the interest of Western scholars has been aroused by findings from psychological studies of meditation practitioners. In particular the possibility that meditation might have short-term therapeutic value has led to a flood of published articles exploring the subject. However, the specific difficulties of research in this area have been compounded by the emphasis on short-term outcome studies which have failed to overcome some major methodological challenges. Furthermore the orientations of researchers have been dictated too infrequently by theoretical considerations; the lack of reflexivity between research and theory in this area has been a major drawback to the advancement of understanding. The quality of research has often been poor and the results sensationalised inappropriately. Attempts to develop typologies of meditation have not been effectively utilized in research and the quest to demonstrate effectiveness of meditation has led to a neglect of the study of processes in meditation. Exploration of the place of meditation in the lifespan of the individual has not been vigorously pursued. Perhaps most importantly there is a need to draw on existing theories of human behaviour in Western psychology, and to explore the implications of Eastern approaches for our understanding of human behaviour, if we are to advance research and theorizing on the psychology of meditation.

The rest of the chapters in this book bring together the very best of research and practice in this area. Existing and new theoretical orientations are also offered in order to light the way for future research on meditation, and to facilitate the development of a greater understanding about the role of meditation in affecting consciousness and behaviour.

2 Meditation in Buddhist psychology

Guy Claxton

> *As stars, a fault of vision, as a lamp*
> *A mock show, dew drops or a bubble,*
> *A dream, a lightning flash, a cloud,*
> *So should one view what is conditioned.*
> *Diamond sutra (Conze 1975)*

Meditation in context

Meditation is a psychotherapeutic practice that is designed to improve the quality of life, and which is undertaken with that intent. But though the practice can be undertaken without any explicit understanding of how it works psychologically, it is nevertheless rare for meditation to be taught in a theoretical vacuum. More usually it is presented within a system of ritual, belief, or interpretation which meditators are expected to study alongside their practice. And after their 'induction' they are as a rule encouraged to keep in touch with a teacher, who can guide practice and answer questions, and/or a group of fellow meditators, all of whom think about what they are doing and converse in a common language of terms, concepts, and intentions.

These conceptual frameworks differ enormously in their nature, degree of elaboration, and explicitness. 'TM' is embedded within a way of thinking (called the 'Science of Creative Intelligence') that encourages meditators to construe their experiences in terms of 'the release of stress' and the achievement of 'finer and finer levels of thought', and to look for the effects of meditation, in the short term, in the success of daily enterprises like business or relationships and in feelings of peace and well-being. Meditation in the Christian mystical traditions draws on the whole apparatus of Biblical thought, especially the Trinity, relies on central organizing concepts like 'the grace of God', and stresses the importance of moral discipline as an accompaniment to meditation. While in the Buddhist traditions we find a huge variety of interpretative systems that place differential emphasis on good conduct, personal happiness, insight, self-discipline, and so on. In addition to all these differences in language, attitude, and conceptualization, meditative practice itself takes many forms. Meditators may be found sitting with eyes open looking at a picture or a candle flame or a blank wall; eyes closed, humming or silently repeating a *mantra*; walking very very slowly, or at normal speed; whirling round and round with arms outstretched for hours on end; or jumping up and down vigorously shouting 'Hoo! Hoo! Hoo!'

Given all this diversity of practice and theory, how on earth are we to make sense of what meditators are up to? Can there be a single, underlying explanation for 'meditation', what it does, and what it achieves? The answer is both 'yes' and 'no'. On the periphery of these traditions, so to speak, we find people attracted for a host of different reasons, who are seemingly trying to achieve quite different goals. The different forms and presentations attract different kinds of people and the expectations aroused are up to a point self-fulfilling (Kapleau 1980). Some people at least come to meditation with the intention of becoming more relaxed or concentrating more effectively or not worrying so much, or 'feeling better', and they get what they want. But it seems that at the heart of each tradition, underneath all the various, and even conflicting, formulations, there is a remarkable consensus (see for example Goleman 1977). Behind the mundane benefits that meditation can bring lies, if a person is willing to undertake it, a deep and very personal journey of enquiry — 'a journey beyond belief' as one meditator (Walsh 1983) has called it — into such profound and perennial questions as 'What is life?', 'What does it mean to be happy?' and, right at the bottom, 'Who — or what — am I?' Nowhere is this bottom line exploration discussed more fully than in the literature of Buddhism, and so in the following pages I shall try to give a psychologically accessible (and acceptable) gloss on the central Buddhist doctrines, in order that we may understand what this journey entails, and the central role that meditation plays therein. Contemporary research on meditation has often ignored the context of belief and intention within which practice takes place, and has sought to establish direct connections between practice and various kinds of outcome. The fact that the results have often been confusing may be due in part to this failure to take into account the cognitive setting.

The chapter first proposes a parallel between Buddhist psychology and constructivist approaches to perception. It then looks at the central Buddhist proposition: 'the doctrine of dependent origination'. This doctrine is then applied to the understanding of self or personhood, which is seen in Buddhism as the crucial area of investigation. Following this there is a discussion of the well-known 'Four Noble Truths', which I will present as distinguishing between two forms of 'suffering', one of which is created by our misapprehensions about our own nature. At this point we can return to a discussion of meditation, seeing it as a training in the 'research methodology' that is needed to undertake the enquiry into self. Finally, we shall review the claims that are frequently made about the effects of sustained meditation within this context, and make some suggestions about future directions for research on meditation.

Buddhist psychology: a constructivist perspective

Buddhist psychology is much more concerned with perception than it is with knowledge, for its diagnosis of 'the human condition' presupposes that much of our experience, while seeming very real, is actually quite inaccurate. This is the root of the problem: we behave badly and live uncomfortably when we do, not because we are evil, but simply because we do not see rightly. Concomitantly the cures that Buddhism prescribes, of which meditation is by far the most important, are designed to cleanse the doors of perception, not to train us to feel or act better. If we can remove the faults in our senses, so we are told, then equanimity and magnanimity will arise quite naturally, just as someone waking from a nightmare sees for themselves that the monster is non-existent and the terror just disperses. It follows that, unlike in many other religious contexts, methods of self-improvement that rely on knowledge, belief, or will are not given great prominence, for the acquisition of understanding or the application of effort mostly have little impact on perception. We cannot as a rule tell ourselves to see differently.

The Buddhist position, because it asserts that perception *is* changeable by psychological practices such as meditation, assumes a 'constructivist' view that is not unfamiliar to Western psychologists. From George Kelly (1955) through Richard Gregory (1966) to Ulric Neisser (1976) and John Anderson (1980) the postulation of a mental model—scheme, cognitive structure, ACT, call it what you will—that subserves and is the source of all experience, decision, and action is commonplace. There is nothing strange in the principle itself. It is even encapsulated in psychological aphorisms: Max Clowes's: 'there is no seeing, only seeing *as*' or Koffka's: 'we see things not as they are but as *we* are'. Nor would most psychologists wish to dispute it. Because it is obvious that we *often* create our own experience—in dreams, hallucinations, visual illusions, and in the perceptual mistakes of segmentation or interpretation that we make every day—it becomes increasingly hard to deny that we *always* have a hand in it.

So the question is not whether our prior experience and beliefs are, as it were, 'dissolved' in our perception, but to what extent and with what results. We now know that our psychology has done a fair bit of selecting—highlighting, deleting, distorting—before the psychology of our own history and goals even comes into it. Having a brain that annotates experience for us, exaggerating edges and movement, attenuating continuity and rest, is obviously to our advantage: we distort our sensation for good reason, and our survival is enhanced thereby. But what *else* have we done to our perceptions and our thoughts before they occur to us? And are the effects of these preconscious interventions always valuable? Where Buddhism goes beyond what is familiar in psychology is in asserting that some of the deep but mostly unexamined and unconscious assumptions that constitute the very foundations of our perception are inaccurate, and that therefore the entire range of experience to which they contribute is ill-founded and misguided. The most important, and therefore the most pernicious, of these assumptions concern our own nature—particularly the ways we view our identity, and even our perception itself.

The nature of concepts

Let us look at our intuitive attitudes to perception first—attitudes that are instantiated in our normal habits of perceptual processing. One of the most significant of these habits is to break up the totality of an experience into bits, and then to interpret these bits as evidence for or against the presence of a concept—or more strictly, of an exemplar or an instance of a concept.

Our approach is to interpret the bits of our experience as *symptomatic*: if enough evidence accrues, I shall decide that I am in the presence of a real donkey, or real love, or a real salami sandwich. Our mental theory assembles elementary regularities in our experience into concepts and we then construe the bits and pieces, in their particular relationships, as evidence *for* the concept. By so doing we create a sense of the concept as existing in its own right, lying behind the world we experience perhaps, but manifesting itself through the attributes that we now believe it to own. Collins and Quillian's (1969) famous diagram of the concept 'Canary' (Figure 2.1) represents this intuition in a stark form. We cannot see 'it' as possessing attributes without at the same time giving 'it' the status of an entity—a thing that has existence in its own right. And this is not just a matter for discussion or intellectual assent. Because this attitude of 'things' 'having' 'attributes', and 'attributes' being 'evidence for' 'things' is embedded in our personal theory, and our personal theory is the mediator and arbitrator of our perception, this attitude permeates the very way we experience the world. Indeed the hardest part of this argument is seeing that there is an alternative.

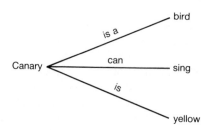

Figure 2.1

When we perceive the bits and pieces of a scene as attributes of, or evidence for, things, we do not therefore see them in their own right, but in the context of the decision we have made about what they are attributes *of*—not a wheel but a chariot wheel; not just a leg but the hind leg of a donkey; not just a look but a meaningful look that tells me how you are *really* feeling. Thus every time I construe something as 'the hind leg of a donkey' I am implicitly confirming and reinforcing the belief that donkeys exist, hind legs exist, and they are related through the possession of the latter by the former.

The relation between attribute and thing is often interpreted as *causal*. If a 'cold' is something other than a runny nose and sneezes, then we can use it to *explain* the runny nose: 'My nose is runny *because* I've got a cold'; 'Spots are *caused* by measles', 'He says things like that *because* he's a bastard'.

The alternative attitude to concepts is that they are simply portmanteau ideas or labels. They are not other than a recurrent conglomeration of experiences, reactions, feelings, thoughts, descriptions, and impulses, woven together. Because they have tended to co-occur in the past our mental theory binds them together so that they become contingent. The presence of some of these features begins automatically to arouse the others. For a young child the sound of mummy's voice may be sufficient to activate a whole set of anticipatory reactions. My experience with cubes leads me to predict that this new one will have a back to it. Notice how language forces us to talk as if there was a 'thing' called mummy that 'has' a voice, or a thing called a cube that 'has' a back. But, says this second view of concepts, we do not need to make this gratuitous inference. All we are justified in claiming is that some features of the world lead me to expect others: a sound readies me for a hug; one conjunction of lines leads me to anticipate another. Thus on this view features are bound together directly with each other, as for example in Hebb's 'cell assembly' model (Hebb 1949), rather than, as in the Quillian depiction, via some common point.

When you have taken a bicycle to bits you have nothing left except the bits. There is no bicycle that 'has' a frame, wheels, handlebars, and the rest: 'bicycle' is just a name for these bits when they are put together in a certain way. Thus bicycles, electrons, sandwiches and measles are not parts of the world but ways of segmenting it and talking about it; like contour lines and county boundaries they exist on the map, not on the ground. They are not entities but notations.

Dependent origination

Buddhism invites one to entertain this second point of view, first intellectually as a psychophilosophical position and then, if one will, as an alternative and possibly preferable basis for our own perceptual processes. It asks us to abandon the view, both intellectually and existentially, that the world is a collection of 'things' that have their own identity and their own individual character, and to explore the so-called 'doctrine of dependent origination' which asserts that the notion of a 'thing' is only an approximation, a counter-factual convenience which violates what is in fact the case — that neither physical nor conceptual segmentation of the world is in the last analysis possible. Nothing can accurately be spoken of *in vacuo*. Any concept is irreducibly composed of, and dependent on, other concepts, and if we forget the seamlessness that underlies our notations and allow that amnesia to percolate into perception then we are apt to confer on these notations and conventions an ontological status that they do not deserve.

Nowhere is this slippery argument better made in the Buddhist literature than by Nagarjuna, a second-century Indian philosopher, in his exposition of the school of *madhyamika*, the 'middle way'. Sprung's (1979) translation of Candrakirti's famous documentary on this exposition puts it like this:

If, in the world which each of us holds together for himself, the causal account is delusory, if, that is, all the things inner and outer which make up a world neither arise nor exist in the realistic, entitative way we naïvely suppose, then the events and sequences which compose life are analogous to a magician's deception: what truly goes on is made to appear like a series of causally dependent events, but is not . . . the indispensible factor in a magician's trick is the false interpretation placed on the evidence of the senses by the spectator. Coins, cigarettes and rabbits are manipulated by the magician strictly in accord with the laws of motion and gravity that govern all objects. It is the spectator who, due to the shallowness of his imagination, penetrates no deeper than his eyesight, and sees these objects passing bewilderingly in and out of nostrils, pockets and top hats. The events making up the trick, the palming of the coin or cigarettes, the collapse of a false bottom in the hat, are not dream, not hallucination, but run of the mill space–time sequences onto which the spectator projects his false expectations.

Edward Conze (1975), commenting on the passage from the *Diamond sutra* which headed this chapter, again appeals to Nagarjuna, who:

shows that ignorance and the products of the magician's art have the following attributes in common: They are neither inside a person, nor outside, nor both inside or outside; they can therefore not be localised with reference to persons; there is nothing real that has been either produced or destroyed; no real event, with an essence of its own, has taken place. And yet, although ignorance is not real it is the condition for all kinds of activity. Similarly the musical instruments conjured up by magic are empty, deceptive, without reality, without objective basis, and yet one can hear their music and see them.

The other obvious metaphor with which to capture the Buddhist conception of our ubiquitous enchantment is the dream. Our normal mode of awareness is to the enlightened, disillusioned consciousness as dreaming is to waking. To quote Nagarjuna for the last time:

(a) there is no reality in a dream, and yet, while one dreams, one believes in the reality of the things one sees in the dream. After one has woken up one recognises the falseness of the dream and laughs at oneself. Just so a man who is plunged into the dreamy state which results from his fettered existence, has a belief in things which do not exist. But when he has found the Path, then, at the moment of enlightenment, he understands that there is no reality in them and he laughs at himself. (b) A dreamer, by the force of his dream, sees things where there is nothing. Just so a man, by the force of the dreamy state which results from ignorance, believes in the existence of all sorts of things which do not exist, such as I and mine, male and female, etc. (c) In a dream one rejoices although there is nothing enjoyable, one is angry although there is nothing to annoy, one is frightened although there is nothing to frighten. So do the beings with regard to the things of the world. (Conze 1975)

The construction of a self

It is impossible to do justice to the elegance and power of Nagarjuna's analysis in a few pages, and even if the reader has followed the argument it is doubtful whether its implications will be clear. 'I think I see what he's on about', you may be inclined to say at this point, 'but I don't understand what all the fuss is about. What has this philosophizing got to do with human happiness — or even meditation?'

The connection is made when we take the doctrine of dependent origination and apply it to one very important concept that sits right at the heart of our personal theories: the one we call 'me', 'myself', 'I'. To what do *these* words refer? What are the salient characteristics that we have bundled together, and chosen to construe as evidence for this underlying entity called 'self'? The first and most fundamental is *separateness*. Our sense of self is individual, localized, personal. It belongs in this little bit of space right here, and what is not right here is not Me. For there to be a me there must be a not-me, and a boundary that separates the two. This boundary may not be sharp, or always well defined, but it must be there. For instance the experiences of perceiving, feeling, doing, and especially thinking seem very central. 'I' see, feel, act, decide. Just as we suppose an electron behind the track, a disease behind the symptoms, a God behind the experience of grace, so we construe thought as evidence for a thinker, acts as evidence for an actor, feeling and perception as evidence for an experiencer. Thus the general tendency to reify our concepts, to grant them existence and reality, is manifest in the way we view our selves.

The other side of me is not-me: if I *am* this, then I cannot also be that. Clearly I am not this table, nor the unfinished hotel I can see from the window, nor you. Much of my experience seems to impinge on me from without. It happens *to* me, but it isn't me. But our attitude to the substance of which we are composed is somewhat ambivalent. *Am* I a body, or do I *have* one? We seem to waver. We allow ourselves to say 'I am tired' and 'I am ill' — but baulk at saying 'I am measles' or 'I am a stomach'. We keep the body at a distance, so to speak, relating to it via possession rather than identification. I *have* a brain and a headache. They are not quite me, but are certainly mine; and it is hard (at least in some cultures) to imagine that 'I' continue to exist when the body does not.

The second characteristic of self is *persistence*. Separateness defines Me as limited in space and content; persistence defines Me as limited in time. 'I' was born; 'I' will die; in between 'I' exist and persist, and some essence continues through my life unchanged, like a thread. Today I am in a different room thinking different thoughts; my body is bigger than it was when I was seven; and yet in some way I am the same Guy Claxton as I was yesterday or 30 years ago.

And the third characteristic, the one most readily observable perhaps, is *autonomy*. Though much of my experience seems to happen to me — I construe my self as a recipient of anger, the baby's cry, and the smell of seaweed — over thought and action in particular I claim to have some control. I don't identify closely with some internal processes: 'I am beating my heart' is not an assertion we would want to defend. But 'I am walking the dog', 'I thought it over and decided not to go', 'I want to go to the zoo tomorrow' all point to an 'I' that is a producer, an author, as well as a spectator. This sense of a self that is the cause, and therefore in control, of at least some of what I think and do is crucial. I reason, I choose, I decide, I intend, I initiate, I evaluate, and sometimes I change my mind. Behind the act there is an actor whose initiative entitles him to any praise or blame that accrues. I am, and feel, responsible.

Thus do I identify and recognize my self: I am different from you; I have a history and a future; and I will and feel, register and act. The next question is: 'What follows from these assumed characteristics?' (We must remember, as we pursue this inquiry, that the sense of self as described is entirely obvious, taken for granted, second nature; it permeates the whole of experience. But we may not take that as evidence for its existence. As we have seen, our beliefs are dissolved in our perceptions; our experience is already theory laden. We cannot therefore accept our experience at face value. If it contains our beliefs, is constructed on the basis of them, then we cannot at the same time accept it as evidence for these beliefs. Because we have decided there is a donkey out there we see this limb as a donkey's hind leg. Because I know this to be a cube, I see this line not *as* a line but as an edge — the edge of a cube. So most of what we take as indicating a self merely indicates a *belief* in a self, and cannot be considered as referential, as pointing to anything that exists as an entity.)

Qua philosophy, Buddhism argues that the general doctrine of dependent origination applies *a fortiori* to the concept of the self. The abilities of memory, thought and prediction exist, as the relative structural circumscription of the body exists, but we need not take these aspects of experience as evidence for an underlying entity, and we reason falsely if we do so. Worse, if we then identify this mental fiction with ourselves, our true natures — if we turn the entity into an identity — then we have made a bad mistake.

While this insight is central to Buddhism, and most clearly articulated therein, it is by no means peculiar to it. It could not be, for if the arguments on which it relies are valid they must be universally available. Thus, just as one example, we have in the Western philosophical tradition David Hume (1888) saying:

for my part when I enter most intimately into what I call *myself*, I always stumble on some particular perception or other, of heat or cold, light or shade, love or hatred, pain or pleasure. I can never catch myself at any time without a perception . . . What we call the mind is nothing but a heap or bundle of different perceptions united together by certain relations.

It is impossible to separate out one part of a bicycle and call it 'bicycle'; in exactly the same way it is impossible to set apart one aspect or component of a human being and call it 'I'. Or we may if we wish, but we do not thereby name any thing. Selves, like pixies, are creatures of our imagination.

The Four Noble Truths

Buddhism, *qua* psychology and psychotherapy, does not, however, stop at defending the idea of the non-existence of self — the 'doctrine of *anatta*' — as a rational position. Indeed Nagarjuna and others assert in the strongest possible terms that if one does take *anatta* merely as an intellectual standpoint one has missed the point completely. For *anatta* contains within itself some bad news and some good news for ordinary human beings everywhere, and the quality of their daily lives. This news, perhaps the most well-known of all Buddhist teaching, is expounded in the so-called Four Noble Truths.

The First Noble Truth, which contains most of the bad news, is the fact of *dukka*, usually translated as 'suffering'. We might distinguish two general classes of suffering (though in doing so I am going beyond the classical formulation in order to bring out most clearly the psychological aspects of the Buddha's words). The first comprises the pain that is an inevitable accompaniment to life: injury, infirmity, bereavement and the approach of one's own death, rejection, the failure of cherished plans, and so on. The implacable law of life is that we must know these forms of suffering, willy-nilly. The fairy-tale possibility of 'happily ever after' is not on offer. We are always prone to such events, and to the pain, hurt, sadness, fear, and grief that are their necessary corollaries.

The second kind of suffering consists of many other feelings that recur throughout life, and which seem to disturb our sought-after happiness: embarrassment, shame, guilt, anxiety, worry, resentment, depression, lethargy, self-consciousness, envy, jealousy, regret, self-doubts, and the common-or-garden sense of being out of sorts or fed up.

The Second Noble Truth asserts the difference between these two classes of *dukkha*. In essence it says that, while the first is truly inevitable, the second is a product of our own *attitude* to life and the deep beliefs that we hold about it. Specifically we do not fully understand and accept the fact that the world, and we ourselves, are changing inexorably, and that loss, bereavement, disappointment, death, and their attendant feelings must be borne. By being committed, deep down, to the belief that perfection, security, and everlasting peace are possibilities we set ourselves at odds with an existence that persists in changing without regard to our wishes. Thus by denying the fundamental fact of impermanence (*anicca*) we set ourselves up for a life of struggle and frustration. We must constantly be judging what happens to see whether it fits with our desires or not. If it does, we cling and defend. If it does not, we resist what is there, and hanker or strive for that which, in terms of our personal set of preferences, would be an improvement. Out of an unconscious resistance to change come the twin goads of attachment and aversion that keep us on the run. And it is precisely this sense of being on the run that denies us the contentment we seek, and brings in to existence all the sufferings of the second kind. Aldous Huxley once summed the situation up by saying that about a third of all human unhappiness is unavoidable, while the other two-thirds are created by the doomed attempt to avoid the first third.

If the first of the Noble Truths detects and diagnoses what Buddhism sees as the most prevalent human epidemic, the second offers us an aetiology. But it does not take us the whole way. It shows us how attachment and aversion are the origins of much that we find tiresome, but it does not tell us where attachment and aversion themselves spring from. Why is it that we are unable to accept at the deepest level the fact of change? What deprives us of the serenity and wisdom that Alcoholics Anonymous speak of in their famous prayer: 'Lord, give me the courage to change those things that can be changed; the serenity to accept those things that cannot; and the wisdom to tell the difference'?

The answer — though it is not normally taught as part of the Second Noble Truth — is: exactly those misconceptions of our own identity that we have been discussing over the last few pages. Having identified my self as separate and bounded, as persisting in essence through space and time, and as at least partially autonomous in thought and action, I have adopted a stance towards life which makes unintended, unanticipated change anathema. By confirming my self within the limits of a body, I have conferred on what lies outside the power to threaten 'me'. By insisting on consistency, I make a hard shell of a self-image for myself that restricts growth and change. By assuming that my mind is in control, I am undermined by, or must ignore, its wilfulness. In fact whatever a person has written, sub- or semiconsciously into their definition of themselves they are thereby required to search for, cling to, or defend.

The Third Noble Truth, which has been implicit in the entire preceding discussion, is that release from the second type of suffering and serenity in the face of the first, is a real, available possibility. If some of our suffering stems from an error of judgement, if we got lost because we misread the map, then if we sit down quietly and study our predicament, and trace the error of our ways, release from that suffering is available. This is the good news of the Buddhist teaching and it sets the scene for the Fourth Noble Truth, which is the Buddha's cure, his prescription for the attainment of release.

This cure, called the Eightfold Path, is Buddhism's do-it-yourself psychotherapy. The eight components of which it consists are, in the usual English translations, Right Understanding, Right Intention, Right Speech, Right Action, Right Livelihood, Right Effort, Right Awareness, and Right Meditation. Right Understanding means mastering with one's mind the Buddhist doctrines: dependent origination, *anatta*, and the Four Noble Truths. Right Intention means being earnestly and honestly committed to exploring their implications in one's own life. Right Speech means noticing the ways in which one's beliefs, assumptions, and attitudes are embedded in the stories one tells to both oneself and others. Right Action means noticing the same thing with respect to the way one behaves. Right Livelihood means organizing one's daily routines, especially how and where one works, so that the spirit of enquiry is fostered and supported. Right Effort means keeping at it, not with intermittent bursts of enthusiasm and despondency, but quietly and relentlessly. Right Awareness and Right Meditation are the real keys for they prescribe the attitude of mind, and how it can be developed, which will generate insight into one's misconceptions and thereby liberation from them. It is with awareness and its training through meditation that the rest of this chapter is concerned.

What is meditation?

One day a man of the people said to Zen master Ikkyu: 'Master, will you please write for me some maxims of the highest wisdom?'

Ikkyu immediately took his brush and wrote the word 'Attention'.

'Is that all?' asked the man. 'Will you not add something more?'

Ikkyu then wrote twice running: 'Attention. Attention.'

'Well', remarked the man rather irritably, 'I really don't see much depth or subtlety in what you have just written'.

Then Ikkyu wrote the same word three times running: 'Attention. Attention. Attention.'

Half-angered, the man demanded: 'What does that word "Attention" mean anyway?'

And Ikkyu answered gently: 'Attention means attention'.

This story, recounted by Kapleau (1980) is one of the most famous of Zen Buddhist stories, and it sums up the heart of meditative practice. There are many different *techniques* for training attention. There are many different *objects* that one can pay attention to. There are different *ways* of paying attention. And there are a variety of different *experiences* that may occur during meditation, and as meditative practice deepens. But in essence meditation is learning to pay attention: simply that. From a very different tradition, that of Christian mysticism, we have St Teresa of Avila, for example, saying to her meditation students: 'I do not require of you to form great and serious considerations in your thinking. I require of you only to look' (LeShan 1983). Thus expressed, stripped of the trappings and connotations that each of the many spiritual traditions of both East and West have given to meditation, it may seem unglamorous or even mundane — as it clearly did to Ikkyu's visitor. And while these attendant systems of belief or interpretation may, in the right hands, be useful to the practitioner, they are secondary and ultimately inessential. The way people understand meditation, and even the sequence of changes that results from consistent practice, does seem to vary from school to school, probably because the culture of each school generates expectations that tend to be, at least in part, self-fulfilling. But at root meditation is a purely psychological technique capable of effecting change in a sceptic just as much as in a believer. It trains awareness in the same way as the learning and automatization of mnemonics train one's ability to remember lists or names.

In Buddhist terms, we might characterize meditation as being like science, and the meditator as a scientist — but a scientist of a particular sort. First he is not collecting data and building a theoretical account of a novel phenomenon. Rather he is like a scientist who comes across a well-developed, widely accepted, almost taken for granted theory, and decides to submit it to renewed scrutiny. Furthermore he is determined that his examination is going to be ruthless. Nothing is going to be taken on trust. Every claim of the theory to provide an adequate account of some phenomenon is going to be checked. Every argument is going to be tested for its logic. Every assertion, every axiom will be explored to see whether it is a necessary component of the overall theoretical structure or not. Is it justified? Is it needed? What does it add?

The scientist who undertakes such a task is up against one major obstacle that the explorer of new territory does not have to overcome. For as well as inspecting the internal logic and consistency of the theory he has to go back to the data and review the theory's explanatory adequacy. And here lies the problem: for a well-established theory such as we are considering will have, as theories inevitably do when they become the orthodoxy, influenced the very way that scientists think about, observe, collect, and select the data. The theory not only provides the content that is to be investigated, but it will have influenced the very processes of experimentation, observation, and interpretation that are to provide the tools for its investigation. Assumptions about what are 'important' or 'relevant' measurements to make, what are the 'sensible' questions to ask, what are 'legitimate' methodologies, and so on, will have become infused into every part of the researcher's *modus operandi*. He cannot therefore trust his own impulses, intuitions, and perceptions, for they may have been contaminated by exactly those presuppositions that he is at pains to unearth and inspect.

It is for just this reason, Kuhn (1970) has argued, that the progress of what he calls 'normal science' is so slow, and the reorganization of scientific thought that takes place during a 'paradigm shift' so dramatic. A scientific revolution always involves uncovering and discarding assumptions about the proper way of doing science, or thinking about it, that one never knew one had made at all. And having shifted a corner-stone, so to speak, the whole edifice must be rebuilt in a new form.

Thus the scientist who undertakes such a task must be constantly critical of his own reactions. He must exercise super vigilance lest a crucial presupposition slips through on the nod. He has to learn to stand outside his reactions and perceptions, to find a vantage point on 'higher ground' which gives him a greater distance and a greater objectivity.

This is precisely the position of the meditator, who has set himself a task of just this sort, and who, in order to have any chance of success, has to exercise just this kind of scepticism and caution. In fact this project is still more difficult, for it is to scrutinize his own personal theory about the world, other people, and himself, which contains the most deeply held and deeply buried beliefs and assumptions of all. He has somehow to look at the commonplaces of his own experience with a fresh eye, and with the suspicion that, if the Buddhist doctrines are right, he is in for some nasty shocks. He must observe the workings of his own mind and start, with scrupulous honesty, to discard beliefs, however cherished or engrained, that turn out to be inaccurate, unjustified, or unnecessary.

Some traditions would dispute this account of the meditator's job, but I think it would find favour with a wide variety of schools. It is close in spirit to the rationales of *vipassana* meditation, which is the practice that Buddha himself reputedly taught, and which aims explicitly for naturally occurring insight into the workings of one's own mind, and the presuppositional framework on which experience is built. Philip Kapleau (1980), a *roshi* (master) in the Zen tradition, says: 'That our sufferings are rooted in a selfish grasping and in fears and terrors which spring from our ignorance of the true nature of life and death becomes clear to anyone compelled by *zazen* (meditation) to confront himself nakedly'. And, to give just one more example from a contemporary Western meditation teacher, Barry Long (1982) says:

there is something that is always sneaking past your guard and getting added to yourself without your scrutiny — your impressions. You have been under a constant bombardment of impressions since the day you were born. They are as subtle and imperceptible as breathing, and the terrible fact is that most of them are false . . . In meditation we start checking for ourselves the validity of our knowledge, all the facts we have been handed in packaged deals since we were children and have used as a 35-inch yardstick ever since . . .

A normal person who treasures an object as being genuine and then discovers it is false will discard it. There is often an embarrassing haste to be rid of it, followed by a feeling of relief or even freedom. You can never cling to what you know is false. It works the same with our impressions of ourselves . . . If you face the fact that what you observe is you and refuse to turn your head by making excuses for it by justifying it to yourself or anyone else, it will start to drop away. And you will feel pain as though a part of you were dying

This quotation raises two other respects in which the meditator's job is even more difficult than that of the sceptical scientist. First, many of the beliefs that he must bring to the surface and evaluate anew are not only cherished, they actually constitute part of the meditator's own identity. If one is committed to an image of oneself as kind, or heterosexual, then thoughts of malice, or homosexual fantasies surfacing unbidden during meditation will be very hard to bear. There is a deep investment in not attending to this unwanted data about oneself, for to do so means abandoning part of the picture of who one thought oneself to be. One has, in Barry Long's terms, quite literally to die a little. And when we get down to those parts of the theory of self — separateness, permanence, and autonomy — that we have discussed above, the sense of threat and the resistance to giving them up can be enormous.

Meditation and psychotherapy

The other major problem for the meditator is that he will slowly have to overcome his deep-seated propensity for 'selective inattention'. To retain one's faith in a theory that both ignores and contradicts aspects of reality requires one to regulate perception so that the theory's inadequaces are tactically ignored. Like a scientist who has become too attached to his point of view we have learnt to conduct only those experiments and register only those data that are consistent with what we already believe. Buddhism agrees with psychotherapy in seeing people as having equipped themselves with defensive habits that may once have served them well, but that now keep them stuck. Recapturing an attitude of 'openness to experience' (Rogers 1961) is seen as being as crucial to the development of spiritual insight as it is to personal growth and the transcendence of neurosis.

There are in fact strong parallels between such systems as gestalt therapy (Perls *et al.* 1973) or rational–emotive therapy (Ellis 1975) and the spiritual traditions that derive from Buddhist teaching. In both, the expansion of awareness is the key: they differ in the areas of personal belief on which this open and non-judgemental awareness is focused. In therapy, clients begin cautiously to examine aspects of their personal theory that state 'I am bad': I am bad because I have unkind thoughts; I am bad because I cling to others; I am bad because I feel things that good people do not feel; and so on. In a context of friendship and trust, these intimidating precepts can be brought to mind and, in the light of the therapist's continued and genuine refusal to provide corroboration for them, re-evaluated or discarded. In this way aspects of experience can be cleansed of their threatening contamination, and be reowned and reintegrated. The boundary of self expands to include them.

The effects of meditation

But the boundary itself remains unexamined and unquestioned in this process. The sense of self is unimpaired, or even strengthened as the pain of inner conflict is resolved. The branches are trimmed, but the roots remain. In meditation, the twin torches of scepticism and receptivity are turned on the boundary itself. The beliefs in a self that is separate, continuous, coherent, and executive are brought to light, and set against the facts of experience. As meditative skill increases and stabilizes, so meditators are able to 'catch' experience before it has been tampered with by the constraints of self. They begin to notice how constant the stream of commentary and judgement is. They see, often with horror, how little control they have over this 'voice'. They see how jumbled and bizarre much of thought is. A steadfast attention to the facts of the matter reveal that the much-prized faculties of reason and choice are corks bobbing on a sea of uncontrolled and unknown influences. In general, experience, caught before the usual beliefs have been stirred into it, like sugar into tea, seems not to be one's own after all, but wells up from an inner spring over which one has neither ownership nor power. And as the questioning proceeds so the premises of self-hood begin to crumble: increasingly one's experience is of a selfless life that at first has an unfamiliar taste (like unsweetened tea), but one which is, though not without some backsliding and some misgivings, acquirable and ultimately preferable. The lies and evasions that have been used to bolster up the self are slowly dropped, and experience becomes thereby more vivid, more exact. The meditator acquires a discernible presence (in the sense of being present, being 'on the ball') and a heightened sensitivity to situations and to people (Shapiro and Walsh 1982). As the preoccupation with one's self, one's identity, and the stratagems for self-preservation start to peel away so one thinks and judges less and one has more time for others. Though the research evidence is scant, the growing interest in meditation as a component of a psychotherapist's training suggests the validity of this claim (see e.g. Welwood 1983; Claxton 1986). And as the inevitability of change and the limits of control sink home, so resistance, resentment, and frustration seem to lessen and simplicity, spontaneity, kindliness, and humour take their place.

Further research

These are the claims of the meditative traditions, whether Buddhist, Christian, Islamic, or Jewish, and though, as I have said, the research evidence (which other chapters in this book review more fully) is scant, they should not thereby be ignored. Rather they need looking into, and in different ways than have commonly been used up to now. As Michael West shows (Chapter 1), the vast bulk of the research has sought to demonstrate immediate effects of meditation in relative novices. Perhaps we should instead be looking for longer-term changes in those who have practised meditation for some years. The course of true meditation, according to many personal accounts (e.g. Goleman 1977; Levine 1979), does not run any more smoothly than that of true love, and we would do better to look for its effects in gradual shifts in attitude and personality over substantial periods of time than in the lowering of heart rate over half an hour. From the Buddhist point of view, the ambiguity of this latter kind of research is to be expected, for the experiential enquiry into the foundations of personal belief is a difficult and scary business. It requires us to look in the eye that from which we have been averting our gaze for most of our lives, and the equanimity that is accruing is going to be punctuated again and again by apprehension, anxiety, and a slipping back into the old familiar ways. Meditation is an archaeological dig into the buried commitments we have made, and it is inevitable that we will be unsettled, from time to time, by what we have unearthed. That is the point.

3   Meditation: contemporary theoretical
     approaches*

Michael M. Delmonte

Introduction

There is a need to examine meditation within a theoretical context in
order to formulate hypotheses about what the meditation experience
may involve and how practice may be therapeutic. Consideration of
these hypotheses, and testing them empirically as well as clinically and
phenomenologically, should lead to a deeper understanding of meditation.
There is now a large corpus of research findings on meditation. Theoretical models are needed to structure them so that we are not left with
an amorphous scattering of data and outcomes about which no
comprehensive deductions can be made.

   No single model may be able to account for the full complexity of
the meditation experience. All models appear to have their strengths
and limitations and have defined 'ranges of convenience'. For this reason
meditation will be examined from theoretical perspectives which are
divergent in emphasis and which focus on different aspects of human
experience and behaviour.

   This chapter will first begin with a series of approaches to meditation including 'information-processing', 'consciousness', and the 'bilateral brain',
before taking these and other aspects of meditation and conceptualizing
them further in terms of psychodynamic, behavioural, and constructivist
orientations. Some general conclusions about the strengths and
limitations of these theoretical approaches will then be discussed as well
as some recommendations for future research and theorising.

Information-processing approaches

Processes of attention are central in any understanding of meditation.
Washburn (1978) describes concentrative meditation as sustained
attention with specific focus, and receptive meditation as sustained
attention without such focus (see Chapter 1 for the distinction between
these meditations). The consequence of this intentional manipulation
of attention is reported to be an increased awareness of mental processes
that are usually unconscious. Washburn posits that during meditation
unconscious operations become known because of the interference with

*An elaboration of 'Models of Meditation'; Delmonte, M. and Kenny, V. (1985). *British
Journal of Psychotherapy*, **1** (3), 197–214.

their normal functioning, whether by their resistance in receptive meditation or by their temporary suppression in concentrative meditation. So, even though the two meditation approaches are distinct they are nevertheless both thought to facilitate insight into mental operations.

Traditionally meditation has been seen as a path leading towards enlightenment. This path is beset with obstacles such as habitual patterns of automatic behaviour, governed by impulses, desires, and the illusion that the self and the rest of the world are separate (the notion of duality). Meditation is seen as a means of overcoming these obstacles by teaching the individual to see the world as it really is, free from preconceptions. Deikman (1966) has called this process 'deautomatization' following Hartmann's (1958) definition of 'automatization' as the building up of motor and perceptual habits. Deikman argues that through meditation there is a deautomatization of automatic perception, cognition, and behaviour, and that in meditation a deliberate attempt is made to perceive all events as novel occurrences. In particular, Deikman believes that cognition is inhibited in favour of perception, and the active intellectual style is replaced by the receptive perceptual mode. Shafii (1973) too sees meditation as a way of helping to free the individual from 'repetitive and automatic behaviour'. The end point of meditation, 'enlightment', is seen as a consequence of this deautomatization, when the meditator permanently transcends ordinary consciousness which is primarily automatic. Thus, the enlightened person is seen to process information phenomenologically, that is, via perception in its 'pure' form 'uncontaminated' by built-up habits (though how can one know if this is really possible?)

Attention is deliberately focused during the concentrative forms of meditation and includes elements of both sensory fixation and sensory limitation. Many objects can serve for the sensory fixation such as a mantra (usually a sacred word), one's breath, a candle flame, repetitive prayer, and a waterfall. In mantra meditation the attention is focused on monotonous repetition of the mantra while sensory input is often limited by the meditator sitting comfortably in a dimly lit and quiet environment. The repetition of the mantra may help to displace and interrupt normal thought processes with a consequent reduction in clear and logical mentation.

It is likely too that the repetition, through a process of inhibition, induces a condition similar to hypnotic trance (Delmonte 1981b, 1984a). Ornstein (1972) suggests that the prolonged focusing of attention on to a single stimulus, which leads to stimulus habituation, may cause the subjective experience of the disappearance of the mantra and all thought, leaving a blank awareness of 'no thought' experience—exactly the experience described by so many mystics. Piggins and Morgan (1977) have noted that steady visual fixation and repetitious auditory input produce altered states of awareness, characterized by the experience of 'no thought'. In meditation such experiences are reported to be accompanied by sensations of great tranquility and 'pure awareness' or 'bare witnessing', without interfering mentation such as the analysis of experience or the drawing of conclusions. However, this state is not easily achieved because throughout meditation there are 'circulating thoughts' which interrupt the focus on the mantra (or other object of meditation). Unpleasant memories, day residues, small worries, and recent positive experiences come into consciousness (West 1980a, 1982). Tart (1971) believes that partially processed experiences are brought back into consciousness during meditation and are reprocessed or 'worked off'.

Non-concentrative forms of meditation accomplish their effects by other means. For example, in the Rinzai school of Zen Buddhism, disciples are instructed to meditate on a *koan* or paradoxical riddle such as 'What is the sound of one hand clapping?'. In the process of attempting to find an answer the disciple may come to the realization that the logical mind cannot clearly comprehend the world and the student spontaneously relinquishes categories and preconceptions at the moment of 'awakening'. In other schools the individual may be asked to contemplate a theme such as 'unconditional love'. In mindfulness techniques the meditator is encouraged to maintain 'a quiet awareness, without comment, of whatever happens to be here and now' (Watts 1957). The objective of mindfulness meditation is 'to come to know one's own mental processes, to thus begin to have the power to shape or control the mental processes, and finally to gain freedom from the condition where the mental processes are unknown and uncontrolled, with the individual at the mercy of his own unbridled mind' (Deatherage 1975, p. 134). Hendricks (1975) sees such introspection as a form of discrimination training which helps meditators observe their own thoughts in a relatively detached way. He speculates that 'since nearly everyone has a certain number of neurotic thoughts, mental health is dependent upon the ability to recognise that they are "just thoughts"' (p. 145).

In summary, many authors contend that the practice of meditation enhances the practitioner's awareness of how perceptual information is processed. Such an awareness is envisaged as leading to greater enlightenment.

Meditation and consciousness

Deikman (1971), who was one of the pioneering researchers on meditation, developed the notion of 'bimodal consciousness', constituting an active and a passive mode. This notion has been invoked in a number of explanations of the process and effects of meditation. The active mode is 'a state of striving, oriented towards achieving personal goals' (p. 481) and is relatively verbal and motoric, engaging the musculo-skeletal system. The receptive mode is inward oriented, introspective, and involves reflexivity and circumspection rather than pre-emption, that is, looking at how one processes reality rather than jumping to conclusions about it. The receptive mode is thus more concerned with perceptual intake than with decisive action. It is largely perceptual and vegetative, with functioning usually occurring at a non-locomotory level. Whereas in the action mode the individual is involved in pursuing goals, the receptive mode tends to be associated with a 'letting go' attitude. Both cognitive and motoric functioning are largely suspended and there is mental and physical quiescence (what Benson *et al.* 1974b call the 'relaxation response'). The action mode, on the other hand, in its extreme form involves what Cannon (1914) called the 'fight or flight' response, where there is acute mobilization of the body's physiological and cortical resources.

Several authors have suggested that one of the consequences of meditation practice is the enhancement of the receptive mode (Maupin 1969; Deikman 1971; Ornstein 1972), since it generally involves developing a receptive or passive attitude. Maupin describes meditation as producing 'a deep passivity combined with awareness' (p. 180). However, the earlier stages of concentrative meditation are sometimes seen as involving the action mode before a quiescent state is reached (cf. Fromm 1977; Washburn 1978). Techniques such as TM and Zen breathing meditation incorporate both concentration and mindfulness elements in what is sometimes called 'passive concentration'. But whatever the technique, the objective is to develop a receptive and non-attached mental set to all experiences occurring during meditation.

The usefulness of the bimodal consciousness concept is that it allows us to see the importance of receptivity (i.e. permeability to new experiences) during the practice of meditation. If meditation were characterized by great activity it is doubtful if one could be receptive to one's internal state, or develop an awareness of the content of one's mind.

Bilateral brain model

Ornstein, following Galin (1974), has argued that meditation is a right cerebral hemisphere mediated experience. He contrasts the left hemisphere mode of experiencing, which he sees as rational, sequential, logical, analytical, verbal, and linear, with the right hemisphere mode, which is seen as intuitive, diffuse, holistic, spatial, and simultaneous. He suggests that the right hemisphere mode corresponds with Deikman's receptive mode and the left with the action mode. Ornstein views meditation as a method for transcending the habitual experience of consciousness through achieving a receptive mental set and experiencing intuitively in gestalts, rather than sequentially and analytically. This leads to the deautomatization of experience, to insight, and ultimately, he proposes, to changed behaviour. Ornstein sees the meditator on a path to transcending the normal selective and restrictive consciousness that characterizes personal construction of reality.

Abdullah and Schucman (1976) and Prince (1978) also contend that during meditation logical analytical thinking is blocked or temporarily discouraged by mantra repetition. Similarly, Davidson (1976) suggests that meditation is an activity which develops 'dormant' right hemisphere capacities. Galin (1974) argues that the non-dominant hemisphere is the repository of unconscious processes and that this material is usually expressed non-verbally through somatic and autonomic symptoms. Thus the insight achieved during meditation involves developing awareness of these unconscious processes of inherited and conditioned behaviours, and of the way in which we construct reality.

However, this 'split brain' model has been challenged by Earle (1981) who concludes that there is no evidence that advanced meditation either inhibits left hemisphere processing or enhances the activities of the right. Rather the evidence suggests that 'in the early stages of meditation, relative right hemisphere activation may be induced through the control of attention, the use of visual imagery and the inhibition of verbal–analytical thought. During the advanced stages of meditation, however, cognitive functions associated with each hemisphere are either automatised or inhibited, leading to a reduction in cortical activity or diminished cortical participation in the generation of mental phenomena' (p. 167).

Warrenburg and Pagano (1982/3) also conclude that there is no evidence that meditation practice over time either facilitates 'globally right hemisphere specialised performance' or impairs left hemisphere performance. On the contrary, they suggest that those who maintain long-term adherence to meditation practice were already predisposed, prior to commencing meditation, to utilize their attention to become totally absorbed in a non-verbal (right hemisphere) mode. In other words, those who are both attracted to and maintain meditation practice have relatively lower levels of left hemisphere processing than other people, and higher levels of right hemisphere processing. They also found that those who maintained regular meditation practice had high scores on tonal memory (a right hemisphere task) and absorption. Finally, there is compelling evidence that the absorption trait is a predictor of a positive response (in terms of practice) to meditation and to relaxation, as well as of self-reports of benefits from practice (Pagano and Warrenburg 1983).

In conclusion, it does not appear that in the long term meditation practice is associated with a shift to right hemisphere dominance. Rather it appears that those who maintain practice already demonstrate relatively high levels of right hemisphere activity.

Psychoanalytic approaches

Many psychoanalytic writers have regarded meditation as a way of inducing regression to more basic psychic functioning, or to what Alexander (1931) called 'a sort of artificial schizophrenia with complete withdrawal of libidinal interest from the outside world' (p. 130). This description derives from the traditional aim of overcoming attachment to desires and drives, and of overcoming the need to gratify the ego. Kretschmer (1962) described meditation as a way of learning to 'control the archetypes' within and to be 'free' from them (p. 80).

Although many authors acknowledge that regression is a feature of meditation they do not describe it as pathological because it is a voluntary condition (e.g. Boals 1978). Several authors distinguish between pathological regression and the adaptive regression of meditation, or regression in the service of the ego (Maupin 1962; Shafii 1973; Fromm 1977). A number of researchers have found that a capacity for adaptive regression and a tolerance for unrealistic experience is related to the practice of meditation (Maupin 1962; Lesh 1970b; Curtin 1973).

Jung (1958) described Buddhist meditation as 'a sort of Royal Road to the unconscious' (p. 508) and saw meditation as a 'surrender' to the collective unconscious. Kretschmer (1962) describes meditation in a similar way: 'Dreams are similar to meditation except meditation gains the reaction of the unconscious by a technique which is faster than depending on dreams' (p. 76). There is clearly much overlap, in terms of both subjective experience and objective indicators between dreams, hypnagogic reverie, hypnoidal states, and meditation (see Delmonte 1981b, 1984a).

Also relevant to the study of meditation is Freud's (1958) suggestion that mental functioning can be differentiated into primary and secondary process. Whereas secondary process mentation is logical, is expressed linguistically and is reality orientated, primary process mentation is characterized by non-verbal imagery and by poor or absent reality orientation. Fromm (1977) has integrated these concepts with her notions of ego activity and ego receptivity and applied them to the understanding of techniques such as meditation and hypnosis. Ego activity is seen as reality orientated, and characterized by conceptualization, focused attention, and a secondary process cognitive mode. Ego receptivity, on the other hand, is seen as involving a primary process cognitive mode, that is, the mode 'typical of preverbal childhood' (p. 374) and rich in imagery as opposed to logical concepts. While most psychoanalysts conceive of primary process as an id mode, Fromm

(p. 374) describes it as 'the cognitive process of the unconscious ego'. Ego receptivity is envisaged as involving unfocused free-floating attention and fantasy, and is supposedly enhanced by meditation and hypnosis. Fromm believes that concentrative meditation initially requires 'unusually great ego activity' (p. 379), but with increased adeptness this gives way to ego receptivity. This fits with descriptions of increased deautomization, receptivity (Deikman 1966; Ornstein 1972), and mindfulness (Brown and Engler 1980), which accrue with meditation practice over time.

Davidson (1976) takes this one step further and postulates a direct link between the meditative state, right hemisphere functioning and primary process cognition 'which characterise the so-called sub- or unconscious mind' (p. 371). He argues that primary process mentation corresponds to right hemisphere functioning and secondary process thinking to left hemisphere activity. Fromm (1981) suggests that for novice meditators there may be an increase in primary process type experience, but that in the advanced stage of meditation all cognitive processing decreases: 'Logic, reasoning, imagery, memory and even anticipation no longer occur' (p. 41). Advanced meditators 'no longer focus on the contents that we call cognitive processes, either Secondary or Primary. . . Instead, they purportedly turn their awareness back on itself, on the very process of the workings of the mind' (p. 42).

In summary, the psychoanalytic approach, with its concepts of regression and primary process cognition, is useful in understanding the numerous reports of non-verbal experiences during meditation. Many of these experiences are habitually repressed but may be expressed during meditation—a topic which will be taken up in the next section.

Behavioural approaches

Behavioural orientations to meditation have led to much concern with the value of meditation as a therapeutic tool (see Chapter 8) and particularly as a stress reduction technique. Meditators from TM groups, for example, often refer to 'unstressing', which is described as the resurfacing of repressed and distressing material during meditation (e.g. feelings of anger or panic). Unstressing can be so strong for some people that they give up meditation (Glueck and Stroebel 1975). Others, especially those with a history of psychogenic disorders, have overt psychotic episodes during meditation (Benson *et al.* 1974a, 1975b; Glueck and Stroebel 1975; Lazarus 1976). Unpleasant physical and emotional sensations, and disturbing thoughts and imagery, during meditation have been reported by a sizeable minority of subjects (e.g. Otis 1974a; Carrington and Ephron 1975a; Kohr 1977, 1978; Walsh and Roche 1979; West 1980a, 1982). However, for many people mild 'unstressing' or release of tension during meditation results in a feeling of well-being after practice.

Goleman (1971) and Otis (1974a) suggest that meditation may be a form of self-paced systematic desensitization with slow exposure to unpleasant memories being accompanied by the relaxed physiological state induced by the practice of meditation. Carrington and Ephron (1975b) describe how the meditator semi-automatically selects material for desensitization according to what: (1) is most pressing emotionally, (2) is most likely to be tolerated without undue anxiety, and (3) is best handled at the present time.

Greenwood and Benson (1977) have argued that meditative techniques are more appropriate than abbreviated progressive relaxation training as reciprocal inhibitors in systematic desensitization. This is because studies of brief progressive relaxation training have not shown it to produce decreased autonomic arousal levels. Research has also suggested that deliberate muscle tensing is no less effective than relaxation in the outcome of systematic desensitization. Furthermore, they argue that it is not clear whether reciprocal inhibition or habituation is the agent involved in systematic desensitization. However, in either case, they suggest that meditative relaxation would be superior to progressive relaxation because it leads both to decreased autonomic activity and to enhanced imagery. Meditation is seen as involving self-paced desensitization to anxiety-evoking mentation while in a relaxed condition.

The suggestion that meditation is a technique that involves reciprocal inhibition and counter-conditioning leading to desensitization of anxiety-evoking thoughts has gained considerable support (e.g. Berwick and Oziel 1973; Otis 1974a; Shapiro and Zifferblat 1976a; Avila and Nummela 1977; Block 1977; Mikulas 1978, 1981). Meditation has also been described using behavioural terms such as 'stimulus control', 'self-instructions', 'non-evaluative self-observation', 'self-contract', and 'behavioural thought stopping' (Shapiro and Zifferblat 1976a). Mikulas (1978) has developed the Buddhist theme that 'life is full of suffering' and that 'the source of suffering is craving' (p. 62). He envisaged meditation as a technique involving 'self-observation and functional analysis of overt and covert behaviours' (p. 63) which leads to relaxation, desensitization, and non-attachment. Carpenter (1977) suggests that meditative exercises provide three therapeutic gains, namely insight into repetitive self-defeating patterns of behaviour and thinking (e.g. cravings), desensitization of painful thoughts, and conditioning of the central nervous system.

Meditation is also popularly seen as a relaxation technique (e.g. Wallace 1970; Wallace and Benson 1972; Shapiro and Zifferblat 1976a). During meditation there is a decrease in physiological arousal (Benson *et al.* 1974a) and many meditators report feeling relaxed during meditation (West 1980a). However, in some forms of yoga meditation (e.g. Raja and Tantric meditations) there is a deliberate attempt to achieve an 'ecstatic' trance which involves arousal rather than relaxation. Das and Gastaut (1955) and Corby *et al.* (1978) observed such high arousal among experienced practitioners during periods of reported yogic ecstacy. Nevertheless, these are exceptions since most researchers report decreased arousal during meditation. This has led Boals (1978) to suggest that relaxation is elicited through a process of classical conditioning when the mantra becomes a conditioned relaxation stimulus. Some research evidence supports this interpretation (Delmonte 1979).

In summary, the behavioural view of meditation tends to see meditation in terms of its possible relaxation effects. Anxiety-provoking thoughts are described as being desensitized while in the relaxed state produced by meditation. Meditation is also seen as a technique of thought control and self-observation. In this sense meditation is envisaged as having a practical value.

Constructivist approaches

Both psychodynamic theory and behaviour theory stem from a realist epistemological and empiricist approach. With this approach it is assumed that a direct understanding of reality can be arrived at by scientific objectification. In more recent years, however, constructivist psychologists have drawn attention to developments in physics and biology which challenge this assumption. 'Objective' reality is postulated to be beyond direct human perception given the constraints imposed by the structure of our sensory equipment and of our nervous system. This section views meditation mainly from the constructivist orientation of George Kelly.

Ornstein (1972) has drawn parallels between Kelly's (1955) formulation of personal construct psychology and his own suggestion that reality is a personal construction. Ornstein suggests that meditation is a technique which facilitates insight into how one processes or constructs reality. Kelly (1955) sees us as living in two realities — firstly the primary reality beyond direct human perception and secondly the interpretations or constructions of this primary reality. For Kelly, we are like scientists developing bipolar constructs in order to make sense of the world by looking for repetitive patterns of similarity and difference among a series of events occurring along a time line. Emerging from past experiences, these constructs organize the anticipation of future events. Even as infants before we acquire language we construe events dichotomously via bipolar discriminations such as 'up versus down', 'mother versus not mother', 'thick versus thin', 'hot versus cold', 'me versus not me', and so forth. These discriminations or constructs are initially preverbal, and although the growing child comes to attach verbal labels to many such discriminations, according to Kelly, much of adult construal remains non-verbal. As each person moves along the dimension of time he modifies his own personal construct system so as to be able to anticipate more accurately the future ahead. Construct systems thus act as templates against which we match our perceptions and experiences of the world.

There is some similarity between the concepts of personal construct theory and those of Buddhist psychology (see Chapter 2). Both acknowledge that normal human understanding of the universe involves the use of dualistic dimensions to make sense of a unitary universe (McWilliams 1984). Buddhist approaches emphasize the need to see through the illusion of duality via techniques such as meditation. On the other hand, constructivist psychologists would focus on the utility of dualistic construing and on the value of elaborating a more sophisticated and effective personal construct system in order to be able to predict events more accurately. Buddhists see suffering as stemming from our desire to force the universe to conform; to our dualistic and egocentric cravings, beliefs, and values, creating divisions and boundaries in a universe that is holistic and unitary: 'to the extent that we attend to conventional, dichotomous, ideas about the universe, we are taken away from direct, immediate experience of the universe' (p. 2). Buddhists believe it is possible to transcend the delusion of our self-invented dualistic world and, in seeing the transparency of our construct system, to experience unity. Such an experience comes from an awareness, cultivated in meditation, of how we personally construct our view of reality. The meditator, by obtaining insight into the workings of the mind, can be viewed as a scientist experimenting with experiences of self and the world, and engaged in a reflexive exploration of his or her own sense-making equipment.

How would constructivists view the processes of meditation? From the Kellian perspective, meditation involves two main 'cognitive sets', namely constriction and dilation. In one set, attention acts to exclude or severely curtail construing by reducing the number of elements to be dealt with to a minimum—as in concentrative meditation. In the other mental set there is a suspension of habitual construing while attending to a wide range of disconnected elements that come into consciousness, as in mindfulness meditation.

Concentrative meditation

Meditators employing concentrative techniques can be viewed as deliberately experimenting with 'constriction' in the Kellian sense, which involves shrinking the perceptual field to a few elements in an attempt to reorganize the construct system so that everything is reduced to one bipolar element which needs little construing (e.g. mantra versus no mantra). Mantra repetition may thus help to block temporarily or limit the emergence of verbally labelled constructs, leading either to 'no thought' or to preverbal construing. Because extreme constriction reduces construing there may be increased concreteness of construing together with regression to preverbal construing (e.g. feelings of sexual arousal, hate, love, fear, aggression, changed body size, and temporal distortion). This preverbal material can be more or less 'neutral' or relatively intense and traumatic ('unstressing').

Very traumatic unstressing is likely to render meditation a rather unpleasant and aroused experience, and may lead to decreased frequency of practice. For some of those who persist, covert reality testing of traumatic constructs during the relaxed meditation state may lead to the desensitization of anxiety-evoking material released during meditation. After meditation one may then develop an alternative construal of past unpleasant experiences. Indeed, it is possible that, as well as emotions, time, space, colour, etc. may acquire new dimensions as a result of the reorganization of one's construct system.

For novices, and during the early stages of meditation, there may be a shift towards relative right hemisphere type activity as the meditator desists from habitual cognitive construal ('secondary process' mentation in psychodynamic terms) and moves to a preverbal level of construal ('primary process' mentation). The constant repetition of a mantra may lead to a trance-like state during which one's repression 'barriers' are weakened by a reduced ability to marshal the cognitive or intellectual defences of a more alert state. It is likely that this trance-like condition will include hypnagogic reverie and loose construal (similar to the strange, surrealistic thoughts we sometimes experience just as we drop off to sleep) typically produced when a low arousal state is coupled with reduced sensory input. Similarly, the preverbal construal which emerges during concentrative meditation is often relatively loose. It is perhaps through such processes that exteroception is severely curtailed and the meditator has recourse to proprioception and interoception.

Mindfulness meditation

The mindfulness techniques can be seen as Kellian 'dilation' whereby the person broadens the perceptual field to include more elements, with the ultimate aim of a more comprehensive organization of the construct system. There is a suspension of habitual cognitive construing (rather than a blocking or an inhibiting as in concentrative meditation), with the self and thoughts construed as elements which are observed in a non-attached or non-judgemental way (i.e. 'bare witnessing'). This non-evaluative free-flowing attention (or 'choiceless awareness') is rather like free association—the spontaneous generation of thoughts and emotions. During mindfulness meditation attention is said to be 'deautomatized', that is, the meditator views the contents of awareness, free from his or her habitual prejudices, as novel events. In a sense the construer takes a 'holiday' from using verbally labelled constructions. As habitual cognitive construal is suspended there is recourse to preverbal construing with the consequent liberation of more vegetative and somatic constructs. Depending on what is in this preverbal reservoir, the meditator explores uncharted areas of the self through experiencing emotions such as fear, anger, anxiety, and sexual arousal, or 'no thought' if the preverbal material has been 'worked through'. The meditator may also experience temperature, temporal, and spatial distortion, hallucinations, and so forth. This 'uncovered' self then becomes part of the conscious self.

In constructivist terms both concentrative and mindfulness meditation therefore lead to a decrease in 'cognitive' construal with a consequent increase in non-verbal construing. Whereas during concentrative meditation 'cognitive' construal is inhibited, during mindfulness it is suspended. Depending on what unresolved emotional material is present, and on the level of adeptness, meditation may be a traumatic experience of unstressing, or a very tranquil experience of 'no-thought', and may involve trance, hypnagogic reverie, and increased suggestibility.

To what extent can this analysis of meditation techniques in constructivist terms be extended to account for some of the phenomena characteristic of meditation such as stimulus habituation, 'unstressing', transcendence, and 'deautomatization'?

Stimulus habituation

Concentrative meditation purportedly leads to a condition of 'no thought' via stimulus habituation. In Kellian terms focusing on a repetitive stimulus means that there will be no perceptual changes (differences or contrasts) and therefore no constructs developed and no anticipation made (since the future is now assumed to be the same as the past and the present). Stimulus repetition means that there is 'no news of a difference' (see Bateson 1980). Similarly, Naranjo and Ornstein (1971) drew an analogy between going 'blank' in the Ganzfeld experiments and the 'no-thought' state during advanced concentrative meditation. In both cases, stimulus repetition leads to stimulus habituation and to inhibition of cognitive construal. Thus, one construes the monotonous stimulus repetition as 'boring' and 'unchanging', and as likely to lead only to more of the same, rather than to any 'news of a difference'. Since our construct system is anticipatory in nature, one anticipates only the lack of need for further anticipation. The person 'switches off' the anticipator attitude since the future is predicted to be identical to both the past and the present. No 'cognitive' constructs are needed.

Unstressing

Unstressing can be conceptualized as the coming into consciousness of repressed material due to the blocking in meditation of habitual verbally labelled construing. During concentrative meditation, the focusing on a monotonous stimulus disrupts thinking and inhibits the mobilization of one's usual defensive constructions, thereby allowing the expression of what psychoanalysts would call 'repressed material'. Repressed material ('suspended elements' in Kellian terms) may be experienced in the form of preverbal constructs such as fear, panic, anger, hatred, irritation, etc. There appear to be many similarities between the cathartic release of preverbal material found during meditative unstressing, and that found in the abreaction of free association. Both may have much in common with the cathartic phenomena found by Grof (1975) in his work with psychedelic drugs and more recently with hyperventilation. It may be that hyperventilation, like relaxation, acts as a 'loosening' exercise at the somatic level and facilitates the expression of preverbal material.

Transcendence

The notion of transcendence, as traditionally understood, is incompatible with personal construct theory. Firstly, Kelly insists on the notion of bipolarity of constructs, that is, one always abstracts on the basis of both similarity and contrast since dichotomy is an essential feature of thinking. This contradicts Zen meditation masters, for example, who continually exhort their students to transcend the illusion of opposites. Kelly says that while we can transcend our biography and not become victims of our circumstances, we only do this through developing alternative constructs. One never escapes from one's construct systems, but always perceives the world through them. Thus, when one transcends a particular bipolarity, one tends to climb to a higher and more abstract level, but a level which, none the less, is structured in bipolar terms.

Transcendence is also understood to mean transcending the split between the experience of self and the universe, that is, becoming one with everything. Again, the Kellian position is incompatible because it argues that we always have two realities: reality as it is beyond direct human perception and our interpretation of reality. Thus, there is always the construer and what is being construed. Since Kelly argues that one cannot transcend one's construct system as a whole, there must always be this duality. In Bruner's (1956) terms, 'you are your constructs', and therefore it does not make sense to talk about transcending one's construct system since this would mean somehow transcending one's self.

It is relatively easy to see how one can transcend verbally labelled constructs, by either blocking them or suspending them, but none the less constructivists would argue that one must still be construing at the preverbal or somatic level. It may be that meditation directly or indirectly elaborates the preverbal construing of the person so that it supercedes the verbally labelled constructions. But this is 'descendence' from the 'mind' to the 'body', rather than transcendence, in which descendence implies moving 'down' from 'cognitive' to preverbal construal (in psychodynamic terms this is akin to adaptive regression, as opposed to psychotic regression). Ascendence, on the other hand, describes a movement 'up' to a higher verbalized bipolar construct, that is to superordinate construal within one's personal construct system. Transcendence, as in 'no thought', might be the feeling of unity or bliss when the meditator has the experience of transcending the bipolarity of all construal. But construct theory would propose that the meditator is nevertheless still construing at a very basic somatic level in terms of balance, posture, respiration, osmoregulation, blood pressure, and other vital aspects of metabolism. Transcendence therefore might be understood in construct theory as the recovery of a preverbal sense of 'oneness' or 'individuality' by not confusing the duality of bipolar construal with the essential unity of reality. Construct theory is not at variance with the notion that during 'no thought' one transcends the habitual cognitive mode of construing typical of adults. But it would argue that the meditator is left with preverbal construing and with a feeling of transcendence of the duality of construal, since much preverbal construal is unconscious or at a low level of awareness.

Deautomatization

In Kellian terms deautomatization implies the construal of reality without biased 'perceptual goggles' or filters. For Kelly, perceiving is conclusion making, and conclusions are likely to be arrived at according to one's perceptual biases or expectations. Such biases are likely to be associated with resistance to invalidating evidence. Meditation is ostensibly characterized by enhanced receptivity (Deikman 1971; Ornstein 1972) or, to use construct terms, an increased permeability of one's constructs to new ideas (elements). Meditation can be conceptualized in this way as a process of falsifiable experimentation (Popper 1959) in which constructs are more open to 'the validational fortunes presented by the flux of reality'.

In summary, the constructivist approach is particularly helpful in conceptualizing many phenomena associated with the practice of meditation such as stimulus habituation, unstressing, transcendence, and deautomatization. It also allows one to compare the concentrative and mindfulness techniques in a useful way. Unfortunately, constructivist psychologists are not on the whole favourably disposed towards empiricism and therefore their ideas are not often put to empirical test. This may be difficult anyway, given the nature of their theories.

Conclusion

In conclusion, the various views of meditation all help to build up a deeper understanding of the meditation experience. The behavioural perspective, although somewhat constrained, is relatively easy to put to the test and there already exists a substantial corpus of research in this area. Psychodynamic and constructivist views do not so readily lend themselves to empirical investigation but appear to have greater powers of description. The advantages of the behavioural approach are its utility, parsimony, and verifiability (see Hall and Lindzey 1978 for their definitions of these terms). On the other hand, the psychodynamic and constructivist approaches appear to have substantial heuristic value — especially when it comes to understanding the *subjective* complexities involved in the meditation experience. A particular feature of the constructivist approach is its comprehensiveness (or broad range of convenience). As a theory about theories (or a metatheory) it can subsume other theoretical formulations under its rubric (see Kelly 1955). However, psychodynamic theory, being more established than constructivist theory, provides useful models of meditation because these can be readily related to the existing body of psychodynamic theorizing.

The approaches discussed in this chapter are not exhaustive. Other perspectives, such as Gestalt theory and Gestalt therapy in particular, may also be helpful in coming to a fuller appreciation of the psychological complexities involved in meditation. Gestalt therapy, like meditation practice, focuses on the 'here and now' of experience. The Gestalt approach may be of special relevance to a further understanding of unstressing, which is akin to the reported emergence of 'incomplete Gestalten' (or 'unfinished business') about which much has been written. One may speculate that from a Gestalt viewpoint meditation techniques facilitate the liberation of repressed incomplete Gestalten so that they may be 'relived' emotionally, that is, 'completed' and integrated psychologically. Meditation could also be examined from a Piagetian theoretical perspective. For example, the integration (or 'assimilation' in Piagetian terms) of novel experiences during meditation, or of repressed material via unstressing, would be viewed as requiring 'accommodation' of existing cognitive structures.

One will probably find a certain overlap between the various theoretical approaches as they must try to account for the subjective experiences reported by meditators, as well as for the research findings. The value of a good theory is that it should help to reconcile research outcome with the phenomenology of meditation. Heretofore, research findings have largely been reported in the absence of clearly defined theory and without reference to the experience of meditators. It is hoped that this chapter will go some way to providing theoretical maps and signposts for researchers exploring this area in the future.

Part II:

Research perspectives

Introduction

Since research on meditation began in earnest in the West over 1000 articles have been published in the professional literature. Many different claims have been made by researchers from a variety of institutions and discerning the overall picture this research has given us is not easy, given the divergence of findings and views. To complicate matters further, studies of meditation have involved measurement on a variety of indices including physiological, personality, task performance, information processing, and clinical, and studies in some areas provide a clearer picture than those in others. Here, it is intended to make the task much easier by presenting balanced and comprehensive reviews of relevant research.

The second part of the book therefore builds on the theoretical bases described in Part I and examines the extent to which their predictions are borne out in research. Ronald Pekala presents the first overview of research on the phenomenology of meditation, critically analysing the studies conducted to date. Generally, he finds them wanting in their degree of methodological sophistication but the review provides details of the experiences meditators report during their meditation. Pekala argues that some evidence is suggestive of meditation being a unique altered state of consciousness but feels it is, as yet, far from definitive. A number of recommendations are offered for refining research in the area.

No greater controversy in this field has been aroused than that caused by the publication of David Holmes' (1984) review of research on somatic arousal reduction during meditation. Here he takes a second look at the evidence and comes to conclusions which will no doubt further fuel the flames of controversy. His analysis of the evidence leads him to conclude that the claims made for meditation have far exceeded the evidence to date. His review focuses not just on arousal reduction during meditation, but also on the claimed stress-inhibiting function of meditation practice. In this chapter he offers rejoinders to the critics of his 1984 review and offers them further challenges.

Peter Fenwick reviews the evidence on brain wave activity associated with meditation practice. He begins by describing the electroencephalo-graph (EEG) and cautions against the temptation to draw unsupported inferences from results of EEG research on meditation. He reviews both the early and the more recent research, discussing in detail the use of coherence analysis in studies. The controversy about whether meditation is sleep by another name is examined and firm conclusions drawn. Finally, theoretical predictions (see Part I) about right hemisphere functioning during meditation are assessed in the light of the research evidence. Peter Fenwick's concluding remarks are based partially on his very extensive experience with the EEG and on his long-standing interest in altered states.

The final chapter in this section reviews the research which has examined personality changes associated with meditation practice. Michael Delmonte presents a hierarchy of studies based on their methodological sophistication and shows that most research interest has focused on the effects of meditation on anxiety. His review of the biochemical evidence reaches somewhat different conclusions from those of Holmes in Chapter 5. He reviews and presents conclusions about research examining the effects of meditation on anxiety, self-esteem, self-actualization, locus of control, introversion–extraversion, depression, and psychosomatic symptomatology. Delmonte cautions that the causes of personality change associated with meditation practice cannot be attributed to meditation itself (as opposed to other non-specific factors) until more sophisticated research is conducted.

4   The phenomenology of meditation

Ronald J. Pekala

Meditation is the process of turning consciousness upon itself to develop attentional control of the processes and contents of consciousness. Given that the focus in meditation involves training the mind to become attuned to specific processes or contents of consciousness, the subjective effects associated with meditation assume primary importance. Yet, despite the last two decades of meditation research, the research involving the phenomenological effects of meditation is still in its infancy.

A primary reason for the lack of research into the subjective effects of meditation is the role that subjective data has played in the history of psychology. At the turn of the century structuralists like Wundt (1897) and Titchener (1898) were investigating the structures of subjective experience, while functionalists like James (1890/1950) and Angell (1907) were trying to decipher the operations and functions of consciousness. Introspection was a common psychological tool. But within 20 years classical introspectionism had vanished from psychology textbooks, and was replaced by Watson's (1913) 'behavioural' approach. According to Boring (1953), a historian of psychology, classical introspection became obsolete due to its failure to demonstrate adequate reliability and validity. Classical introspection 'went out of style after Titchener's death in 1927, because it had demonstrated no functional use, and also because it was *unreliable* (my italics)' (p. 174).

The emergence of cognitive psychology in the 1960s and 70s and a simultaneous renewed interest in consciousness have brought a return of introspection as a quasi-acceptable methodology. However, introspection as currently used in cognitive–behavioural and consciousness research is unlike the self-reflection practised by the turn-of-the-century introspectionists. The new introspection is of the phenomenological variety in that it is 'a free commentary on whatever cognitive material the subject is aware of' (Hilgard 1980, p. 10). Subjects do not have to be extensively trained in the practice of introspection, and neither do they need to be restricted to the rigid criteria used by the classical introspectionists to define and report internal experience. As with descriptive phenomenology (Husserl 1913/77), the new introspection involves a 'detailed description of [the phenomena of] consciousness as they appear in consciousness' (Ashworth 1976, p. 364). As such, it has been labelled phenomenological observation or phenomenological assessment.

Reliability, validity, and artefact in phenomenological assessment

As in the past, there is currently much controversy over introspective or phenomenological reports. Nisbett and Wilson (1977) have indicated that introspective access of cognitive processes 'is not sufficient to produce generally correct or reliable reports' (p. 233). Smith and Miller (1978), on the other hand, suggest that cognitive processes may not be as inaccessible as Nisbett and Wilson indicate. Lieberman (1979) has argued for a limited return of introspection, citing the classical and modern literature which has shown that introspective 'data can be highly reliable and useful, helping not only to predict specific behavior, but to discover fundamental principles of learning and performance' (p. 332). From a somewhat different perspective, Ericsson and Simon (1980) have argued that verbal reports (involving introspection) are data just as behavioural observations are data and inaccurate phenomenological reports appear to 'result from requesting information that was never directly heeded, thus forcing subjects to *infer* rather than *remember* (my italics) their mental processes' (p. 215).

The question of reliability suggests that validity may be difficult to confirm. Although the data presented by Ericsson and Simon (1980), Klinger (1978), and Lieberman (1979) indicate that introspective data can be both useful and valid, Rachlin (1974) and Skinner (1974) have strongly questioned the value and validity of introspective reports and have gone so far as to proclaim them superfluous. In relation to this controversy, Klinger's (1978) advice is apropos:

In the observation of inner experience, as in such other procedures, the validation process resides in ruling out artifacts, in replications, and ultimately, in the usefulness of data and theory for making possible other forms of prediction and perhaps, control. (p. 227)

Given the various phenomenological processes and contents of consciousness available for self-report (Battista 1978), any significant phenomenological assessment should also attempt to be comprehensive including such contents and processes of consciousness as imagery, internal dialogue, positive and negative affect, memory, volition, attention, rationality, etc.

One artefact that may be detrimental to a comprehensive assessment of the phenomenological effects of meditation is the effect of *demand characteristics*. First given succinct definition by Orne (1962), demand characteristics refer to the 'totality of cues which convey an experimental hypothesis to the subject' (p. 779). The determination of demand characteristics allows for the isolation of the effects of the experimental setting from the effects of the experimental variables. The study of demand characteristics first assumed prominence in hypnosis research. Given that meditation may be similar to hypnosis (Bärmark and Gaunitz 1979), similar attempts to control for demand characteristics in research on meditation should be made.

Another artefact that may be of crucial important in meditation research involving subjective reports is *introspective sensitization*. Introspective sensitization, is, to my knowledge, a term that was first used by Hunt and Chefurka (1976) to describe the unusual nature of subjective reports that may occur when a person is asked to intro-spect into his or her subjective experience. Hunt and Chefurka's thesis is that:

'describing the bare features of momentary awareness without any refer-ence to the consensual world of objects, persons, and meanings, should itself elicit patterns of anomalous awareness typical of standard altered state settings'. (p. 868)

Hence the phenomenological effects of meditation need to be assessed and compared with the phenomenological effects of introspection, possibly by comparing meditation (with eyes closed) with a baseline condition such as introspection during eyes-closed-sitting-quietly.

Given the previous review, if research into the phenomenology of meditation (and by this I mean the subjective or phenomeno-logical effects associated with the processes and contents of consciousness during meditation) is to continue into the mainstream of psychological research, phenomenological meditation research will need to address the reliability and validity of phenomenological reports of meditation and do so in a comprehensive fashion, while attempting to control for demand characteristics and introspective sensitization.

The following sections will review the studies that I have been able to locate that examined phenomenological effects associated with meditation. For organizational purposes, I have grouped these studies into four general categories: single case studies, studies involving meditation groups only, studies involving meditation and control groups, and studies involving meditation groups versus other groups (such as hypnosis, relaxation, etc.) and / or control groups.

Each section will summarize the studies and describe some of the more interesting or salient phenomenological reports. Tables (for all but the single case studies) will summarize the more technical aspects of the studies and will also indicate to what extent the five criteria for evaluating the adequacy of phenomenological research have been satisfied, that is, reliability, validity, comprehensiveness, and control for demand characteristics and introspective sensitization. Each section will then conclude with a summarization and critique subdivision.

Following the review, I will summarize what phenomenological state effects can be said to be definitively associated with meditation and offer suggestions for future research.

Single case studies

Review

Tart (1971) has described his experiences as a psychologist who practised TM for about a year (after having tried other types of meditation). Tart noticed that poorly processed material from the previous day or two would surface during meditation, and hence the meditation appeared to act as a 'psychic lubricant' by allowing partially blocked psychic material to be fully processed. He also noticed a 'large increase in my ability to cease thinking, to put my mind in a condition where it is alert to incoming stimuli, but is otherwise still' (pp. 138–9).

Walsh (1977, 1978, 1984) presented a description of his first 2 years of meditation while practising *vipassana* or insight meditation for 1 or 2 hours a day, along with 6 weeks of intense meditation during meditation retreats. After several months of insight meditation, Walsh reported on the incredible chaotic fantasies which filled his mind. In his first meditation retreat he estimated spending over 90 per cent of his time in 'mindless fantasy and agitation'. The lack of self-control over his stream of consciousness, his attachment to material wants and needs, his incessant internal dialogue, and a slow but significant increase in perceptual sensitivity and short periods of intense peace and tranquility appeared to have been salient characteristics of his experience of meditation. For Walsh, meditation 'provided a range of experiences, insights, and developments formerly totally unknown' (1984, p. 264).

Hendlin (1979) elaborated on his subjective experiences during a Zen intensive meditation retreat. After a beginning day of excrutiating pain, Hendlin experienced a tremendous variety of somatic, visual, auditory, gustatory, affective, and cognitive sensations in the following week, such as an activation of energy at the base of his spine that flowed upward and ended in a 'beautiful display of golden light' and 'celestial music'. Various visual experiences with eyes open and closed were also reported, including a 'faint glow around others' bodies' and 'fireworks in my mind's eye'. Although there were also negative experiences (paranoia and self-aggrandisement), the meditation retreat brought for Hendlin 'a state of consciousness that I had previously believed to be possible only through the use of psychedelic drugs' (p. 42).

Summary and critique

These case studies suggest that meditation can have profound effects in terms of reported subjective experiences. Although none of the case studies reported on the reliability or validity of the introspective reports, both Walsh and Hendlin tended to be rather comprehensive in their phenomenological observations. Whether their reports were due to the meditation process or were the result of introspective sensitization, compounded by sensory deprivation and experimental demand, is unknown. But case studies, by definition, do not control for such influences, and that is why experiments are done. It is to an examination of these that we now therefore turn.

Studies involving meditation groups only

Review

In one of the earliest and best-known phenomenological studies of meditation, Deikman (1963) had subjects meditate on a blue vase. Subjects reported alterations in the perception of the vase, alterations in state of consciousness, decreases in distractions, personal attachment to the vase, and pleasurable feelings. Individual subjects reported: merging with the vase, a feeling of radiating heat and being sexually excited, dedifferentiation of the landscape (viewed after the meditation session) where the visual perception of the landscape became unorganized, and a transfiguration experience, with objects becoming luminescent and visually enhanced (after the meditation session).

Maupin (1965) had subjects practise a breathing technique daily during a 2-week period. Based on an interview conducted after the meditation sessions, five hierarchical patterns were distinguished. These patterns were: dizziness and fogginess, relaxation and calmness, pleasant body sensations, vivid breathing sensations, and concentration and detachment. Correlations between tolerance for unrealistic experience and adaptive regression with meditation level were found, but no relationship was evident between the attentional measures and meditation level. The significant correlations suggest some concurrent validity for the classification of meditation level based on the subjects' phenomenological reports. Nevertheless, the lack of significant correlations between attention and meditation appears to suggest that meditation level as assessed was not mapping attentional level, but rather ability to relinquish control, which is a variable highly correlated with hypnotic susceptibility (Kumar and Pekala 1986a, b), which was not assessed.

Lesh (1970b) compared meditators who practised a Zen meditation technique with two control groups. Unfortunately, subjective reports were available only from the experimental subjects. The meditators were asked to record their experiences, which were subsequently rated by judges into one of several response patterns. The resulting data indicated that 21 per cent of the subjects had difficulty concentrating, 27 per cent had 'befogged consciousness', and 27 per cent experienced definite calmness. Similar results were obtained by West (1980a) who conducted a survey of people who had learned TM and assessed subjective experiences during meditation. Twenty-one per cent of the respondents reported unpleasant sensations during meditation, and 30 per cent reported feelings of physical relaxation and stillness.

Osis *et al.* (1973) conducted several experiments to determine if different meditation techniques will engage the same types of core phenomenological processes. Subjects practised their own diverse types of meditation. Before meditation they completed a mood questionnaire and after the meditation session a questionnaire assessing phenomenological experiences. Varimax factor analyses were then conducted on the data obtained, with subject session as the unit of analysis. The authors found six factors that appeared in either three or four of the four experiments. These included: self-transcendence and openness, mood brought to the session, an intensification and change in consciousness, meaningfulness, forceful exclusion of images, and general success of meditation. The authors concluded that they were successful in mapping core factors associated with meditation experience across subjects who practised a variety of meditation techniques.

Extending Osis *et al.*'s research, Kohr (1977) invited participants to investigate the change in the quality of their subjective experience during meditation over a 28-day period by completing a modified version of the Osis questionnaire after each meditation session. The results indicated that the quality of meditation experience improved from the first to the second 2-week period, with items comprising the factor of 'intensification and change in consciousness' exhibiting the greatest change. Meditators who had the highest adherence to the programme reported the 'higher quality meditation experience'. Kohr (1984) factor analysed the data, attempting to generate the same results obtained by Osis *et al.* Three factors — intensification and change in consciousness, psychological state prior to session, and negative experience — were replications of factors previously identified by Osis *et al.* He concluded that 'the meditation experience is more than just an intensified day residue and more than merely physical relaxation' (p. 278). His results also appear to support Osis *et al.*'s conclusion that there appear to be certain core meditation experiences, which are common to different meditation practices.

Van Nuys (1973) compared subjects' recorded lapses in consciousness or intrusions in concentration during two meditation exercises and correlated the number of intrusions with hypnotic susceptibility and two other personality measures. Significant negative correlations between the number of intrusions and susceptibility measures suggested a relationship between absorbed attention during meditation and a person's hypnotic susceptibility. The author concluded that there is a 'relationship between attention deployment and altered states such as hypnosis and meditation' (p. 67).

Greenfield (1977) investigated individual subjective responses to three types of meditation. Forty-five females practised mantra meditation, visualization, and bare attention over a 10-week period. Subjective experiences were comprehensively assessed. The results indicated several significant differences in subjective experience across the three meditation techniques, although mystical experience was not significantly different across the techniques. The mystical experience dimension indicated, however, that meditators were consistent in rating their experience along phenomenological domains that included high ratings for unity, noetic feelings of reality and truth, a sense of sacredness, deeply felt positive mood, paradoxicality, a transcendence of space and time, transiency, and, to a lesser extent, ineffability.

Summary and critique (see Table 4.1)

None of the 'meditation groups only' studies assessed the reliability of reporting on phenomenological experience, except for the Van Nuys (1973) and the Greenfield (1977) studies. In several studies, subjects were divided into subgroups based on individual differences measures, and differences among subgroups were found, suggesting discriminant validity for the measures assessed. Unfortunately, none of these studies controlled for demand characteristics or introspective sensitization by the use of appropriate control procedures. Hence the phenomenological effects specific to meditation cannot be determined.

These studies *suggest* that meditation is associated with certain core phenomenological effects, that appear to occur more so for certain groups than others. However, we do not know whether these effects are due specifically to the meditation experience, or are non-specific effects associated with the practice of meditation. The most commonly reported effects are increased relaxation and calmness, increased absorption, alteration or intensification of consciousness, and unpleasant sensations or negative experiences.

Meditation versus control groups

Review

Banquet (1973) studied 12 TM subjects and 12 matched controls under several conditions. A push button with a code of five signals permitted subjects to indicate a variety of psychological events during meditation: body sensations, involuntary movements, visual imagery, deep meditation, or transcendence. However, no comparisons of the different types of psychological events recorded by meditators versus controls are reported, except for the observation that 20-cycle beta waves were

Table 4.1 Meditation groups only

Author(s)	Year	No. of Ss	Length¹ of sessions	No of sessions	Method	Results	Reliab.	Valid	Comprehensiveness	Control of demand char.	Control of intro. sense
Deikman	63	4 & 4	usu. 15 min.	12 & 1	Meditation on a blue vase	Alterations in affect, perception, attention, and cognition	No	No	No	No	No
Maupin	65	28	45 min.	10	Breath meditation	Five hierarchical patterns of subjective experience found	No	Yes	No	No	No
Lesh	70	16	30 min.	20	Breath meditation	21% difficulty concentrating, 27% 'befogged consciousness', 27% calmness	No	Yes	No	No	No
Osis et al.	73	84	30 min.	17 av.	Ss practised own type of meditation	Six core factors found associated with meditation	Yes	No	Yes	No	No

Author	Year	N	Length[1]	Sessions	Type	Findings					
Van Nuys	73	47	15 min.	2	Breath and candle meditations	'Relationship between attention deployment and altered states'	Yes	Yes	No	No	No
Greenfield	77	45	unknown[2]	unknown	Mantra, bare attention, and visualization	Mystical experience the same across all three meditations	Yes	Yes	Yes	No	No
Kohr	77	141	20 min.	28	Specific meditation exercise	Change in subjective experience over time	No	Yes	Yes	No	No
West	80	83	N/A	N/A	Meditation survey of subjective experience of TMers	29% unpleasant sensations, 39% physical sensations and stillness	No	No	Yes	No	No
Kohr	84	145	20 min.	28	Factor analysis of '77 study	Replicated three factors: intensification of consciousness, mood prior to session, negative experiences	Yes	No	Yes	No	No

[1] Refers to length of meditation session.
[2] Data taken from secondary source.

associated with deep meditation or transcendence (which was not further defined) for four meditators.

Kubose (1976) had introductory psychology students divided into one of three groups: a meditation group instructed to perform a breath-counting task, and two control groups. The meditation group subjects were instructed to press a key to indicate a lapse in attention (after Van Nuys' 1973 procedure) while all subjects completed a brief inventory after the fifth, 10th, and 15th sessions. The key pressing indicated concentration decreased within each session but increased across sessions for the meditating subjects, while the questionnaire data (based on rank orderings) indicated that meditating subjects were more 'present centred' while control subjects were more 'past or future centred'.

Somewhat similarly, Spanos *et al.* (1979) compared four groups of trained meditators with a group of non-meditators. All subjects signalled 'intrusions of thoughts into their attention' in the manner of Van Nuys' (1973) instructions, while attempting to focus non-analytically on a self-generated subvocal, nonsense sound. The results indicated that meditators reported fewer intrusions and reported 'deeper' levels of meditation than non-meditators. Number of intrusions and meditation depth was found not to be related to length of meditation practice. A follow-up study (Spanos *et al.* 1980) compared two groups of subjects who attended non-analytically to a nonsense sound. Whereas one group was given instructions in meditation in the TM tradition, the second group was instructed in 'non-analytical attending'. A self-rating scale and Van Nuys' (1973) method were used to measure degree of attending. The results suggested that attitudinal, expectancy, and motivating variables may play a role in the subjective reports of intrusion rate.

Demand characteristics were also investigated in a study of Zen meditation by Malec and Sipprelle (1977). Whereas a control group were asked to 'just sit there', the three other groups were instructed to meditate after viewing a video tape demonstrating a 'counting-breaths' Zen meditation exercise, and depicting three different outcomes: a relaxation outcome, an arousal outcome, or no specific outcome. Profile analysis of a mood scale assessing pleasantness, activation, and dominance 'did not reveal effects for treatment groups or for the interaction of groups and periods on any factor' (p. 340). However, across the three periods for the three treatment groups, pleasantness decreased, activation increased, and dominance was lower after the treatment period than the other periods. The authors concluded that experimental demand did not affect self-report.

Kanas and Horowitz (1977) investigated the effects of TM meditation using a control group, a premeditation group, non-teaching meditators, and meditation teachers. In a rather complex design, non-meditators (the controls and the premeditators) sat quietly for 10 minutes while the teaching and non-teaching meditators were requested either to sit quietly or to meditate. After the meditation/sitting-quietly condition, all subjects wrote down their mental contents (for the meditation/sitting-quietly period), and ranked their stress and affect levels. The results indicated no significant differences across all four groups during the meditation/sitting condition regarding intrusive thoughts, although there was a trend for premeditators to score lowest on intrusive thoughts. Premeditators were also significantly higher in reported stress and negative affect than the other three groups during the meditation sitting condition (no significant differences were reported between meditators and controls). During the meditation/sitting period, there was a tendency (not significant) for meditating meditators to have fewer intrusive thoughts than the sitting meditators and to rate themselves higher on positive affects and lower on negative affects. The lack of significant results (although several tendencies were reported) appears not to support the distinctiveness of meditation versus sitting quietly, in terms of the variables assessed.

Corby *et al.* (1978) investigated Tantric (Ananda Marga) meditation by comparing a control group with a trainee and an expert group. All subjects experienced a baseline state, paying attention to breathing, and meditation on a word. After the session, the subjects filled out a questionnaire on their subjective experience during the sessions (the details of this self-report instrument was not described). No statistically significant results were reported: 'the three subject groups were remarkably similar in their reports of subjective experience' (p. 575).

Holmes *et al.* (1983) have examined the physiological and subjective effects of TM. On 4 successive days, experienced meditators engaged in relaxation, meditation, and relaxation, while subjects with no experience in meditation experienced relaxation, rest, and relaxation. Self-report (retrospective) measures of somatic arousal, cognitive arousal, and somatic and cognitive relaxation were obtained for the premeditation and prerest periods, and the meditation and rest periods. Reliable increases in relaxation from the premeditation to the meditation period were reported by meditators, although change in somatic and cognitive arousal did not reach significance (possibly due to a 'floor' effect). The authors compared reports of subjective arousal between meditators and non-meditators and found that the 'data offered no evidence that meditation was more effective than resting for reducing subjective arousal' (p. 1250).

Kornfield (1979) reported on a phenomenological study involving intensive insight meditation. Subjects participating during silent meditation retreats (involving 12 or more hours of daily meditation) were compared with control subjects 'who received identical talks and instructions but who practiced meditation only one or two hours a day' (p. 44). The retreat meditation subjects produced phenomenological reports vastly more unusual and different than that of the controls. Unusual experiences included: spontaneous movements; alterations in body image; 'energy' flow experiences; unusual breathing patterns;

changes in the perception of pain; unusual visual, auditory, gustatory, and olfactory experiences, including various sense modality hallucinations; rapture and bliss; equanimity; time changes; concentration changes; 'out-of-the-body' experiences; effortless awareness; and 'psychic' experiences.

Brown and Engler (1980) conducted a study of insight meditation involving participants who experienced a 3-month retreat, advanced Western meditators, and a meditation 'master'. Data consisted of responses to the Profile of Meditation Experience (POME) inventory (Maliszewski *et al.* 1981) and the Rorschach. Differences in perceptual changes across the meditation subjects' groups for the Rorschach led the authors to conclude that 'meditation concerns itself with a thorough analysis of all mental operations — ideational, affective, and perceptual' (p. 189).

Brown *et al.* (1984a) tested the visual sensitivity of subjects who practised 16 hours of mindfulness meditation daily before and after a 3-month retreat. A control group who meditated only 2 hours a day were also tested. The phenomenological reports of meditators indicated that the meditators after the retreat were more capable of distinguishing perceptual stimuli and perceptual-biasing factors than before the retreat. Forte *et al.* (1984) also used a tachistoscopic paradigm to explore the perceptual experiences of advanced meditators. Several volunteer meditators, believed to have possibly attained the 'first level' of enlightenment, were compared with three simulating controls in terms of their phenomenological responses to tachistoscopic presentations of light flashes. The resulting data indicated that, although there were certain similarities between meditators and simulators, advanced meditators reported phenomenological effects very different from those of simulators. Reports unique to meditators included: an increased ability to discriminate successive moments of awareness; a heightened sense of the contextual background; an increased awareness of perceptual biases; a shift in the locus of awareness; and voluntary control over the locus of awareness.

Summary and critique (see Table 4.2)

A review of the studies of this section reveals conflicting results. Although meditation was not associated with a decrease in intrusive thoughts for one study (Kanas and Horowitz 1977), it was for another (Spanos *et al.* 1979). Interestingly, no significant differences between meditators and non-meditators were found by Corby *et al.* (1978), and Holmes *et al.* (1983) found that meditation was no different from resting in decreasing subjective arousal. On the other hand, Kornfield (1979) showed very pronounced differences in the phenomenological reports of meditators in intensive meditation retreats versus controls, while Forte *et al.* (1984) demonstrated that there were significant differences between the phenomenological reports of 'enlightened' meditators and simulators.

These conflicting results may be related not only to the different types of meditation assessed, the length of meditation practice, and the skill of the meditators, but also to methodological inadequacies evident across all the studies that were reviewed. Only two used reliable self-report methodologies (see Table 4.2), although even with these the reliability data is not given and the reader is referred elsewhere. Several of the studies used Van Nuys' procedure for observing intrusions. Although Van Nuys reported reliability data when he used this procedure, the other studies cited in this section did not and the study by Spanos *et al.* (1980) even questions its validity.

Most of the self-report measures of phenomenological experience also used rather circumscribed measures of phenomenological experience, except for the POME (Maliszewski *et al.* 1981). The lack of significant findings generally reported between meditation and control groups may be reflective of the lack of a comprehensive phenomenological assessment tool. On the other hand, studies that controlled for introspective sensitization (the Kanas and Horowitz and the Holmes *et al.* studies) appear to suggest minimal differences between meditation and a sitting-quietly/rest period. Several of the studies tried to assess the role of demand characteristic. Although Malec and Sipprelle found that experimental demand did not affect self-report, the second Spanos *et al.* (1980) study implicated demand characteristics as having an effect.

The Kornfield and Brown and Engler studies found vast differences between long-term meditators and controls, but neither study controlled for expectancy, subject selection, or introspective sensitization. The very interesting study by Forte *et al.* controlled for demand character-istics by using simulators. Unfortunately, these simulators knew nothing of insight meditation. It would have been more useful perhaps to compare meditators who had attained the first level of enlightenment against meditators who had not attained such a level, but were told to simulate this attainment. Quantification of subjects' phenomenological reports and a blind review process would have further strengthened this study.

Meditation versus control and other groups

Review

Morse *et al.* (1977) compared meditation, self-hypnosis, and relaxation across four subject groups and six conditions. For the subjective evaluation, subjects were asked to rate the phenomenological states associated with the stimulus conditions on dimensions of euphoria, dissociation, depth, and most effortless induction (how these terms were defined to subjects is not mentioned). For all four subjective measures, meditation and autohypnosis were found to be better when

Table 4.2 Meditation versus control groups

Author(s)	Year	Total No. of Ss	Length[1] of sessions	No. of sessions	Type of groups	Method	Results	Reliab.	Valid	Comprehensiveness	Control of demand char.	Control of intro. sense
Banquet	73	24	30 min.	1	12 TMers & 12 Ss about to learn TM	Ss tested during rest, meditation, post-meditation, and concentration	20 Hz associated with deep meditation and transcendence	No	No	No	No	No
Kubose	76	27	16 min.	15	Breath-counting group, two control groups	Meditation group performed breath-counting	Meditating Ss more present centred	No	Yes	No	No	No
Malec and Sipprelle	77	40	15 min.	1	3 meditation groups, 1 'sitting there' control	Ss experienced baseline, treatment, and recovery periods	Experimental demand did not affect self-report	No	No	No	Yes	No
Kanas and Horowitz	77	58	10 min.	1	4 groups: controls, pre meditators, teaching and non-teaching meditators	Complex design: meditators versus non-meditators during various conditions	No differences across groups regarding intrusive thoughts	Yes	Yes	No	No	Yes
Corby et al.	78	30	20 min.	2	3 groups: non-meditators, meditation trainees and experts	SS experienced baseline, attention to breathing, mantra meditations	'Subject groups were remarkably similar' in subjective reports	No	No	No	No	Yes
Spanos et al.	79	50	15 min.	2	25 TMers and 25 non-meditators	SS attended non-analytically to a mantra	Meditators reported fewer intrusions and deeper meditation	No	Yes	No	No	No

Study	Year	N	Length of session[1]	Duration	Design	Procedure	Findings					
Spanos et al.	80	34	15 min.	20	3 groups: meditators versus non-analytically attending controls	SS attended to 'mantra' or nonsense syllable	'Attitudinal, expectancy, and motivational variables' may be involved	No	Yes	No	Yes	No
Kornfield	79	163+		2 wks or 3 mos	Intensive meditators or controls (who only meditated per day)	SS surveyed as to nature of subjective experiences	Intensive meditators much different from controls	No	No	Yes	No	No
Brown and Engler	80	40	N/A	N/A	5 groups: depending on meditation experience	SS responded to Rorschachs	Phenomenological reports of advanced meditators much different	No	No	Yes	No	No
Holmes et al.	83	20	20 min.	4	TMers versus controls	Ss experienced relaxation, meditation or rest, relaxation	Meditation no more effective than rest in decreasing arousal	Yes	Yes	No	Yes	Yes
Brown et al.	84a 84b	32	16 h	3 mos	Meditators versus controls who meditated only 2 h per day	Visual sensitivity tested before and after 3-month period	Meditators more capable of distinguishing perceptual biases	No	No	No	No	No
Forte et al.	84	10	N/A	N/A	7 meditators & 3 simulating controls	Meditators compared tachisto-scopically against simulators	Phenomenological reports of meditators much different from simulators	No	No	No	Yes	No

[1]Refers to length of meditation session.

compared with relaxation, but there were no statistically significant differences between meditation and autohypnosis.

Bärmark and Gaunitz (1979) compared TM and relaxation–heterohypnosis across experienced meditators and highly susceptible hypnotic subjects. The results indicated that:

during meditation, (*vis-à-vis* baseline), subjects paid less attention to their body posture, felt more relaxed, experienced the body becoming lighter, felt warmer, experienced a weaker subject–object differentiation, and experienced time as passing more quickly. During hypnosis (*vis-à-vis* baseline), subjects paid less attention to the environment, to body posture, and to their respiration. They felt more relaxed, experienced a weaker subject–object differentiation, felt more concentrated, and reported an enhanced vividness in their imagery. (pp. 231–2)

Comparing differences between meditation and hypnosis revealed only one significant difference — hypnotic subjects reported experiencing more vivid imagery. The authors concluded that 'transcendental meditation is a phenomenologically altered state of consciousness which resembles the hypnotically altered state' (p. 237).

Lehrer *et al.* (1980) assigned volunteers to one of three conditions: progressive relaxation, clinically standardized meditation (Carrington 1979), or a waiting-list control. Five to six weeks after the study the experimental subjects were tested and asked to rate how often and how intensely they experienced various thoughts and sensations. The results indicated that items discriminating the progressive relaxation subjects from the other groups 'tended to be descriptive of physiological or muscular sensations, while items that discriminated the meditation group from the other groups tended to be descriptive of cognitive experiences' (p. 300).

Credidio (1982) randomly assigned female subjects to three groups: patterned biofeedback (given feedback to reduce electromyographic activity levels and increase skin temperature simultaneously), clinically standardized meditation, or a control group. All subjects received weekly training and were encouraged to practise on their own. Although the meditation group demonstrated the most positive subjective reports, the author indicated that having to attend to two biofeedback signals may have been anxiety provoking for the biofeedback subjects.

Brown *et al.* (1982) surveyed the phenomenological reports of persons involved in either self-hypnosis, mindfulness meditation, or waking dreaming (trying to re-experience 'a significant or highly emotionally charged element from a recent night dream', p. 298). Phenomenological experience was quantified by means of the TIME (profile of Trance, Imaging, and Meditation Experience) questionnaire which assessed 11 a priori categories. Discriminant function analyses were conducted for each of the sections of the TIME inventory, attempting to classify subjects correctly into each of the groups. The authors concluded that:

while self-hypnosis involves self-referential thinking, memory changes, and intense emotions, waking-dreaming emphasizes the immediate impact of emerging images, which unfold in a thematic manner and have a sense of their own reality. Mindfulness meditators have difficulty managing distractions, but with experience learn greater awareness of bodily processes, and experience changes in the perception of time and self; mental processes seem to slow down, and awareness assumes an impersonal quality. (p. 292)

Pekala and Levine (1981, 1982) developed a questionnaire, the Phenomenology of Consciousness Questionnaire (PCQ), for mapping and statistically assessing the intensity of and pattern variations in phenomenological experience associated with various stimulus conditions. They assessed the states of consciousness associated with sitting quietly (experienced twice), relaxation/meditation, and reading erotica. Thirty-seven of the PCQ's items reliably and validly mapped 19 (sub)dimensions of phenomenological experience. The results indicated that relaxation/meditation, compared with eyes open, was associated with a significant decrease in internal dialogue, self-awareness, imagery amount and vividness, positive and negative affect, volitional control, and memory. It was also associated with a significant increase in altered state of awareness, altered experiences, increased absorption, and a more inward attentional focus. Almost identical results were obtained upon comparing relaxation/meditation with reading erotica. The relaxation/meditation condition, compared with the other conditions, was also associated with a significantly different pattern structure. Diagraming this pattern structure via *psygrams* (graphs of the psychophenomenological states associated with given stimulus conditions, Pekala 1985a) suggested that the relaxation/meditation condition was an altered state of consciousness from baseline, when using Tart's (1975) definition of an altered state of consciousness.

Thapa and Murthy (1985) compared altered states of consciousness among meditators, schizophrenics, and epileptics. Phenomenological experience was assessed using a self-report information schedule that was based on Ludwig's (1972) and Tart's (1975) criteria for altered states of consciousness. The meditative altered state of consciousness (ASC) was characterized by body image changes, disturbed time sense, change in emotional expression, change in meaning and significance, feelings of rejuvenation and alteration in thinking, perceptual distortions, and loss of control. The epileptic ASC, on the other hand, was characterized by perceptual illusions, and hallucinations; while the psychotic ASC was characterized by perceptual distortions, changes in body image, changes in meaning and significance, alterations in thinking, hyper-suggestibility, and alterations in time sense.

Summary and critique (see Table 4.3)

Two studies (Morse *et al.* and Bärmark and Gaunitz) found few pheno-menological differences between meditation and hypnosis, whereas differences between progressive relaxation and meditation were found

Table 4.3 Meditation versus control and other groups

Author(s)	Year	Total No. of Ss	Length of condition	No. of sessions	Type of groups	Method	Results	Reliab.	Valid	Comprehensiveness	Control of demand char.	Control of intro. sense
Morse et al.	77	48	6–8 min.	1	4 groups: trained in TM, self-hypnosis, both or neither	6 conditions: baseline, relaxation, 3 hypnosis conditions, meditation	'TM does no better than other forms of relaxation'	No	No	No	No	Yes
Bärmark and Gaunitz	79	42	30 min	2	23 meditators & 19 high susceptible Ss	Ss experienced baseline and meditation or hypnosis	TM is an altered state that resembles hypnosis	No	No	Yes	No	Yes
Lehrer et al.	80	34	About 1 h	4	3 groups: progressive relaxation, meditation, controls	SS had 4 training sessions & told to practise on their own	Relaxation found different from meditation	No	No	No	No	No

Credidio	82	30	about 20 min.	7	3 groups: bio-feedback, meditation, controls	SS had 7 individual sessions and encouraged to practise on their own	Biofeedback Ss had trouble attending to 2 signals simultaneously	No	No	No	No
Brown *et al.*	82	122	Varied	Varied	3 groups: self-hypnosis, meditation, waking dreaming	Survey of Ss practising 3 different methods	Practices were significantly different from one another	Yes	Yes	Yes	No	No
Pekala and Levine	81 82	249	30 min. relx/med.	1	249 Ss experienced 4 conditions	Ss experienced eyes closed (twice), relaxation/ meditation, reading erotica	Significantly different intensity and pattern differences among conditions	Yes	Yes	Yes	No	Yes
Thapa and Murphy	85	46	N/A	N/A	3 groups: meditators, epileptics, schizophrenics	Survey of each of subject groups	Ss pheno-menologically different from one another	No	No	Yes	No	No

by Lehrer *et al*. None of these studies, however, met the five criteria proposed at the beginning of this chapter to evaluate methodological adequacy.

Of the seven previously reviewed studies in this section, only Pekala and Levine and Brown *et al*. gave reliability data on their instruments, although Brown *et al*. only give test–retest reliability and do not mention a measure of internal reliability. In terms of comprehensiveness of phenomenological assessment, three of the studies tapped at least 10 dimensions of phenomenological experience. Several of the studies used instruments that have demonstrated discriminant validity (both the TIME and the PCQ differentiated different stimulus conditions). Unfortunately, for Thapa and Murthy's information schedule we are given only descriptive validity data. There is similar uncertainty about the validity of the scale used by Bärmark and Gaunitz. Only the Bärmark and Gaunitz and the Pekala and Levine studies attempted to assess for introspective sensitization. Although the results of both studies suggest that meditation is phenomenologically different from sitting quietly with eyes open/closed, in contrast to several of the studies of the previous section, neither study controlled for demand characteristics by using a credible attention-placebo condition. The Brown *et al*. study also failed to control for demand characteristics, subject selection, and expectancy.

Hence, we do not know the extent to which reported differences between meditation, hypnosis, and imagining or even meditation and sitting quietly may be due to differences inherent in the nature of these procedures, and how much may be due to demand characteristics. In any event, the data suggest that meditation and hypnosis may be much more similar than different in terms of reported phenomenological characteristics.

Conclusions

A critical evaluation of research on the phenomenology of meditation suggests that definitive knowledge is sparse. None of the studies reviewed in this chapter met the five criteria: adequate reliability and validity, a comprehensive phenomenological assessment, and control for introspective sensitization and demand characteristics.

Failure of studies to meet the above criteria is also compounded by the fact that different meditation techniques may produce or be associated with different phenomenological effects, and the studies reviewed here have assessed meditation techniques ranging from concentrative to insight-oriented approaches. Meditation studies involving naïve to 'enlightened' practitioners, and utilizing formats from several minutes to many hours per day over periods from 1 day to several months would also be expected to produce very different subjective effects.

In summary, the data to date, when controlling for expectancy, introspective sensitization, demand characteristics, and related variables do not support the statement that meditation induces or is associated with a unique altered state of consciousness significantly different from hypnosis or even sitting quietly with eyes closed. That that may indeed be the case, at least for some people, is *suggested* by the evidence, but tighter and more comprehensive research is needed to definitively assess and document that. The data, however, do suggest specific issues that will need to be addressed if the phenomenological effects of meditation are to be understood by behavioural scientists.

Recommendations for research on the phenomenology of meditation

Psychology's goal is the 'prediction and control of behavior' (Watson 1913, p. 158). If phenomenological meditation research is to abide by that goal, the phenomenological assessment of meditative 'states' must be reliable, valid, and comprehensive. Such assessment can only be judged reliable and valid if phenomenological data are quantifiable. To distinguish between the type of phenomenology that is needed to help define the subjective states associated with not only meditation, but also hypnosis and other 'altered states' (Tart 1975), and to distinguish further this type of phenomenology from that of classical introspection (Angell 1907) and phenomenological psychology (Valle and King 1978), I have elsewhere named such a comprehensive approach a *psychophenomenological approach* (Pekala 1980, 1985a, b). A psychophenomenological approach to meditation would utilize phenomenological observation but combine that observation with traditional psychological theorizing, empirical research, and quantification and statistical analysis, to yield a comprehensive, quantifiable data-base on the phenomenology of meditation.

The PCQ (Pekala and Levine 1981), revised to what is now the PCI (Pekala 1982), the POME (Maliszewski *et al.* 1981), and the TIME (Brown *et al.* 1982) are retrospective psychophenomenological instruments that can be used, and may form the prototype for other, more refined, instruments, in mapping phenomenological effects associated with meditation. Using such instruments in retrospective phenomenological assessment should, however, be compared with concurrent phenomenological approaches (or concurrent verbalization as Ericsson and Simon 1980 label it) to assess concurrent validity. To date, little research has been done comparing retrospective and concurrent verbalization (Kendall and Korgeski 1979; Hurlburt 1980), and none in reference to meditation.

To determine if such states are indeed different from sitting quietly with eyes closed and introspection, future meditation research must develop strategies to assess and control for introspective sensitization and demand characteristics and see how such influences may modify, change, or determine the phenomenology of the meditation experience. In addition, more research needs to be done comparing meditation against hypnosis, relaxation, waking fantasy, and related states. Future phenomenological meditation research should also attempt to control for individual differences. Individual differences research has indicated that low, medium, and high absorption and hypnotically susceptible individuals report significantly different intensities and patterns of phenomenological experience (as assessed by the PCI) in hypnosis and even in eyes-closed-sitting-quietly (Pekala *et al.* 1985; Kumar and Pekala 1986a, b; Pekala and Kumar 1986). Non-significant differences in phenomenological experience across relaxation, meditation, and hypnosis may become significant if individual differences measures are used. This may be especially true in reference to hypnotic susceptibility and its influence as a moderator variable, since it has already been implicated in differential responsivity to meditation (Van Nuys 1973) and biofeedback (Miller and Cross 1985).

The data reviewed in the present chapter suggest that the phenomenology of meditation may depend on the type of meditation practised, the personality (individual differences) of the meditator, and non-specific effects, among other factors. It is probably this richness which not only makes research into the phenomenology of meditation quite complex and arduous, but also leads to man's continued fascination and preoccupation with a discipline probably thousands of years old. Although the human mind has externalized itself into the fascinating technology of the present century, the mind itself remains an enigma. Perhaps the scientific study of the phenomenology of meditation will allow consciousness to confront itself, resulting in better prediction and control of human behaviour and experience.

5   The influence of meditation versus rest on physiological arousal: a second examination

David S. Holmes

Over the past 20 years there has been widespread interest in the use of meditation, with the most publicized and popular technique being TM (Maharishi Mahesh Yogi 1963). It appears that many persons use meditation to reduce physiological arousal, and because of its purported effects on arousal, meditation is used to treat numerous disorders which stem from or involve hyperarousal.[1] For example, meditation has been used to treat hypertension (Benson and Wallace 1972a; Benson *et al.* 1973; Blackwell *et al.* 1975; Michaels *et al.* 1976; Simon *et al.* 1977), asthma (Wilson *et al.* 1975), inflammation of the gums (Klemons 1977); drug abuse (Benson and Wallace 1972b; Shafii *et al.* 1974), alcohol abuse (Shafii *et al.* 1975), insomnia (Miskiman 1977a, b), stuttering (McIntyre *et al.* 1974), and a variety of psychiatric disorders (Bloomfield *et al.* 1975; Glueck and Stroebel 1975). Furthermore, meditation has been suggested as an alternative to progressive muscle relaxation training (Boudreau 1972).

Because of the potential importance of meditation as a technique for reducing physiological arousal, in 1983 three of my students and I conducted a simple experiment in which we compared the arousal-reducing effects of meditation and rest (Holmes *et al.* 1983). In that experiment, 10 experienced meditators and 10 other persons who had no experience with meditation came to my laboratory for individual appointments on each of 4 days. Each subject was first asked simply to sit quietly for 5 minutes. Meditators were then asked to meditate for 20 minutes, whereas non-meditators were asked to rest for 20 minutes. Following the meditation/relaxation period, all of the subjects were again asked to simply sit quietly for another 5-minute period. The results of that experiment were very striking: meditation and rest resulted in decreases in arousal, but, contrary to what is generally expected, *meditation did not result in greater reductions in arousal than did the rest*. In considering these results it is important to recognize that the meditators were highly trained (certified teachers of TM and/or trained in the Sidhi type), and thus the findings could not be attributed to lack of skill on the part of the meditators. These findings raised serious questions about the effects and value of meditation.

As it turned out, we were not the first investigators to compare directly the effectiveness of meditation and rest for reducing physiological arousal. In fact, an initial examination of the literature revealed a variety of similar experiments, and *those experiments failed to provide any reliable evidence that meditation was more effective than simply resting for reducing physiological arousal!* I was intrigued by the sharp contrast between the widely held view of the effects of meditation and the fact that there was a substantial body of evidence that meditation was not more effective than rest for reducing physiological arousal. An examination of the research that was cited by the advocates of meditation quickly revealed the basis for the widely held but apparently erroneous conclusion concerning the effects of meditation on arousal. The findings cited by the proponents of meditation were based on uncontrolled investigations in which the investigators simply compared the arousal levels of subjects *before* they meditated with their arousal levels *during* meditation. They found (as did I and my colleagues) that arousal decreased when the subjects began meditating. The problem with those investigations is that they did not include a condition in which non-meditators simply rested, and therefore *the investigators could not determine whether meditation was more effective than rest*. It is of interest to know that meditation reduces arousal, but it is of more interest and importance to know whether meditation is more effective than simple rest for reducing arousal. Indeed, it is meditation's alleged incremental value that is its *raison d'être*.

To clarify the situation, in 1984 I published an article in the *American Psychologist* in which I systematically reviewed the research on the differential effectiveness of meditation and rest for reducing physiological arousal (Holmes 1984). In that article I concluded that 'at the present time there is no evidence that meditation is more effective for reducing somatic (physiological) arousal than is simply resting' (Holmes 1985, p. 6). As the saying goes, 'the rest is history'. To put it bluntly, there was a storm of protest from meditators and professionals who employ meditation as a technique for reducing arousal. I received hundreds of requests for the article, I was invited to participate in numerous 'talk' shows to defend my position; the controversy attracted interest in numerous newspapers across the United States including the *New York Times*, and a series of six articles was published in a subsequent issue of the *American Psychologist* in which objections to my conclusions were raised and I responded to the objections (Benson and Friedman 1985; Holmes 1985a, b; Shapiro 1985; Suler 1985; West 1985).

I was exceptionally pleased when Dr West invited me to contribute to this volume because this chapter will give me an opportunity to do two important things. Firstly, I will be able to present a revised review of the research concerning the effects of meditation versus rest on physiological arousal. Specifically, I will be able to incorporate into the review the additional research that has been brought to my attention since I wrote the original article and delete from the review research which subsequent investigation has revealed to be flawed. Secondly, this chapter will provide me with an opportunity to summarize and respond to the concerns that were raised by critics of my original review article, thus making an overall evaluation easier for the reader.

The remaining portion of this chapter is divided into five sections. In the first section conceptual and methodological issues will be discussed, thus providing a perspective within which to evaluate the research. The second section comprises a review of the research on the differential physiological effects of meditation and rest. In the third section attention is focused on the question of whether persons who meditate show less physiological response to threat than do persons who do not meditate. The concerns and criticisms that were raised about my earlier review are discussed in the fourth section, and overall conclusions and implications are presented in the fifth section.

Conceptual and methodological considerations

Types of investigations

Case study. At the outset it is important to recognize that the research on meditation can be divided into three rather distinct groups. The first group contains case studies of the effects of meditation. Those accounts provide a rich source of hypotheses concerning the effects of meditation, but because they are lacking in controls they cannot be used as empirical tests of the effects of meditation, and consequently they will not be considered here.

Own-control. The second group contains investigations in which the *own-control* research design was employed (e.g. Wallace 1970; Wallace *et al.* 1971; Wallace and Benson 1972; Beary and Benson 1974; McCuaig 1974; Benson *et al.* 1975c; Younger *et al.* 1975; Bakker 1977; Hebert 1977; Janby 1977; West 1977). In this type of investigation, subjects are first asked to simply sit quietly without meditating, then they are asked to meditate, and finally they are asked again to simply sit quietly. The pre- and postmeditation periods are used as 'control' periods, and the levels of arousal evidenced during those periods are compared with the level of arousal evidenced during the meditation period.

The results obtained with the own-control design have consistently indicated that subjects had lower arousal while meditating than they did before or after meditating, and those results have been generally accepted as evidence for the effectiveness of meditation for reducing arousal. It is important to recognize, however, that those investigations suffer from a serious limitation. Specifically, *those investigations do not indicate whether or not meditation is more effective than other arousal-reducing strategies such as simply resting*. Indeed, subjects who sit and then rest may show the same decrease in arousal as subjects who sit and then meditate. Because it is generally assumed that meditation results in different effects than does simple rest, and because those proposed differences have a variety of important theoretical and practical implications, it is essential to compare directly the effects of meditation to the effects of resting. Therefore, in this review reliance will not be placed on the data from investigations in which the own-control approach was employed.[2]

Experimental-control.   The third group contains those investigations in which the *experimental-control* approach was used. With that approach, a group of subjects who are trained in meditation are asked to meditate, whereas another group of subjects who are not trained in meditation are asked to rest, and then the arousal levels of meditating subjects is compared with the arousal levels of resting subjects. This is generally the most effective approach to studying the effects of meditation and so the present review relies on the results of experiments in which this approach was used.

Before concluding this overview of approaches, it should be noted that some investigators have used a combination of the own-control design and the experimental-control design. In one case, the subjects participated in a sit/meditation/sit sequence on some days and in a sit/rest/sit sequence on other days, thus making it possible to compare meditation and resting within the same subjects (Pagano *et al.* 1976). Unfortunately, if this approach did not yield differences between the meditation and rest days, it could be argued that on the rest days the meditators 'slipped into' their meditative state. In another group of investigations, subjects' arousal levels were assessed while resting before they had been taught to meditate, and then 3 to 4 months later, after the subjects had been taught to meditate, their arousal levels were assessed while meditating (Jevning *et al.* 1977, 1978a, b, c). With that approach, however, the meditation vs. rest comparison is confounded with factors such as time, history, laboratory experience, etc., thus making the conclusions drawn from the data subject to alternative interpretations.

Methodological issues

Although the experimental-control design is generally the best approach for studying the effects of meditation, many of the investigations in which that approach was used suffer from one or more potentially serious methodological problems, and some brief attention should be given to those problems before undertaking the review of the data.

Amount of training/experience with meditation.   One potential problem revolves around the nature and amount of training and experience the meditating subjects had with meditation. Obviously, if the subjects in the meditation condition were not adequately trained or experienced with the technique, the comparison with the non-meditating subjects would be meaningless. It has been asserted that almost anyone can learn the TM technique in only a few training sessions (Maharishi Mahesh Yogi 1963), but a number of investigations have revealed differences between novices and advanced meditators (cf. Jevning *et al.* 1977, 1978a, b, c; Lang *et al.* 1979). Certainly, if subjects with limited training or experience served in an experiment that did not reveal differences between meditating and resting subjects, the lack of a difference might be attributed to an ineffective manipulation of the independent variable, that is, meditation. With regard to the training/experience issue, it might be noted that in some investigations the meditators had as little as 2 or 3 weeks of experience (see Parker *et al.* 1978; Boswell and Murray 1979), whereas in others the subjects had between 3 and 5 years of experience and/or were qualified as teachers of TM (cf. Jevning *et al.* 1979, 1978a, b, c; Holmes *et al.* 1983).

Subject selection. It is of course desirable to assign subjects randomly to conditions, but if subjects are randomly assigned it may be practically impossible to conduct and maintain the experimental manipulation (learning and practising meditation) over the number of weeks, months, or years that may be necessary to assure that the meditators receive sufficient training and experience. Consequently, in the investigations that involved prolonged training or experience, subjects were not randomly assigned to conditions. Instead, persons who earlier had voluntarily elected to become meditators and who had maintained the practice for some time were compared: (1) with a matched group of non-meditators, (2) with a randomly selected group of non-meditators, or (3) with a group of non-meditators who had recently elected to learn meditation but who had not yet learned or practised the technique. Those procedures may introduce problems because persons who elect to learn to meditate and who continue the practice for many years may differ in some ways from persons who do not elect to learn to meditate or who do not continue with meditation once it is learned.

Analyses of data. The major statistical problem encountered in this body of research revolves around the failure of investigators to control for the influence of initial differences in arousal between meditating and non-meditating subjects (i.e. the law of initial values; Lacey 1956; Wilder 1962). Initial differences between meditating and non-meditating subjects can influence subsequent scores directly (e.g. in the absence of any change, subjects with lower initial arousal may appear to have decreased their arousal at subsequent times relative to subjects with higher initial arousal) and can inhibit the degree to which subjects can change their arousal (e.g. ceiling and floor effects). The effects of initial differences are particularly pronounced with physiological measures, and it has been demonstrated that even non-reliable initial differences can create or obscure subsequent reliable differences (Kinsman and Staudenmayer 1978). Simple difference scores are insufficent for controlling for the effects of initial differences, and therefore either covariance or residualization procedures must be employed (Benjamin 1967; Cronback and Furby 1970). Unfortunately, these controls have been used only rarely. In the absence of those corrections, at a minimum it would be necessary to conduct a conditions (meditating subjects vs. resting subjects) by trials (pre-meditation/pre-rest period vs. meditation/rest period) analysis of variance in which a conditions by trials interaction is predicted (e.g. greater reduction in arousal across trials for meditating than resting subjects). Regrettably, in most cases the investigators simply compared the meditating and resting subjects during the meditation/rest period.

Physiological arousal during meditation

Having identified the types of investigations that have been conducted and the various potential methodological problems, in this section attention will be focused on the question of whether subjects who are meditating evidence lower levels of arousal than subjects who are resting.[2] Table 5.1 contains a summary of the experimental findings concerning heart rate, electrodermal activity, respiration rate, blood pressure, EMG activity, skin temperature, oxygen consumption, and blood flow. The findings concerning biochemical factors could not be efficiently summarized in tabular form because so many substances have been examined, and therefore a summary of the experimental findings concerning biochemical factors is presented in a subsequent paragraph. The information in Table 5.1 and the paragraph on biochemical factors make it possible to examine the effects of meditation on any one response across experiments and to examine the effects of meditation across responses within any one experiment.[4]

Heart rate

In none of the 18 experiments in which heart rate was monitored did the meditating subjects evidence reliably greater decreases in heart rate than did the resting subjects. On the other hand, in five of the experiments the meditating subjects actually evidenced greater increases in heart rate than did the resting subjects (Goleman and Schwartz 1976; Travis *et al.* 1976; Elson *et al.* 1977; Michaels *et al.* 1979; Puente 1981).[5]

Table 5.1 Experiments indicating reliably lower somatic arousal among meditating than resting subjects during meditation/rest periods

Experiment	Heart Rate	Electrodermal	Resp.	Blood Pressure	EMG	Other
Bahrke and Morgan (1978)	No					O$_2$, No Temp., No
Boswell and Murray (1979)	No	No				
Cauthen and Prymak (1977)	No	No	No			Temp., No
Credidio (1982)					Yes	Temp., No
Curtis and Wessberg (1975–6)	No	No	No			
Dhanaraj and Singh (1977)	No		No			O$_2$, Yes Tidal vol., Yes
Elson et al. (1977)	No[1]	Yes[2]	Yes			Temp., No
Goleman and Schwartz (1976)	No[1]	No				
Hafner (1982)				No		
Holmes et al. (1983)	No	No	No[1]	No		
Lintel (1980)		No				
Malec and Sipprelle (1977)	No[1]	No		No	Yes	
Michaels et al. (1979)	No[1]	No		No		
Morse et al. (1977)	No	No	No		Yes	
Orme-Johnson (1973)		No				
Parker et al. (1978)	No			Yes		
Peters et al. (1977b)	No					
Puente (1981)	No[1]	No	Yes			
Raskin et al. (1980)	No	No			No	
Routt (1977)	No	No	No		No	Blood flow, No
Travis et al. (1976)	No[1]				No	HR var., No
Walrath and Hamilton (1975)	No	No	No			
Zuroff and Schwartz (1978)	No					

Notes: [1]Reliably *higher* arousal was observed in meditating than in resting subjects.
[2]Meditating subjects were initially more aroused, and hence their greater decrease in arousal may have been due to regression to the mean.

Electrodermal activity

Of the 14 experiments in which electrodermal activity was measured, only one provided reliable evidence that meditating subjects achieved greater decreases in arousal than did resting subjects. Caution must be exercised in accepting the results of that investigation, however, because the meditating subjects began with considerably higher arousal than did the resting subjects ($t(20) = 1.48$, $P = 0.15$; test computed by the present author based on data in the original report; Elson *et al.* 1977, Table 1, p. 55). Indeed, at the end of the meditation/rest period, the meditating subjects showed only slightly lower arousal than the resting subjects (Elson *et al.* 1977, Figure 2, p. 55), and the decline in arousal evidenced by meditating subjects can probably be attributed to regression to the mean.

In considering the findings concerning electrodermal measures, some attention should be given to the often-cited work of Orme-Johnson (1973). The results of his investigation indicated that experienced meditators showed reliably fewer spontaneous galvanic skin responses (GSR) while meditating than non-meditators did while resting, and thus it was concluded that meditation served to reduce arousal. It is important to recognize, however, that the meditators also showed reliably fewer spontaneous GSR responses than did the non-meditators when the two groups of subjects were simply asked to sit quietly (i.e. during a period in which the meditators were *not* meditating). In fact, the difference between the groups during the sitting period was almost identical to the difference between the groups during the meditation/rest period, thus clearly indicating that the meditation did *not* serve to *reduce* arousal from the initial level. Of course, it could be argued that the long-term practice of meditation had served to reduce the chronic levels of arousal of meditators, but the other research reviewed in Table 5.1 has not supported that possibility (i.e. the other research has not generally revealed differences between experienced meditators and non-meditators in resting levels of arousal). Therefore, it is most likely that the effects noted in this investigation were due to subject selection factors. In any event, this investigation did not provide evidence that the act of meditating reduced subjects' phasic levels of arousal, although it did highlight the importance of controlling for initial levels of arousal (see earlier discussion).[6]

Respiration rate

The nine comparisons of the changes in respiration rates which are associated with meditation and rest revealed only two cases in which the meditating subjects evidenced a reliably greater decrease in respiration rate than did resting subjects (Elson *et al.* 1977; Puente 1981). Interestingly, there was also one experiment in which meditating subjects showed reliably higher respiration rates than resting subjects (Holmes *et al.* 1983).

Blood pressure: systolic and diastolic

Only one of five experiments in which blood pressure was measured indicated that decreases in blood pressure were greater with meditation than with rest (Parker *et al.* 1978). It might be noted, however, that the one set of positive findings was based on 10 alcoholic subjects who had been exposed to meditation for only 3 weeks (the amount of practice time in that period is not clear from the report). In view of the fact that other investigations with larger samples of more experienced meditators did not reveal changes in blood pressure, one must question both the replicability and the generalizability of the one set of positive findings.

EMG activity

Electromyogram (EMG) activity was assessed in six experiments, but only three of those provided evidence that meditating subjects experienced less muscle tension than did resting subjects.

Other variables

In none of the four experiments in which skin temperature was measured were reliable differences found between meditating and resting subjects; in the one experiment on blood flow, no differences were found between meditating and resting subjects; and in only one of two experiments dealing with oxygen consumption was it found that meditating subjects evidenced reliably lower levels than resting subjects.[7] Finally, in one comparison for each variable, meditating subjects were found to have reduced respirator tidal volume but not different heart rate variability than resting subjects.

Biochemical factors

Of the 29 comparisons that were made over 27 substances in six experiments, only four reliable differences between meditating and resting subjects were found. Specifically, no reliable differences were found in plasma renin or aldosterone (Michaels *et al.* 1979); noradrenaline or adrenaline (Michaels *et al.* 1976); vanillylmandelic acid (VMA), urine adrenaline, urine noradrenaline or plasma adrenaline (Lang *et al.* 1979); growth hormone (Jevning *et al.* 1978b); testosterone (Jevning *et al.* 1978a); plasma lactate (Michaels *et al.* 1976, 1979); threonine, serine, asparagine, glutamic acid, glutamine, glycine, alanine, citrulline, valine, isoleucine, leucine, or tyrosine (Jevning *et al.* 1977). Some comments should be made concerning the four reliable differences that were found. First, one investigation yielded a difference in plasma cortisol (Jevning *et al.* 1978a), but another did not (Michaels *et al.* 1979). Second, levels of plasma prolactin were found to differ between meditating and resting subjects, but the difference did not appear until the rest period after the meditation period (Jevning et al. 1978b). Third, meditators were found to have higher levels of plasma noradrenaline (Lang *et al.* 1979). Fourth, meditating subjects were found to have higher levels of phenylalanine than resting subjects, a finding which reflects high arousal in meditators and a finding the authors described as 'unexpected' (Jevning *et al.* 1977). Overall then, these findings do not provide evidence that meditation reduces arousal as measured by various biochemical factors.

Comments and conclusions

A number of comments should be made concerning the results of the experiments in which the levels of arousal of meditating subjects were compared with the levels of arousal of resting subjects. Firstly, from Table 5.1 and the accompanying discussion, it is clear that *across* experiments there is not a measure of arousal on which the meditating subjects were consistently found to have reliably lower arousal than resting subjects. Indeed, the most consistent finding was that there were *not* reliable differences between meditating and resting subjects. Furthermore, there appear to be about as many instances in which the meditating subjects showed reliably *higher* arousal as there are instances in which they showed reliably lower arousal than their resting counterparts.

Secondly, it is clear that *within* any one experiment there is no consistent evidence *across measures* that meditating subjects have reliably lower arousal than resting subjects. In fact, of the 23 experiments that involved more than one measure of arousal, only two experiments revealed reliably lower arousal of meditating subjects on more than one of the measures which were considered (Dhanaraj and Singh 1977; Elson *et al.* 1977), and in the latter of those two experiments the meditating subjects evidenced reliably higher arousal on one of the other measures obtained.

Thirdly, it is very important to recognize that the results of one well-done experiment can outweigh the results of numerous less well-done experiments, and thus, in addition to simply counting findings, the quality of the research must be considered. With the present set of experiments, considering those with more or fewer problems does not change the patterning of results. Furthermore, as noted in the preceding paragraph, there is not one experiment that provided consistent evidence that meditating subjects were less aroused than resting subjects, and thus the possibility that there is one good experiment confirming the utility of meditation for reducing arousal is precluded. Indeed, there does not even appear to be one bad experiment which offers consistent evidence that meditating reduces arousal more than resting.

Fourthly, in this review we are able to draw conclusions only from published research, and, given the differential difficulty associated with publishing confirming results vs. null results, the incidence of null results summarized here is probably an underestimate of those which have actually been found.

Fifthly, it should be mentioned that, although in the majority of experiments the meditating subjects use the TM technique, there are experiments in which other techniques were used but they did not yield appreciably different results (Elson *et al.* 1977; Bahrke and Morgan 1978). Although it is possible that other meditation techniques might be more effective for reducing somatic arousal than those which were reviewed here, at the present time there are no data to support that speculation.

Sixth and finally, it is worth noting that, although the investigations in which the experimental-control procedure was used did not provide evidence for the arousal-reducing function of meditation, the investigations in which the own-control procedure was used did provide such evidence (see earlier citations). As noted earlier, however, the own-control procedure does not permit the appropriate comparison. With regard to the difference in conclusions drawn from investigations which employed the own-control comparison versus the experimental-control comparison, it might be noted that in one investigation the data were analysed both ways and thus a direct comparison of the two approaches was provided (Holmes *et al.* 1983). The own-control comparison indicated that meditation reduced arousal from the premeditation level, but the experimental-control comparison indicated that meditation did not reduce arousal more than did resting. The sharp difference in findings illustrates the importance of the methodological issue and the distinction between the types of research should be kept in mind when evaluating the research findings and the conclusions of authors.

Overall then, it appears that there is no measure which across experiments reflects lower arousal in meditating than resting subjects, and that there is no experiment which across measures reflects lower arousal in meditating than resting subjects. In view of those results we must conclude that at the present time there is no evidence that meditation is more effective for reducing somatic arousal than is simple rest.

Meditation and control of somatic arousal in threatening situations

In this section, attention will be focused on the question of whether subjects who practise meditation are better able to control their arousal in threatening situations than are subjects who do not practise meditation. There are three reasons why it is important to answer that question. Firstly, it is *practically* important. Indeed, one of the reasons why meditation is often used as a psychotherapeutic technique is that it is widely believed that meditation will facilitate the control of arousal in threatening situations.

Secondly, an examination of the ability of meditators and non-meditators to control arousal in threatening situations might reflect on differences in the *processes* involved in meditating and resting. Consider the following: In the previous section it was found that meditating and resting subjects evidenced comparable reductions in arousal, but it is possible that the meditating and resting subjects achieved their comparable reductions through different processes. Specifically, in resting subjects the arousal reductions may have been due to adaptation, whereas in meditating subjects the reductions may have been due to adaptation and/or to something the meditating subjects learned as a consequence of their meditation. It is unlikely that the adaptation that the resting subjects experienced would be of any value in a subsequent threatening situation, but it is possible that the meditating subjects learned something as a consequence of the meditation which they might be able to apply in the subsequent threatening situation. Differences in arousal levels between meditators and non-meditators under stress might then reflect on the interpretation of the results that were reviewed in the previous section.

Thirdly, if there are differences in the ability to control arousal between meditators and non-meditators, the differences may be more likely to be apparent in threatening situations because the opportunity for differences in arousal are greater in threatening situations than they are in non-threatening situations. For practical, theoretical, and methodological reasons then, the ability to control arousal in threatening situations provides an excellent test of the effects of meditation.

Surprisingly, despite the importance of experiments on the effect of meditation on arousal in threatening situations, there are only seven such experiments. Because these experiments are more complex than those in the previous section and because it is important to consider the types of threats that were used, in this section consideration will be given to each experiment individually.

Review of the research

The first experiment in this series provided a test of the effects of meditation in a threatening 'real-life' situation that was personally relevant for the subjects (Kirsch and Henry 1979). Specifically, 38 speech-anxious subjects were each asked to give a speech and their heart rates were assessed immediately before the speeches were given. For 3 weeks following the speeches, the subjects participated in one of four conditions: (1) systematic desensitization in which the subjects used progressive muscle relaxation training, (2) systematic desensitization in which meditation replaced the muscle relaxation training, (3) meditation, or (4) no treatment. Following the treatment period, each subject was asked to give a second speech and again heart rates were assessed. Comparisons of subjects' speech-related heart rates before and after the treatments revealed that only the subjects in the desensitization with relaxation-training condition evidenced a reliable decrease in heart rate. That is, meditation did not result in a decrease in heart rate. (It should also be noted, however, that comparisons among the groups indicated that the change observed in the desensitization with relaxation-training conditions was *not reliably greater* than the changes observed in the other conditions.) These findings did not provide any evidence for the utility of meditation for controlling arousal in threatening situations.

In the second experiment in this series, each of 80 subjects was randomly assigned to one of four conditions: (1) a TM-like mantra meditation condition, (2) an antimeditation (placebo) condition in which the subjects walked actively and concentrated on problems, (3) a muscle-relaxation-training condition, and (4) a no-treatment condition (Boswell and Murray 1979). The treatments were practised for 15 minutes twice a day for 2 weeks. In the stressful situation which followed the training period, the subjects were required to take a college level IQ test and a digits backwards test, and the subjects were led to believe that they had performed poorly on both tests. To assess stress, data on spontaneous GSR, skin conductance, and heart rate were collected during the stressful situation. Comparisons of the subjects in the four conditions on those measures failed to reveal any reliable differences, and thus again meditation was left without any support for its hypothesized stress-reducing function.

A third experiment in which the stress-reducing function of meditation was tested involved a comparison of the effects of: (1) TM, (2) behaviour therapy consisting of progressive muscle relaxation training and cognitive restructuring, (3) self-relaxation training, and (4) no treatment (Puente and Beiman 1980). The treatments were conducted over a 4-week period. In the stress-testing sessions that occurred before and after the treatment/no-treatment period, the subjects were shown slides of medical/surgical stimuli that in a pilot study had been found to elicit physiological and subjective stress responses. While the subjects watched the slides, their heart rates were recorded. Only the subjects in the behaviour therapy and the self-relaxation conditions evidenced reliable reductions in heart rate responses from pre- to post-treatment measurements. The results of this experiment suggest then that, contrary to what is usually assumed, training in meditation may be *less* effective for controlling arousal in threatening situations than is training in behaviour therapy or relaxation therapy, and no more effective than no treatment.

The fourth experiment to be considered is somewhat different from the others in that, although it was designed as an experiment, it was not analysed as such (Goleman and Schwartz 1976). Specifically, 30 experienced meditators were randomly assigned either to a meditation condition or to a non-meditation condition, and 30 non-meditators were also randomly assigned to the meditation and non-meditation conditions. Apparently subjects were randomly assigned to the conditions so that the responses of subjects in the meditation condition could be compared with the responses of subjects in the non-meditation condition, but those comparisons were not reported. Instead, responses of experienced meditators were compared with the responses of non-meditators regardless of the conditions in which the meditators and non-meditators had served. Obviously, although the investigation was designed as an experiment and gives the initial appearance of an experiment, it is in fact a correlational study with the potential problems attendant thereto. Despite this problem, the results of this investigation deserve attention because they are frequently cited as evidence for the stress-reducing effects of meditation.

In this investigation, the responses of meditators and non-meditators were compared while the subjects watched a stressful film. The film portrayed three industrial accidents: 'the fingers of a worker are lacerated, a finger of another is cut off, and an innocent bystander is killed by a wooden plank driven through his midsection as a result of carelessness' (Goleman and Schwartz 1976, p. 458).

Contrary to what might be expected, first it was found that during the minute prior to each accident (i.e. when the subjects were anticipating what was going to happen), the meditators showed reliably *greater* increases in skin conductance response frequencies than did the non-meditators. The authors acknowledged that generally such a finding would be interpreted as evidence that meditators showed a *greater* stress response in the face of threat than did non-meditators, but the authors chose to interpret the findings as evidence for a 'defensive reaction' (i.e. vigilance) on the part of the meditators which might facilitate coping reactions. That is certainly an interesting speculation, but, as the other findings will indicate, it is without support in this investigation.

The second finding was that immediately after each accident the meditators showed a reliably greater decline in skin conductance response frequencies than did the non-meditators, but it is important to recognize than those declines simply brought the meditators down from their high level of arousal to the level of arousal of the non-meditators. That is, the greater decline evidenced by the meditators did *not* result in a *lower* level of arousal. The authors pointed out that the greater postaccident decline in arousal by meditators may have been due to simple regression from their initially higher levels, but argued that that was not the case and suggested instead that the decline was due to a more rapid habituation on the part of the meditators. No evidence was offered for that interpretation, however. Furthermore, even if the declines were due to faster habituation, the faster habituation did not in any way improve the position of the meditators relative to the non-meditators because the habituations did not take the meditators to a lower level of arousal than the non-meditators had achieved.

The third finding of this investigation involved heart rate. Although data concerning heart rate were collected, they were incompletely and inconsistently reported, thus making it difficult to draw conclusions concerning the reliability of the differences in heart rate between the meditators and non-meditators. Inspection of the figure presented by the authors (Goleman and Schwartz 1976, p. 462, Figure 3) indicates, however, that throughout the stressful film the meditators had *higher* heart rates than did the non-meditators. In summary, this investigation provided no evidence that experienced meditators can achieve or maintain lower levels of arousal in threatening situations than non-meditators. In fact, the reverse seems to be the case.

Another experiment reported 4 years later yielded comparable results (Lehrer *et al.* 1980). In that experiment, 36 subjects were randomly assigned to conditions in which they learned progressive muscle relaxation, meditation (similar to TM), or received no training (waiting-list control). After 4 weeks of training or waiting, the subjects participated in a laboratory session in which they were exposed to '5 very loud tones'. The results indicated that, while anticipating the stressful tones, the subjects 'trained in meditation showed greater increases in EMG activity (forearm and frontalis) and higher heart rates than did subjects trained in muscle relaxation or those who received no training. Additionally, the subjects trained in meditation evinced greater heart rate deceleration in response to the tones, an effect that was attributed to a greater orienting response on the part of those subjects. (There were not reliable differences in skin conductance or EEG alpha.) Overall then, these results reflect a *higher* level of response, arousal, and sensitivity to stimulation on the part of meditators, and they offer no evidence that experience with meditation serves to attenuate the physiological response to stress.

In the sixth experiment subjects' responses to a stressful film (see previous description) were assessed during a pretest and a post-test (Bradley and McCanne 1981). During four sessions (pretest, two intervening sessions, post-test) subjects practised meditation or muscle relaxation. Half of the subjects in each of those conditions were given information that generated positive expectations regarding the effectiveness of the technique (meditation or muscle relaxation) for reducing stress, whereas the other half of the subjects were given negative expectations. Subjects assigned to a control condition did not practise any technique and were not given expectancies.

The results indicated that in general the subjects who were given training in meditation *and* positive expectations had lower heart rates during the stress than did other subjects. It is noteworthy that the effect did not improve between the pre- and post-test. (Neither treatments nor expectancies influenced electrodermal responses.) The authors concluded that in so far as meditation has any effect on the response to stress it is due to the 'subjects' expectancies about the utility of a meditative treatment' (Bradley and McCanne 1981, p. 249), an effect that has been demonstrated in other research (Smith 1976).

Finally, in what appears to be the most recent experiment in this series, 30 subjects were randomly assigned to meditation or control conditions and either practised meditation or sat quietly twice a day for 30 days (Hoffman *et al.* 1982). During pre- and post-testing sessions, heart rate, blood pressure, and noradrenaline were measured while subjects were exposed to isometric stress (handgrip tests at 30 per cent and 100 per cent of maximum strength). The results indicated that the 60 sessions of meditation did not reduce heart rate or blood pressures (systolic, diastolic) relative to subjects who rested, but did result in higher levels of noradrenaline. It is important to recognize, however, that higher levels of noradrenaline reflect *higher* levels of arousal.

Summary and conclusions

The results of the seven experiments in which meditators were compared with non-meditators during stress consistently indicated that the meditators did not show lessened physiological responses to stress than did non-meditators. In so far as differences were found, they suggested that meditators might be *more* responsive to stress than non-meditators, and there was no evidence that the hyper-sensitivity on the part of the meditators was in any way adaptive. Overall then, these results provide no evidence whatsoever that training in meditation facilitates the physiological response to stress.

Concerns, comments, and replies

Having reviewed the evidence concerning the differential effectiveness of meditation and rest for reducing physiological arousal, and having concluded that meditation is not more effective than rest for reducing physiological arousal, we can now consider the concerns that have been raised regarding the review and the conclusion. These concerns were originally raised in response to my earlier review and conclusion (Holmes 1984), but because there is little difference between the two reviews and conclusions the concerns are relevant here.

1. Meditation does reduce arousal

A number of critics expressed concern about my original conclusions and asserted that *meditation does reduce physiological arousal* (e.g. Shapiro 1985; Suler 1985; West 1985). Yes meditation does reduce arousal, and I never meant to suggest that it did not. Indeed, even my own data demonstrate that meditation reduces arousal (Holmes *et al.* 1983)! The important point to recognize, however, is that the question is *not* whether meditation reduces arousal, but whether meditation reduces arousal *more* than does rest. Meditation reduces arousal, but there is no evidence that meditation reduces arousal more than does rest.

2. Meditation reduces arousal more than rest, but the effects of meditation have been obscured in the research

One commentator suggested that 'we should also consider other important psychophysiological phenomena that may complicate or obscure the effect of meditation such as autonomic response specificity and directional fractionation' (Suler 1985, p. 717). The argument the commentator made was that although the data do not show any differences between the effects of meditation and rest, the effects of meditation may be obscured or reduced by processes that are not influencing the effects of rest. Unfortunately, the commentator: (a) did not offer any suggestions as to how such processes might obscure the effects of meditation, (b) did not indicate why those processes would not also influence the effects of rest, (c) and did not offer any data to support his speculation. There is always the possibility that some time in the future some additional effects will be found that will lead us to conclude that meditation is more effective than rest for reducing arousal, but at the present time it does not seem appropriate to imply that the effects are there but are hidden by some unspecified process that only affects the responses of meditators.

3. Meditation is not adequately defined

When the results of an investigation fail to confirm a hypothesis, one strategy for saving the hypothesis is to assert that the variable in question (in this case, meditation) was not properly defined. If that is the case, the variable of interest may not actually have been studied and thus the results may be irrelevant. This has been suggested as one explanation for why 'meditation' was not found to be more effective than rest for reducing arousal (Suler 1985).

In my original empirical research (Holmes *et al.* 1983), I did not attempt to define meditation *conceptually*. Instead, I defined meditation *operationally*: meditation was what meditators did, and meditators were persons who were adequately trained in TM. No one had seriously questioned whether TM was meditation (the authorities always referred to the practice as meditation), and therefore it seemed appropriate to define the practice of TM as meditation.

In my review of the research (Holmes 1984), I did not limit myself to investigations that were based on TM, but instead considered any practice that was labelled as 'meditation'. It was necessary to include all forms of 'meditation' so as not to limit the findings artificially. It is always possible that a predetermined conceptual definition will preclude the consideration of a very effective technique. Most of the research I reviewed was based on the practice of TM, but the findings based on TM were not noticeably different from those based on other techniques, and none of the other techniques that were defined as 'meditation' proved to be more effective than rest for reducing physiological arousal. It appears then that the definition of meditation has not limited or biased the investigation of the process.

Finally, if what I and others studied was not meditation, then it is the critics' responsibility to tell us what meditation is and to demonstrate that 'it' (whatever they define meditation to be) is more effective than rest for reducing arousal. In this case, the burden of proof is clearly on the critics, and their argument collapses under that burden.

4. We must not ignore the fact that meditation has been practised for centuries

A question I have encountered many times since publishing my review is that meditation has been practised for centuries, and who am I to question it? For example, one author wrote:

Meditation is an ancient therapeutic technique that has been studied and practised by many individuals of far-reaching intellect and insight. It has endured the rise and fall of civilizations, and predates both science and psychology by many centuries. As scientists who sometimes do not bother climbing onto the shoulders of our predecessors, let us carefully examine any conclusions about its ineffectiveness. (Suler 1985).

In response to this criticism I must point out three things. Firstly, the history of therapeutics is riddled with treatments that were used for many years before adequate research proved them to be useless (blood letting, for example), and the fact that a treatment was used for many years is not evidence that it was effective. Secondly, I am not arguing that meditation is 'ineffective', only that *it is not more effective than rest*. Thirdly, I must suggest that if 'the individuals of far-reaching intellect and insight' had had the experimental evidence that we now have, they might have given up the practice of meditation more readily than some of its current proponents.

5. We should not throw the psychological effects out with the physiological effects

Numerous persons have cautioned that even if we conclude (reluctantly) that meditation is not more effective than rest for reducing physiological arousal, we should not then conclude that meditation does not have other benefits. For example, one author wrote: 'If it is indeed true that meditation does not affect somatic activity [more than rest], let us be careful to avoid conclusions that its effectiveness in other realms must therefore be restricted' (Suler 1985).

My review of the evidence concerning the effects of meditation was limited to its effects on physiological arousal, but the findings revealed by my review do have important implications for other realms. That is the case because many of the other effects that are attributed to meditation by its advocates are predicated upon or mediated by the reduction of physiological arousal. It is also important to note that, although those other effects are beyond the scope of this review, a variety of research has indicated, for example, that the psychotherapeutic effects of meditation can be attributed to the placebo effect (Smith 1975, 1976). Indeed, it has been found that when an 'antimeditation' technique (pacing and focusing on problems) was presented to subjects as 'meditation' it was effective in reducing the subjects' self-reports of anxiety. From those results it was concluded that 'the crucial therapeutic component of TM is *not* the TM exercise' (Smith 1976, p. 630). Unfortunately, a thorough examination of these effects is beyond the scope of this chapter.

6. There may be differences between persons who elect to learn meditation and those who do not, and those differences may have influenced the results of the investigations of meditation

Many of the investigations in which the responses of meditators were compared with the responses of non-meditators are in fact only *quasi*-experiments because subjects were not randomly assigned to the meditation and rest conditions. Instead, years before the various investigations were conducted the subjects self-determined whether or not they would learn to meditate, and that decision determined the group in which they would serve later. Therefore, it is possible that the subjects in the meditation and rest conditions differed on some factor other than meditation and that factor may have influenced the results (West 1985). Consistent with that possibility, there are reports indicating that persons who elect to learn to meditate are more 'neurotic' and 'anxious' than the general population (Williams *et al.* 1976; Fehr 1977; Rogers and Livingston 1977). If such differences are pervasive, they could pose a problem. However, their potential effects have not been demonstrated, and the *true* experiments that were reported (those in which random assignment was used) did not generate results that were different from the quasi-experiments.

7. Resting is actually a 'self-regulation strategy', and therefore it does not provide an appropriate control against which to compare the effects of meditation

It has been asserted that a condition in which subjects simply rest is not an appropriate control condition with which to compare the responses of subjects in a meditation condition (Shapiro 1985). Instead of being a control procedure, simply resting may be a 'self-regulation strategy' through which one can 'access a relaxation response, similar to what occurs during meditation' (Shapiro 1985, p. 7). That being the case, it is the critic's position that in comparing meditating subjects to resting subjects we are not comparing meditation with a *control* and finding *no difference*, but rather we are comparing *two treatments* to one another and finding that *they are both effective for reducing arousal*. Voila! The sow's ear has just been turned into a silk purse!

I disagree with that analysis of the situation, and I think that the problem can be approached and solved on two levels. On one level, in the true experimental sense resting does serve as an excellent control in experiments on meditation because resting involves everything that meditation does except the act of meditating (the use of a mantra, etc.). The fact that resting and meditating have the same physiological effects indicates that 'meditation' adds nothing.

On another level, I agree that resting does reduce physiological arousal, and that as such it can be an effective means of temporarily reducing physiological arousal. I think that calling resting a 'self-regulatory strategy' is stretching the usual use of the term a bit, but, as Humpty Dumpty has pointed out, our words can mean what we want them to mean (Carroll 1960). Therefore, for now I will accede to the critic's position and call resting a 'self-regulatory strategy'. The question then arises, are resting and meditation *both* effective self-regulatory strategies? I have acknowledged that resting is, and the answer concerning meditation is both yes and no. Yes, meditation is an effective strategy if by meditation you mean the *whole treatment package which includes resting*. However, the answer is no, meditation is not an effective strategy if by meditation you mean the *meditation component* (mantra, etc.) of the treatment package because it has been consistently demonstrated that the meditation component adds nothing to the effects achieved by the other components of the package (i.e. resting). Indeed, meditation does not even appear to have a placebo effect for physiological responses. One might argue that the meditation component cannot be meaningfully removed from the treatment package and that it is the total package that must be evaluated, but that argument misses the point. The point is that *the effects of the package do not change regardless of whether the meditation component is included or not, and therefore the meditation component is superfluous*. I may be convinced to call resting a self-regulatory strategy (it does reduce arousal), but then I can not be convinced to call meditation a self-regulatory strategy because the meditation component of the package clearly does not contribute to the reduction of arousal.

8. Other problems

Finally, it is important to note in that commenting on my original review a number of critics made statements that were simply wrong and served to confuse the issue. For example, after acknowledging the importance of the distinction between own-control and experimental designs, one pair of critics (Benson and Friedman 1985) stated that 'Beary and Benson (1974) carried out a study that fulfilled Holmes's requirements of having simple resting controls to which the effects of meditation were compared' (p. 726). The critics then went on to describe how arousal levels were lower in meditating than in resting subjects. However, on page 116 of the article to which they referred it was clearly stated that 'Each subject served as his *own control* ' (emphasis added; Beary and Benson 1974). Those same critics also suggested that an investigation by Peters *et al.* (1977a) provided evidence for the physiological effects of meditation, but inspection of the report reveals that no physiological data were collected! It is unfortunate that these and other errors were introduced, and for a complete discussion of them the reader is referred to my earlier comments (Holmes 1985a, b).

Overall conclusions and implications

This revised review of the published experimental research on the influence of meditation on physiological arousal did not reveal any consistent evidence that meditating subjects attained lower levels of physiological arousal than did resting subjects. Furthermore, the review did not reveal any consistent evidence that subjects who had meditated had a lessened physiological response to stressful situations than did subjects who had not meditated. These conclusions are in sharp contrast to the widely held beliefs about the effects of meditation.

The conclusions generated by this review of the experimental research have implications for the personal and professional use of meditation as an antidote for high physiological arousal. Clearly, *such use is not justified by the existing research*. This is not to say that the practice of meditation might not have other effects, but any such potential effects could not be due to the usually assumed effect of meditation on physiological arousal. Obviously, that limitation greatly limits the range of potential effects of meditation.

The review also illustrated the need for careful attention to methodological issues and problems when considering research in this area.

Indeed, the original conclusion that meditation resulted in a unique reduction of physiological arousal was undoubtedly based on the uncritical acceptance of conclusions from 'own-control' comparisons rather than from experimental tests involving appropriate control conditions.

If professionals interested in controlling physiological arousal are to be effective and maintain professional and public credibility, it is essential that they do not promise more than the data permit. There can be no doubt that the claims made for meditation have far exceeded the existing data, and it is time to bring our promises and practices into line with the evidence. It is also time for the proponents of meditation to develop the methodological sophistication that is required for the production, evaluation, and presentation of research so that readers will not be misled by their reports. For my part, since completing my research programme on meditation I have turned my attention to studying the effects of physical (aerobic) fitness on physiological arousal in stressful and non-stressful situations. That line of research has produced some exceptionally strong findings (heart rate response to stress can be reduced by as much as 29 b.p.m.!). In view of that, I can strongly recommend that persons who are interested in reducing arousal spend their time *exercising* rather than *meditating or resting.*

Notes

[1] It should be recognized that not all forms of meditation are designed to reduce arousal. Indeed, some types of meditation such as the Mevlevi, or whirling dervish, involve considerable bodily activity and serve to increase arousal. The present review is focused on the more passive forms of meditation which are designed to reduce arousal. For a discussion of the types of meditation, see Naranjo and Ornstein (1971).

[2] It might be noted that to overcome some of the limitations of the typical own-control procedure, a multiple activity own-control procedure could be used in which, for example, subjects sat quietly, meditated, sat quietly, rested, sat quietly, rested, and sat quietly. Unfortunately, this procedure has not been used to study meditation, although an own-control with different acitivities on different days has been used (see the discussion of the research of Pagano *et al.* 1976 in the next section).

[3] It might be noted that the influence of meditation on arousal has been examined in a number of previous reviews (Akishige 1968; Gellhorn and Kiely 1972; Kanellakos and Lukas 1974; Woolfolk 1975; Davidson 1976; Rigby 1977; West 1979b; Schuman 1980; Shapiro 1980). Unfortunately, the conclusions drawn in previous reviews generally cannot be accepted because the authors were selective in the investigations they cited; disregarded methodological problems in drawing conclusions from investigations; and/or indiscriminately mixed results of case studies, uncontrolled investigations, and appropriately controlled experiments in drawing conclusions.

[4]It should be noted that research which was reported only in an abstract was not considered in this review because those reports rarely contain sufficient information to enable an adequate evaluation of the procedures and results. Results concerning blood pressure in an experiment by Peters *et al.* (1977b) were not summarized in Table 5.1 because different conclusions were drawn when different analyses were conducted and therefore it was not clear whether or not there was a reliable difference between meditating and resting subjects. The results of two other experiments (Rogers and Livingston 1977; Zaichkowsky and Kamen 1978) were not summarized in Table 5.1 because the appropriate statistical tests were not conducted, thus making it difficult to draw conclusions. However, inspection of those data did not suggest that meditation was more effective than rest for reducing arousal. Finally, it should also be noted that research concerning EEG responses was not considered in this review. That research was excluded because adequate ways of quantifying and comparing EEG activity in different groups were not available or used.

[5]Heart rate was considered in one other experiment involving meditating and resting subjects, but the measurement of heart rate did not occur until after the meditation/rest period and thus the data do not reflect directly on the meditation (Corey 1977).

[6]In one other experiment it was reported that meditating subjects evidenced lower arousal as measured by skin resistance than did control subjects (Laurie 1977). In that experiment, however, the control subjects were told to 'meditate' (rather than to rest) but they had not had any experience with meditation and were not instructed in how to meditate. Under those circumstances, complying with the instructions might have been difficult or anxiety provoking for the control subjects, and thus the arousal of those subjects may not have declined as much as if they had been asked to simply rest.

[7]Oxygen consumption was also measured in one other experiment, but in that case the control subjects listened to classical music rather than simply resting and it is likely that the music influenced respiration (Fenwick *et al.* 1977).

6   Meditation and the EEG

Peter Fenwick

Introduction

Ever since Western scientists began to investigate the nature of consciousness they have looked for answers in the study of the functioning of
the human brain. However, advances in neurophysiological techniques,
such as the implantation of micro-electrodes into the nerve cells within
the brain, have only underlined the fact that neurophysiological instruments are limited to the measurement of brain function. Consciousness
eludes them.

Attempts to use the EEG to look for clues to the nature of consciousness
have succeeded to some extent. However, most brain rhythms are non-
specific, and thus any particular pattern can refer to numerous subjective
states. So difficulties are likely to arise when one moves from description
to interpretation. It is never possible to attribute specific meaning to
gross brain rhythms such as the EEG, which is the wide spatial average
of millions of brain cells doing fairly similar things. Neither is it possible
to interpret what the cells are doing from the pattern of the EEG except
in a very broad way. It is an even further leap to move from there to
the content and quality of consciousness. Understanding why this is
so requires a knowledge of the genesis of the EEG.

The genesis of the cortical EEG

The EEG is generated by the cells in the superficial layers of the cortex
and is a spatial average of their activity. The EEG activity would sum to
zero if certain groups of cells were not linked together and fired
synchronously. This synchronous driving of the cortical cells arises in the
thalamus, and is then conducted to the cortex, so that the EEG generator
can be seen as a cortico-thalamic unit. The thalamus, in its turn, is olled
by the reticular activating system. There is thus diffuse control of cortical
cells which generate the EEG, as they are linked to the thalamus, which
in its turn is modified by the reticular activating system. The scalp EEG
is a spatial average of these small cortical areas; the larger the cortical
area involved in synchronized activity, the higher is the amplitude of
the EEG. Cooper *et al.* (1965) estimate that it requires 6 cm^2 of
coherent activity on the surface of the cortex to be 'seen' in the scalp
EEG (Creutzfeldt *et al.* 1966, Fenwick 1981).

Thus, the EEG rhythms are very 'blunt' indicators of underlying brain activity. They are the result of the synchronization of huge pools of cells, and thus their appearance reflects diffuse regulatory processes which are non-specific. Any EEG picture will have multiple causation, and many different states can lead to similar EEG pictures. The alpha rhythm, for example, is found in the relaxed waking state, but also in deepest coma just prior to death. An alert, high frequency EEG may indicate an attentive, analysing mind, but the same EEG picture may also represent 'coma vigile', in which the patient is totally unresponsive to any form of stimulation. Thus, extrapolating from EEG rhythms to mental states is likely to be both hazardous and haphazard.

The analysis of EEG records is heavily dependent on statistical theory, but as the conditions of such theory are seldom met, the results of frequency analysis require caution in their interpretation. In recent years the method of coherence analysis has become very popular with meditation research workers, and extravagant claims about states of consciousness based on coherence analysis have been made. Coherence is the frequency correlation coefficient, and represents the degree to which the frequency profile of two areas of the head are similar. There is nothing magical about coherence, and it is not possible to argue from coherence values to underlying brain states or brain functioning. Coherence values will always depend on the width of the frequency band being estimated. Coherence analysis is also subject to another pitfall. If the activity of two scalp areas is referred to a common third scalp area, a change in coherence may show itself between the two cortical areas when no change has occurred. This is because the activity in the reference area has increased, apparently enhancing the similarity of the activity in the other two areas. Thus altered coherence should be interpreted cautiously, and if common reference recording is involved interpretation becomes very difficult.

Early studies in meditation

In the 1950s, it was hoped that the EEG would be the 'open sesame' to an understanding of brain function, personality, and mental illness. It was thus not surprising that as EEG machines became smaller, and almost portable, those scientists interested in consciousness, meditation, and the esoteric should apply this new measurement method to genuine yogis fresh down from the Himalayas. Das and Gastaut (1955), Bagchi and Wenger (1957a, b), Anand *et al.* (1961), and Kasamatsu *et al.* (1957) were the first workers in this field.

Das and Gastaut examined seven Indian meditation experts, and demonstrated a decrease in alpha amplitude and an increase in alpha frequency during meditation, and suggested that meditation was an 'alerting' procedure. They also detected generalized bursts of spindles of fast activity at the time that their practitioners claimed to be entering *'samadhi'* (the ultimate goal of meditation). This early view of meditation as an 'alerting' phenomenon is now thought to be incorrect, and it is possible that the fast activity they detected was due to interference from the scalp muscles. However, the paper describing their results was not sufficiently detailed to indicate whether this was in fact so. Several subsequent papers, reviewed below, have mentioned the appearance of fast activity in the ultimate state of meditation.

Bagchi and Wenger (1957b) lugged their EEG machines and portable generators up into the mountain caves of several 'genuine' Indian yogis, whose EEG they recorded during the meditation sessions, while banging cymbals behind them, flashing lights in their eyes, and plunging their feet into baths of cold water. They report that in some cases the alpha rhythm was unresponsive to this maltreatment. Thus, the second important concept arose, that of sensory withdrawal during the meditation period. These two ideas, fast rhythms during *Samadhi* and sensory withdrawal during meditation, are the foundation concepts of work on the EEG features of meditation.

In 1966, Kasamatsu and Hirai used as subjects 48 Japanese priests and their disciples whose meditation experience ranged from 1 to more than 20 years. The EEGs were recorded during *zazen* meditation, the practice of which, while differing between monasteries, was essentially similar. *Zazen* consists of passive mindfulness with the eyes open, detachedly watching the ebb and flow of the mind without interference. Frequently, the procedure is carried out looking at a blank wall. At the commencement of the meditation, fast alpha activity appeared with a frequency of 11–12 Hz. The appearance of this alpha activity with the eyes open is similar to alpha activity normally seen when the eyes are closed, suggesting that the state of *zazen* is a less aroused state than ordinary eyes-open wakefulness. This position is reinforced by the finding that the alpha amplitude then increased while the alpha frequency decreased, mainly in the frontal and central regions. After some time, occasional rhythmical theta runs at 6–7 Hz appeared. The authors found that there was a direct relationship between the length of time the priests had practised meditation and the EEG changes that occurred in the meditation session. The more experienced meditators, those with over 20 years experience, always showed runs of theta activity. Of considerable interest also was the finding that the EEG changes corresponded to the Zen master's categorization of his disciples as 'low', 'middle', or 'high' in their degree of advancement on the Zen pathway. This method of classification was better than classifying the subject according to their number of years of meditation experience. It was found that many disciples who had been meditating for a number of years had little theta in their EEG, and had also not advanced far along the Zen pathway in the master's rating. Thus, EEG analysis appeared to tap some fundamental process of brain activity which correlated with the pupil's advancement in Zen meditation.

The presence of theta activity could suggest that Zen meditation was a form of sleep, a point which was taken up by the authors:

The rhythmical theta train appears in some Zen priests during Zen meditation. The theta train is also seen in the sleep pattern, but electrographical differences exist between the theta waves in sleep and the rhythmical theta train in Zen meditation. This difference is evident in the following example: a rhythmical theta train is clearly seen on EEG during a certain Zen master's meditation. At this point the click stimulus is given, the rhythmical theta train is blocked by the stimulation and reappears spontaneously several seconds later. The alpha arousal reaction, which is often seen by the stimulation in a drowsy state, is not observed.

They went on to argue that both the EEG features and the mental state of sleep are different from that of meditation. This clear explanation by Kasamatsu and Hirai should have been sufficient to dispose of the argument that sleep and meditation were similar but controversy subsequently developed and this is reviewed below.

One further finding from this study, as yet unreplicated, was that the alpha activity which arose when the eyes were open did not show habituation of the blocking response (i.e. the alpha activity blocked for the same length of time following a repeated auditory stimulus, without habituation). Kasamatsu and Hirai offered the following interpretation: 'A kind of concentration subserves the maintenance of a certain level of consciousness on the one hand, and the sitting meditation form supports the centripetal sensory inflow at a certain level on the other. In these circumstances it would be supposed that the alpha blocking becomes less susceptible to habituation.' It is not entirely clear what the authors meant by this, although their description of the Zen state is clear: 'The Zen masters reported to us that they had more clearly perceived each stimulus than in their ordinary waking state. In this state of mind one cannot be affected by either external or internal stimulus. Nevertheless, he is able to respond to it.' This implies that each stimulus, although a repetition, is perceived by the central nervous system as new, indicating that brain function is altered during Zen meditation.

The author (Fenwick 1969) was one of the first workers to carry out a controlled study of meditation. It involved a comparison of the EEG changes seen during drowsiness with the changes occurring in meditation. Detailed computer analysis of the statistical characteristics of meditation was carried out, again compared with drowsiness, and this showed that the two states were quite separate. Subjects were native Londoners who had been taught a technique of mantra meditation similar to TM. Subjects were asked to meditate for 30 minutes or to drowse for 30 minutes, and the order was randomized. Results indicated a pattern of an initial increase in alpha amplitude followed by bursts of theta activity at the height of the meditation session; occasional bursts of fast activity were intermixed with theta rhythms. Independent blind rating of the EEG showed that it was possible to separate meditation from drowsiness reliably with a high level of statistical significance. Computer analysis of three subjects confirmed that the statistical properties of the frequency and amplitude profiles of the EEG during drowsiness and meditation are quite different.

By the dawn of the 1970s, the scientific literature already contained many of the basic concepts relating meditation to EEG rhythms which are still with us today. In 1964, the Maharishi Mahesh Yogi had started on his mission to spread meditation throughout the world and a young PhD student, Keith Wallace, who came across the Maharishi's ideas in the late 1960s, carried out a study on the physiology of this form of Raja Yoga (TM). The results of this study were published in the *American Journal of Physiology* and subsequently reprinted in numerous periodicals with much publicity (Wallace 1970; Wallace *et al.* 1971). These papers mark the beginning of a greater scientific awareness of meditation. They also drew research workers' attention to the existence (on their doorstep rather than in the Himalayas) of easily available meditating subjects who were keen to take part in scientific experiments.

Expansion of meditation research

Basic findings

TM meditators were the subjects in several EEG studies of meditation conducted by Wallace (1970), Wallace *et al.* (1971), Banquet (1972, 1973; Banquet and Sailhan 1974), and Fenwick *et al.* (1977), all of whom came to essentially the same conclusion. At the beginning of meditation the alpha rhythm increases in amplitude and then generally slows in frequency by 1–3 Hz before spreading forwards into the frontal channels. In some meditators, bursts of theta activity are seen bitemporally, which may alternate with a recurrence of the alpha rhythm. In some studies only, bursts of beta spindling, mainly frontally, are seen in the deeper stages of meditation, and it has been suggested that these are concurrent with 'transcendence'. All these changes are suggestive of lowered cortical arousal. Beta spindling is frequently seen in non-meditators who have become drowsy and passed into stage 1 sleep. Thus, the EEG changes point towards a behavioural state which is on the dimension of alertness to drowsiness. However, it must be remembered that EEG changes are non-specific, and it is not possible to argue from them to mental state. But physiologically this pattern of changes is not unique to meditation alone. Thus we cannot conclude on the basis of these findings that the meditation state is physiologically unique, but neither can we infer that the mental state of meditation is not distinct from low arousal states of drowsiness and light sleep.

Coherence analysis

In the early 1960s, Walter (1963), Walter *et al.* (1966), and Walter and Brazier (1969) experimented with correlation analysis of the EEG waveforms, and were the first to use coherence analysis. Levine (1976) and Levine *et al.* (1977) applied the method of coherence analysis to meditation. They were able to show that coherence values increased during meditation, both homolaterally and bilaterally, between central and frontal electrode placements. They interpreted this raised coherence as indicating evidence for 'long range spatial ordering' of the central nervous system during meditation. Haynes *et al.* (1977) confirmed the presence of increased coherence, and found a correlation between this and the subjective experiences of the transcendental experience. They extended the idea that increases in coherence were consistent with 'coherent ordering of brain function during transcendental meditation' and went on to say that 'the TM technique provides a basis for creative ability and holistic growth'. It should be recognized that what these authors have demonstrated by a change in coherence is either that activity at the common reference electrode was increasing (both Levine *et al.* and Haynes *et al.* used linked mastoid electrodes as a reference), or that there was a similarity in frequency profile between the two electrode derivations. A similarity in frequency profile should not be interpreted as an increase in order, as this would indicate that the final state of order is one in which the frequency profiles of each electrode derivation are similar. Such a state could be achieved either during an epileptic seizure, or during delta coma, or even during death. High coherence values have been found, for example, in schizophrenia, and none of the authors have argued from this that schizophrenia is beneficial and that these high coherence values indicate long range ordering of the schizophrenic's mind. What can be argued, and this is certainly not without interest, is that there is synchronization and spreading out of spindling within thalamic structures, thus causing an increasing similarity of spectral profile in different cortical areas, and thus a higher coherence. The question then becomes, what is the mechanism that leads to increased thalamic spindling, and how can this be correlated with mental state?

Farrow and Hebert (1982) studied coherence values in one subject practising TM by focusing on the period of breath suspension which occurs when subjective mental activity is at its lowest. They reported the interesting finding that just prior to this period delta and beta coherence were low and alpha and beta coherence were high in most electrode derivations, and that the high coherences decreased towards the end of the breath suspension period. They interpreted this as suggesting that the coherence values, together with the other parameters measured, had to attain a certain value for the finer states of meditation to arise. The drift away from this would then indicate that the episode was over. This would certainly be consistent with a form of partial arousal at the end of such an episode, leading to a change in thalamic spindling.

Dillbeck and Bronson (1981) have shown that subjects practising meditation for regular sessions on a long-term basis show increased coherences, particularly in the alpha band. This confirms the previous work on biofeedback, which shows that alpha amplitude can be conditioned by practice.

An interesting extension of the idea of EEG coherence is provided in a feet-off-the-ground study by Orme-Johnson *et al.* (1982), who attempted to show that EEG coherence could be affected by a group of 2500 students meditating a thousand miles away. They took three different pairs of meditators and measured coherence between the pairs. They report that coherence in the alpha and beta frequencies increased significantly on the days when the distant subjects were meditating, compared with the control days when they were not. Unfortunately, what could have been an extremely interesting experiment was so poorly controlled that it is impossible to gain any useful information from it. The most likely explanation for the changes found by the experimenters was that the subjects knew when they were meditating with the distant group and when they were not. It is therefore likely that the quality of meditation was different on the two occasions, without having to postulate a parapsychological explanation. If this experiment were repeated with the necessary controls, and proved to be a real effect and not due to chance variations between subjects compounded by their knowledge of the experimental conditions then the laws of physics would need rewriting.

Meditation and sleep

The question of the similarity between sleep and meditation has occupied a disproportionate amount of the literature. It is often suggested that meditation and sleep are similar (Lukas 1973; Otis 1974b; Williams and West 1975; Younger *et al.* 1975; Pagano *et al.* 1976; Fenwick *et al.* 1977; Hebert and Lehmann 1977; Warrenburg *et al.* 1980). However, reports of the subjective experience of meditating subjects differentiate meditation from sleep. Kasamatsu and Hirai tackled this point in their foundation paper:

In the course of EEG recording during Zen training, the disciples sometimes fall into a drowsy state which becomes clear on the EEG pattern. At this time, the click stimulus is given, then the drowsy pattern turns into the alpha pattern, and alpha arousal is observed. This electrographical change is usually accompanied by a floating consciousness from sleep to wakefulness, according to the disciple's introspection. This state is different from the mental state in Zen meditation. The sleepiness, which is called '*konchin*', is suppressed in Zen meditation.

Clearly some meditators will sleep during their meditation if they are tired. Indeed it is not unusual for subjects carrying out any one of a number of relaxation techniques to go to sleep, but this does not mean that relaxation and sleep are the same thing.

Much the most interesting question is whether the neurophsyiological processes underlying meditation are in some respects similar to those of sleep. As has already been pointed out, it is never possible to argue back from an EEG picture to a mental state. There is a difference in mental state between meditation and sleep. However, if the same constellation of factors is found in both meditation and sleep, then it is possible that the same neurophysiological mechanisms are involved in both processes. As already described, the slowing and spreading forward of the alpha rhythm, intermittent bursts of theta activity, intermixed with alpha, and the occurrence of slow, rolling eyeball movements with the additional reported occurrence of myoclonic jerks during meditation (Banquet 1973; Fenwick 1974; Fenwick *et al.* 1977) all suggest that cortical arousal is decreased along the dimension of relaxed alertness to stage 1 sleep. Most of the phenomena indicate stage onset (not stage 1, but drowsiness) sleep. Stigsby *et al.* (1981), in an excellent study, carried out a computer analysis of EEGs during meditation, drowsiness, and sleep. They found that meditation was similar, in its spectral profile, to waking and drowsiness, but was quite different from stage 1 and 2 sleep, thus confirming the findings of Fenwick *et al.* (1977). There are other crucial differences between meditation and sleep. Firstly, an average subject not practising a technique of meditation cannot hold himself in the deepest stages of drowsiness, just before the onset of sleep, without rapidly falling through it into stage 1 sleep. Secondly, some features of the meditation experience are alien to those of deep drowsiness. For example both the subjective experience during meditation and the changes in rate and rhythm of breathing are atypical of stage 1 sleep or deep drowsiness. Thus one is forced to conclude that although the meditating state is in the direction of lowered cortical arousal it is different from that of deep drowsiness and stage 1 sleep in several significant respects.

Attenuation of alpha activity

In the 1950s, before sophisticated electronics were available, it was usual to examine the responsiveness of a subject by measuring the response of his alpha rhythm to click and flash stimuli. This measure was chosen as the alpha is easily seen in the raw record and it was possible to measure the alpha-blocking time in response to stimulation. The normal response is a standard habituation curve, with total habituation of the blocking response by the 10th to 15th trial. Before the mechanism of generation of the alpha rhythm was fully understood, it was assumed that absence of a blocking response indicated an isolation of the cortex from the periphery, and lack of habituation showed a fundamental alteration in the response of the cortex to new information, with an alteration of the usual learning process. Subsequent work, particularly in the evoked potential field, has shown that considerable voluntary control can be exercised over the amplitude and latency of evoked potentials, and that the manipulation of attention is the most important factor (Mesulam and Geschwind 1978; Bumgartner and Epstein 1982).

Bagchi and Wenger (1957a) and Das and Gastaut (1955) were the first to report that alpha blocking was absent during meditation in their studies of practised yogis. They argued that this indicated an isolation of the cortex from the environment. On the other hand, Kasamatsu and Hirai (1966) reported that the alpha blocked equally to click stimuli on each trial, and that there was no alteration in blocking time during a stimulation session. This indicated that the cortex was responding to each stimulus as new, and the idea coincided well with the Zen view of the world in which each moment is said to be perceived independently of those which have gone before.

These two observations form the basis of subsequent studies. But the situation still remains confused. Delmonte (1984c), in an excellent review article, speculated that yoga meditators whose attention is directed inwards will fail to block, while Zen meditators, who practise 'mindfulness' will fail to habituate. However, as he goes on to point out, this does not happen. Wallace (1970) found blocking and no habituation, whereas Banquet (1973) usually found no blocking; and Williams and West (1975) reported increased alpha blocking (all these studies were on TM meditators).

Subsequent carefully conducted studies (Lehrer *et al.* 1980; Becker and Shapiro 1981) examined alpha blocking during Zen, yoga, and TM in naïve and experienced meditators, and in control subjects. These studies showed that alpha blocking occurred in all groups, although there were slight differences between groups, supporting West's (1980b) suggestion that the depth of meditation is important. This idea of depth can be taken further, as what is now clear is that specific techniques which train attention (and meditation is one) can alter not only the frequency profile of the EEG rhythms but also the way the cortex responds to novel information. It is thus likely that meditation is not a specific method for altering cortical responsiveness, but rather that the mechanics of meditation affect those systems which mediate arousal and the blocking response.

Meditation — a right hemisphere experience?

There is now evidence from both the neurological and the psychological literature that the right hemisphere plays an important part in the synthesis of emotion (Gainotti 1972; Wechsler 1973; Gasparini *et al.* 1978; Finkelstein *et al.* 1982; Bear 1986) the adding of emotion and rhythm to speech — prosidy — (Tucker *et al.* 1977; Ross 1981; Ross and Rush 1981); and in the memory and structure of the three-dimensional and spatial aspects of our world (Fedio and Mirsky 1969). There is also evidence, both psychologically and neurophysiologically, that the right limbic system is particularly involved with ecstatic experience. (Cirignotta *et al.* 1980). Although only one experiment has been carried out, the findings suggest that musical concordance activates right hemisphere hippocampal functioning, whereas discordance activates the left (Wieser and Mazzola 1985).

Dysprosidy and aprosidy are respectively the altered ability and the inability to attach emotion and rhythm to speech, or to appreciate the emotion behind gestures and facial expressions. They result from right hemisphere damage which extends into the temporal lobe and the right, deep, mesial temporal structures (Tucker *et al.* 1977; Ross 1981; Ross and Rush 1981). Many meditation methods specifically make use of rhythm as a means of entering the meditative state. The repetition of the mantra, drum beats, singing, and chanting are examples. Thus, to this extent, meditation can be thought of as a means to activate right temporal structures. It has been suggested by workers studying patients with epilepsy that those who have right temporal lesions show specific behavioural traits which correlate with increased emotional attachment (hyperemotionality) to the everyday world. A consequence of this is a religious and cosmic view of the world. This view is particularly supported by neurologists of the Harvard school (Waxman and Geschwind 1975; Bear and Fedio 1977; Bear 1979; see for a review Fenwick 1983), although the extent to which this does occur has been questioned by other authors (Herman and Riel 1981; Mungus 1982). Thus, activation of the right hemisphere, and consequent alterations in subjective experience may be one of the important outcomes of meditation practice.

Further evidence that the right temporal lobe is particularly important in the genesis of the mystical experience comes from the epilepsy literature. Cirignotta *et al.* (1980) quote the case of a patient with right temporal lobe epilepsy and an ecstatic aura (onset of the fit). They said:

Seizures generally come on when he is relaxed or drowsy. The subjective symptoms are described by the patient himself as "indescribable", words seeming to him inadequate to express what he perceives in those instants. However, he says that the pleasure he feels is so intense that he cannot find its match in reality. Qualitatively, these sensations can only be compared with those evoked by music. All disagreeable feelings, emotions, and thoughts, are absent during the attacks. His mind, his whole being, is pervaded by a sense of total bliss. All attention to his surroundings is suspended: he almost feels as if this estrangement from his environment were a *sine qua non* for the onset of seizures. He insists that a comparable pleasure is that conveyed by music.

The meditation literature also has an example. A paper by Persinger describes the onset of abnormal discharges limited to the temporal regions during an ecstatic episode occurring during a meditation session. Because a bitemporal pair of electrodes was used, it is not possible to say whether it was the right or the left hemisphere which was involved. This paper does, however, add weight to the concept that temporal activation occurs during the meditation session. Further evidence for a right temporal location for mystical experience in non-epileptic subjects comes from a paper by Fenwick *et al.* (1985), who studied a group of psychic sensitives. They found a correlation between poor performance on psychometric tests relating to the right hemisphere and mystical experience.

Ornstein (1971, 1972), Schwartz (1974), and Davidson (1976) all support the idea that meditation is predominantly a right hemisphere function, whereas Abdullah and Schucman (1976), Prince (1978), and Ehrlichman and Wiener (1980) suggest that it is left hemisphere inactivation during the meditation session which leads to right hemisphere dominance. There is very little evidence from the meditation literature that EEGs show significant asymmetry, or that right hemisphere activation specifically occurs, partly because few workers have set out to test this assumption directly. Westcott (1974) showed that there was greater right hemisphere activity in meditation than in controls, and he, together with Glueck and Stroebel (1975), showed that there was an increased alpha amplitude in the left hemisphere at the beginning of meditation which later spread to the right. These findings are however, far from answering the question about specific hemisphere activation, as it is difficult to relate specific hemisphere activation to changes in alpha activity. Pagano and Frumkin (1977), using the Seashore Tonal Memory Test (thought to be a test of right hemisphere function), showed enhanced performance in a group of TM meditators compared with controls. They interpreted this as an indication that TM enhanced right hemisphere functioning. Other workers (Bennett and Trinder 1977; Brown *et al.* 1977; Earle 1977) have failed to show any differences of symmetry between meditation and baseline resting conditions. Indeed, Warrenburg and Pagano (1982–3), after a series of experiments, concluded that there was no evidence that meditation practised over time either facilitated right hemisphere performance or impaired left hemisphere function. They even went on to suggest that a capacity for right hemisphere absorption prior to meditation led to the subjects continuing with the practice of meditation, and thus self-selection might be the important explanatory factor.

Earle (1984), in his review of hemisphere asymmetry, concluded that the:

data on meditation does not fully support the right hemisphere hypothesis. What it does seem to suggest is that in the early stages of meditation relative right hemisphere activation may be induced through the control of attention, the use of visual imagery, and the inhibition of verbal analytical thought. During the advanced stages of meditation . . . [there is] . . . a reduction in cortical activity or diminished cortical participation in the generation of mental phenomena. The degree of asymmetry exhibited by meditators in the early stages of meditation may vary according to the type of meditation they are engaged in, the particular object or objects of meditation they are utilising, and individual differences. (p. 408)

Clearly there is a need for a further series of experiments designed to examine the state of hemisphere activation during meditation. There is sufficient evidence from the neurological literature that the right hemisphere is involved with the deeper emotional aspects of our psychic life, and thus should have relevance to the meditation experience.

Formulation and conclusion

This chapter set out to examine the contribution that EEG analysis has made to the study of meditation. Quite clearly, electro-encephalography has advanced our understanding of the effects that meditation has on the central nervous system. Unfortunately many of the early studies were carried out by naïve experimenters who had little conception of the normal range of changes that occur in ordinary physiological and pathological states. There was initially a tendency to attribute differences, either between controls and meditators, or between pre- and postmeditation sessions for same subject experiments, to an effect of meditation rather than to the non-specific changes in alertness, arousal, and attention which occur in the meditation session. As mentioned by numerous reviewers, subject selection, type of meditation, and control procedures were poorly thought out, making interpretation of the exper-imental results difficult. It has never been possible in EEG work to argue from alterations in EEG pattern or spectral profile to changes in mental state, as patterns and profiles are non-specific, and may occur with a variety of different sets of brain functioning, each of which can support a different cognitive state.

However, having said that, some generalization is clearly possible. Meditation of most (possibly all) types leads to a change in thalamic spindling which is characteristic of that produced by a reduction in reticular activating tone. Thus alterations in alpha frequency and an increase in theta activity with a change in scalp distribution are almost universally described features of the changes seen in the cortical EEG. Another feature produced by this alteration in reticular activating system tone relates to the occurrence of beta spindling, which is common in the general population, and is not specific to meditation, although it may have a specific connection with some meditation techniques. Sitting quietly with eyes closed, drowsiness, and sleep onset are all quite different behaviourally from any of the meditation techniques, and it is of little interest to compare meditation with these states. Comparison with relaxation methods, where a task is given which is behaviourally similar to that of meditation, has led overall to the interesting finding that most of the electrophysiological differences disappear, though some still remain. However, tighter control of subject selection and experimental design is still required.

That meditation alters cerebral rhythms on a long-term basis has been adequately demonstrated. However, biofeedback literature also has numerous examples of such changes, which are thus not specific to meditation. As meditation clearly has effects on thalamic spindling, persistent practice will produce long-term changes in EEG spectral profiles. There is also always a danger of attributing such a non-specific change to the meditation itself when it may be related to the alterations in lifestyle and other non-specific effects which are part of the meditation training programme.

Meditation is practised for the changes in cognition which occur during the meditation session, and for the long-term benefit which may accrue to the practitioner. What is clearly needed now is a more refined set of questions, designed to investigate the functioning of specific cortical areas rather than directing attention to the more global and generalized changes characterized by the EEG.

Speculation

The cognitive and emotional changes produced by meditation seem to be part of what meditators seek. Meditation is, after all, a spiritual discipline leading to a greater understanding of the world. Two analogies of the process of change are often offered. The first uses the image of a dusty mirror, and meditation is likened to the action of polishing it. When the process is complete there is no difference between the mirror and the world, as the reflection is perfect, and thus man's mind is seen as taking on the property of universal mind. The second compares the mind to mercury, forever darting about and on the move. Again, meditation stills the mind, and leads to the transmutation of mercury into silver, and then, with the addition of 'magic herbs' (emotion) into gold. This change involves a diminution of the personal ego, together with a reduction in specific ego aims. Those events which happen to an individual are seen to be less related to his own individual sense of 'I', and more related to the universal aspects of nature. Thus, in his everyday life, the individual is freed from the imperative demands of his own desires, and becomes more responsive to the events around him and more appropriate in his actions. This refining of his nature proceeds to the point at which the ego collapses, and a holistic view of the world supercedes. Many systems of philosophy describe the moment of the collapse of the psychological structures which make up the personal self as the moment of enlightenment, or *satori*. The characteristic of enlightenment is a permanent freeing of the individual from the illusion that he is 'doing'.

How then might meditation bring this about? Clearly the joining of a meditation group and the practice of its philosophy can in itself help to broaden an individual's understanding of the world so that it encompasses a more holistic view. The practice of the meditation then has two major effects. The periods of meditation are partially spent 'thinking' about the philosophy of the group, and this helps to reinforce the meditator's motivation and desire for change. The meditation session also has a physiological effect resulting in a change in brain functioning, and thus a world perceived differently. It would seem as if periods spent meditating, with the discursive mind 'silent' and the activation of the cortex hovering around stage onset sleep, lead to a weakening of left hemisphere cognitive structures. This sets the scene for the final moment when the cognitive structures relating to self collapse, and the world is seen in its 'suchness'. We have some evidence, from detailed neurophysiological and psychological investigations of a Zen master, that in the Zen state although both right and left hemispheres function as normal on straightforward intelligence testing, on dynamic testing an almost entirely right hemisphere strategy is used in dealing with the world. This would seem to support the view that the subjective description of the moment of enlightenment as a collapse in the cognitive structures which represent the 'self' in the outside world is reflected in an altered neurophysiological functioning of the brain, such that the individual responds to any situation almost entirely with the right brain. This results in a three-dimensional view of self as not separate from the world, and thus actions are seen to arise in response to the prevailing circumstances and not from individual will. The person is now holistic.

7   Personality and meditation

Michael M. Delmonte

Introduction

Few would contest that external environmental factors play a role in personality development. However, little consideration has been given to various 'internal' techniques such as meditation and the extent to which they influence the expression of personality. Meditation is a self-generated experience, or an autogenic technique, which modifies our internal environment temporarily and it may be that this deliberate interference with subjective experiences is associated with measurable personality change. Are the effects of meditation limited to subjective experiences during practice, or are there also more long-term changes such as those reflected in personality scores? The response to this question is of interest for both theoretical and clinical reasons. If the answer is affirmative, and if observed changes are in the direction of improved psychological health, then this would provide important evidence that individuals can actively engage in covert health-promoting experiences.

Most studies investigating the effects of meditation on personality have focused on neuroticism and anxiety. This allows the relationship between practice and psychological health to be investigated in the context of an extensive corpus of theory and scientific evidence. This chapter therefore begins with an examination of the effects of meditation on psychometric measures of anxiety and neuroticism. Then the effects of meditation on other corroboratory (but non-psychometric) measures of anxiety are reviewed. These include biochemical, motoric, and physiological indices of anxiety and arousal. The influence of meditation on self-esteem, depression, psychosomatic symptomatology, self-actualization, locus of control, and introversion is also reviewed and discussed.

Shapiro (1982) described three broad groupings of attentional strategies in meditation: a focus on the whole field (wide-angle-lens attention) as in mindfulness meditation, a focus on a specific object within a field (zoom-lens attention) as in concentrative meditation, and a shifting back and forth between the two as in integrated meditation. Of these, concentrative meditation is the most widely practised in the West. Thus those forms of meditation in which focused attention plays a large role (such as TM, Zen meditation and their non-cultic or clinically adapted derivatives) will form the basis of the review. It may be that the various meditation techniques are associated with different outcomes. However, the limited number of comparative studies in which the effects of different techniques are contrasted makes definitive comment on this issue difficult.

Meditation and anxiety

Hamilton (1959) and Buss (1962), by factor analysing anxiety scores obtained from psychiatric patients, obtained two factors ('psychic' and 'somatic' anxiety) which accounted for the major portions of the variance in anxiety questionnaire scores. Schalling *et al*. (1975), and Schwarz *et al*. (1978), having extensively reviewed the literature, similarly hypothesized that anxiety is made up of cognitive and somatic components. Davidson and Schwartz (1976), with their 'multiprocess' model, postulated that somatic and cognitive components of arousal would differentially respond to different forms of relaxation. More precisely, they posited that the different relaxation techniques (i.e. primarily cognitive versus somatic) 'will be more effective in reducing same mode vs. other mode anxiety' (p. 426). Similarly, Schwartz *et al*. (1978) argued in favour of 'differential effects of a somatic (physical exercise) and a cognitive (meditation) relaxation procedure' (p. 321). In other words, they contended that specific subcomponents of anxiety may be differentially associated with relaxation techniques engaging primarily cognitive versus somatic subsystems. They offered weak evidence showing that subjects practising physical exercise retrospectively reported relatively less somatic and more cognitive anxiety than meditators (however, the two groups were neither matched nor formed by random assignment). The multiprocess model is opposed by the older unitary relaxation response model of Benson *et al*. (1974a), who posit that the various relaxation techniques all elicit a general relaxation (trophotropic) response involving all physiological systems in concert. According to this model, meditation is only one of several techniques which leads to the relaxation response, that is, to general physiological and cognitive quiescence.

There has been a paucity of research on personality variables and their relationship to the practice of meditation except in relation to anxiety and neuroticism, which have been examined in approximately 40 studies on meditation. It will not be possible to give detailed accounts of these studies here; rather, a general overview will be presented. Unless otherwise specified state, trait, cognitive, and somatic anxiety, together with neuroticism, will be collectively referred to as 'anxiety'. Similarly, the word 'anxious' will include 'neurotic' unless otherwise indicated. Anxiety can be measured along a number of dimensions (e.g. behavioural, psychophysiological, and psychometric). To begin with, we focus primarily on the effects of meditation on psychometric (i.e.

self-report) ratings of anxiety. The studies examined range from the methodologically weak to the more sophisticated:

(1) Cross-sectional designs with various degrees of matching;
(2) Simple pre–post designs;
(3) Pre–post designs with prospective meditators as controls;
(4) Random assignment to meditation and control groups;
(5) Random assignment to meditation and comparison groups with controls for credibility and expectancy.

A major problem with cross-sectional studies is that individuals attracted to meditation may differ in certain respects from those who are not so inclined. Hence, differences found between meditators and non-meditators may not be attributable to practice *per se*. This problem can be partly overcome by using prospective meditators as controls, or by randomly assigning meditation-naïve subjects to meditation and control groups, in pre–post research paradigms. However, with this design there still remains the problem that those assigned to the meditation and control conditions will have different expectations. Random assignment to meditation and comparison groups with controls for expectancy of relief is the most methodologically sophisticated research design we consider here.

Studies with cross-sectional design

A number of studies show that experienced meditators are significantly less anxious than comparison groups of controls (Hjelle 1974; Goleman and Schwartz 1976; Van den Berg and Mulder 1976). Since in these studies the control subjects were either prospective meditators (Hjelle 1974; Van den Berg and Mulder 1976) or 'interested' in meditation (Goleman and Schwartz 1976) they controlled for predisposition to meditation. However, they did not control for self-selection as attrition from meditation practice may account for the experienced meditators being different from the control subjects. Those who drop out of practice may have been different from the 'continuers' before taking up meditation. These studies do not therefore provide evidence that meditation practice actually decreases anxiety.

Studies with pre–post design

Several researchers have reported decreases in anxiety amongst those learning and practising meditation for periods ranging from one to 16 months (Tjoa 1975; Blackwell *et al.* 1976; Williams *et al.* 1976). However, none of these studies included a control group so explanations other than meditation being the effective change agent are possible. For example, there is considerable evidence to suggest that prospective meditators are significantly more anxious than those in the general population and are more anxious than control groups (Otis 1973; Ferguson and Gowan 1976; Williams *et al.* 1976; Kanas and Horowitz 1977; Rogers and Livingston 1977; Delmonte 1980; West 1980a). Furthermore, those subjects who drop out (between 30–50 per cent after 1 year) tend to be significantly more anxious than those who continue (Otis 1973; Williams *et al.* 1976; Smith 1978; Delmonte 1980; West 1980a). These findings are consistent with reports that those who drop out of meditation score significantly higher on measures of psychopathology (Smith 1976, 1978; Nystul and Garde 1979) and lower on measures of self-esteem (Rivers and Spanos 1981). Observed differences between meditators and controls may therefore be due simply to the high anxiety group dropping out. The question remains, can the pre–post change in anxiety be totally accounted for by this self-selection process or is the regular practice of meditation *per se* associated with reduction in such scores? Otis (1973) stated that 'the people in each of these groups (i.e. "regulars", "irregulars" and "drop-outs") may have differed from each other in those particular attributes before starting TM' (p. 7). In other words, those low on anxiety may maintain practice more so than anxious subjects.

In attempts to address this question, both meditators and controls have been pretested prior to meditation instruction for the 'treatment group' and followed up for periods ranging from 6 to 10 weeks (Ferguson and Gowan 1976; Van den Berg and Mulder 1976; Rogers and Livingston 1977). Use of this procedure has shown significant reductions in anxiety among meditators but not control subjects. However, subjects have not always been randomly assigned to the meditation and control conditions. The problems of subject volunteer status and predisposition to meditation were thus not overcome, though in the study by Van den Berg and Mulder the problem was partially met by using prospective meditators as control subjects. However, subjects in these studies were not randomly assigned to conditions, so even here, predisposition to change would be likely to account for differences between those learning meditation and those having no intervention (see Chapter 9 for a fuller discussion of such problems).

Pre–post designs with random assignment to groups

Several authors improved on the above designs by randomly assigning subjects to either meditation or comparison procedures. On follow-up (which varied from 1 to 12 months later) only meditators showed significant pre–post test reductions in anxiety (Puryear *et al.* 1976; Zuroff and Schwarz 1978; Bali 1979; Carrington *et al.* 1980; Lehrer *et al.* 1980). This finding is particularly interesting in the case of the Zuroff and Schwarz and the Lehrer *et al.* reports because, as well as control groups, these studies employed parallel progressive relaxation groups, the members of which showed no significant changes in anxiety.

Several authors who also allocated subjects at random to either meditation or comparable interventions found significant reductions in anxiety for both meditation and comparison conditions, including the following: 30 minutes of rest—the dependent measure being state anxiety (Bahrke and Morgan 1978; Michaels *et al.* 1979); 2 to 5 weeks of progressive relaxation (Parker *et al.* 1978; Boswell and Murray 1979; Busby and DeKoninck 1980); 6 weeks of muscle biofeedback (Raskin *et al.* 1980); 3 weeks of rest using alcoholics as subjects (Parker *et al.* 1978); and from 1 week to 6 months of credible 'antimeditation' or 'mock meditation' (Smith 1976; Boswell and Murray 1979; Goleman *et al.* 1979). Thus, although the meditators demonstrated significant decreases in anxiety, these decreases were not greater than those found with established relaxation techniques, physical exercise (Bahrke and Morgan 1978), or with highly credible control procedures. This finding contradicts other, already cited, reports that the practice of meditation, unlike that of progressive relaxation is associated with significant decrements in anxiety.

Studies in which random assignment was used showed not only that meditation experience—ranging from 1 to 18 weeks—was associated with significant reductions in anxiety, but also that this reduction was significantly greater than that observed in a parallel control group, the members of which engaged in eyes-closed rest practice over 2 weeks (Dillbeck 1977) or which formed a no-treatment comparison group (Linden 1973; Heide *et al.* 1980). The Linden study also included 18 weeks of counselling as a comparative intervention. Meditation was significantly superior to counselling in reducing (test) anxiety. In conclusion, the above studies show meditation to be either equal or superior to other interventions in reducing anxiety.

Clinical studies

There have been several reports of decreased anxiety following meditation practice in a clinical context (Candelent and Candelent 1975; Daniels 1975; Glueck and Stroebel 1975; Shapiro 1976; Kirsch and Henry 1979). Some studies were poorly designed and were more like case histories, but in four studies both random assignment and longitudinal design were used. Benson *et al.* (1978b) found that meditation, relaxation, and self-hypnosis were equally effective over 8 weeks in reducing anxiety in patients with anxiety neurosis. Patients who had moderate–high hypnotic responsivity, independent of the technique used, improved significantly. Kirsch and Henry (1979) found that meditation, systematic desensitization, and systematic desensitization with meditation replacing progressive relaxation did not differ in their efficacy in reducing anxiety. Smith (1976) found that meditation, although effective in reducing anxiety in anxious college students, was no more so than highly credible procedures which were designed to control for expectation of relief and for the ritual of sitting twice daily.

Raskin *et al.* (1980) reported that, although meditation was effective in reducing chronic anxiety, it was not superior to muscle biofeedback in this respect. There are, therefore, at least four longitudinal studies, with random assignment of high anxious subjects, in which substantial decrements in anxiety were reported following meditation practice. It thus appears that meditation is as effective as some other clinical interventions in reducing elevated levels of anxiety, but that expectancy and ritual may at least in part account for these findings.

In a study without control subjects, Girodo (1974) used a simulated TM technique with nine patients diagnosed as anxiety neurotic. After 4 months, five patients improved significantly and the remaining four showed no appreciable decline in anxiety. Girodo's analysis showed that meditation tended to be beneficial for those patients with a short history of illness (an average of 14.2 months) and not for those four subjects with a long history (an average of 44.2 months). Raskin *et al.* (1980) argued that the effectiveness of meditation in the treatment of chronic anxiety is limited in that only 40 per cent of their subjects showed 'marked clinical improvement'. However, Raskin *et al.*, unlike Girodo, did not investigate the role of chronicity in intervention outcome.

The clinical evidence is thus promising and again suggests that meditation practice is associated with anxiety reduction though the research designs are inadequate to allow for more definitive conclusions (see Chapter 9). To what extent can one attribute the decreases in anxiety to regular meditation practice? Even if frequency of practice is related to such decrements, is it meditation per se that is the critical agent or must we look more carefully at 'non-specific' effects associated with practice?

Decreases in anxiety have been found to be positively related to frequency of practice by some authors (Tjoa 1975b; Williams *et al.* 1976; Fling *et al.* 1981) and not by others (Zuroff and Schwarz 1978). Delmonte (1981a) found that both decrements in anxiety and improved 'present-self' images were correlated with frequency of practice. It is possible that, although practice frequency is in general related to the benefits claimed, there may be a 'ceiling effect' above which little further improvement is reported. For example, Peters *et al.* (1977a) found that less than three practice periods per week produced little change, whereas two daily sessions appeared to be more practice than was necessary for many individuals to achieve positive change. Similarly, Carrington *et al.* (1980) reported that 'frequent' and 'occasional' practitioners did not differ in terms of improvement.

Smith (1978) found that those who maintain meditation practice and who display the greatest reduction in trait anxiety score high on the 16PF factors of sizothymia and autia. Sizothymic individuals tend to be 'reserved', 'detached', and 'aloof' whereas autia describes a tendency to be 'imaginatively enthralled by inner action', 'charmed by works of the imagination', 'completely absorbed', and to demonstrate a capacity to dissociate and engage in 'autonomous, self-absorbed relaxation'. This report is consistent with findings that subjects high on hypnotic responsivity are more likely to show substantial decrements in anxiety consequent upon learning and regularly practising meditation (Benson *et al.* 1978b; Heide *et al.* 1980). It is also relevant to note that suggestibility increases during the practice of meditation *per se* (Delmonte 1981b).

Both credibility of intervention and expectancy of benefit are positively related to improved self-reports. Highly credible control procedures have been found to be as effective as meditation in reducing anxiety (Smith 1976). In a very careful study, Smith randomly assigned subjects to meditation or to a placebo condition which was designed to match 'the form, complexity, and expectation-fostering aspects of TM' and involved simply sitting quietly twice daily. Both interventions were equally effective in reducing trait anxiety, striated muscle tension and skin conductance reactivity. However, it could be argued that just sitting is also a standard form of meditation (see Watts 1957). Smith also compared two other groups exposed to similar fostering of expectation. Again, he found no significant differences between the groups on the outcome measures even though one group practised a 'TM-like meditation exercise' and the other 'an exercise designed to be the near antithesis of meditation' (p. 630). The latter exercise involved deliberate cognitive activity such as 'fantasy, day dreaming, storytelling and listening'. Delmonte (1981a) found that expectancy of benefit from meditation practice assessed prior to initiation is related both to the frequency of practice and to the reported benefits of such practice. Similarly, Kirsch and Henry (1979) reported that high credibility of rationale for meditation was significantly related to reduced anxiety. It could, therefore, be argued that the reductions in anxiety associated with meditation practice simply reflect a quasi-placebo effect. Only Zuroff and Schwarz (1978) found that expectations of benefit were not significantly correlated with such reductions (though this finding could be explained by the relatively broad assessment of expectancy employed). In conclusion, a strong case can be made for taking 'non-specific' factors into account in any conceptualization of the effects of meditation on personality.

So far, we have considered self-report psychometric measures of anxiety, but the effects of meditation on other more objective measures of anxiety can be reviewed.

Studies of biochemical, motoric, and physiological measures of anxiety arousal

It is worth noting that reductions in self-reported anxiety following meditation practice are not always accompanied by decrements in behavioural or physiological measures of anxiety. For example, Raskin *et al.* (1980) found that, although meditation, relaxation, and muscle biofeedback were all associated with reductions in clinically assessed chronic anxiety, these reductions were not related to changes in EMG. Kirsch and Henry (1979) randomly assigned speech-anxious subjects to: (a) meditation, (b) desensitization with meditation (replacing progressive relaxation, as suggested by Greenwood and Benson 1977), (c) systematic desensitization, or (d) no treatment, and found that all three treatments were equally effective in reducing self-reported anxiety and produced a greater reduction in self-reported anxiety than found in the untreated subjects. However, there were no concomitant improvements in behavioural measures of anxiety, and reliable changes in physiological (heart rate) manifestations of anxiety were found only in subjects who rated the treatment rationale as highly credible. Zuroff and Schwarz (1978) randomly assigned subjects to TM, muscle relaxation training, or no treatment. Whereas all three groups improved on a behavioural measure of trait anxiety, only the meditation group showed significant decreases on a self-report measure of anxiety.

These last three studies demonstrate that meditators readily show decreases on self-report measures of anxiety but that these decrements may not be validated by concurrent reductions on more objective indices. If the effects of meditation are mode specific, as the multiprocess model of anxiety (Schwarz *et al.* 1978) would predict, then it may be that the effects of meditation are more readily apparent with self-report (predominantly cognitive) than with behavioural or physiological measures. The outcomes of these studies appear to be consistent with the multiprocess model which predicts some desynchrony between and within physiological, cognitive, behavioural, and biochemical indices of anxiety and arousal. The more parsimonious interpretation is that it is easier to 'fake good' with self-report than with behavioural, biochemical, or physiological markers of anxiety. However, the outcome of the Zuroff and Schwarz study, in which only the meditation group reported significant reductions in both self-report and behavioural measures of anxiety, is not consistent with this interpretation.

Most investigations of biochemical markers of relaxation–arousal associated with the practice of meditation have examined state effects — those immediate responses precipitated during meditation. Reviews suggest that meditation is only marginally superior (at most) to eyes-closed rest in terms of reducing biochemical levels of activation. The reported decreases in lactate, cortisol, dopamine beta hydroxlase, renin, aldosterone, and cholesterol, and the reported increases in phenylalanine and prolactin, although of interest, are not unique state effects of meditation. The most strongly supported long-term (i.e. trait) effect of meditation is a reduction in serum cholesterol levels. This finding is in accord with the rather compelling evidence that the practice of meditation is associated with long-term reductions in blood pressure (see Delmonte 1985a for review). No significant effects were obtained using testosterone, growth hormones, and catecholamines as indices of change.

The outcome of another extensive review — this time of studies with physiological markers of arousal — will be summarized here, as it also offers cross-validational evidence on meditation as an intervention strategy (see Delmonte 1984b). Meditation practice is associated with lower activation in both state measures such as frontalis EMG and respiratory indices (oxygen consumption, carbon dioxide elimination, and respiration rate) and trait measures such as blood pressure. However, these effects are no greater than those produced by other relaxation procedures.

The outcome of these two reviews is consistent with Benson's relaxation response theory. Benson *et al.* (1974a) postulated that a unitary relaxation response can be precipitated by one of several relaxation procedures (including meditation) incorporating certain minimal components such as closed eyes, low muscle tonus, a 'mental device', a passive attitude, and a quiet environment. However, as we have seen, self-reported reductions in anxiety are not always validated by concurrent reductions on behavioural or physiological indices of activation. This suggests that the effects of meditation are largely mode specific, in that somatic components of anxiety (as measured by physiological and behavioural indices) are less responsive to a 'mental' technique than the cognitive components of arousal assessed by self-reports. If further evidence substantiates this view then there will be increased support for the Schwarz *et al.* (1978) multiprocess model which predicts that meditation would be more effective in reducing cognitive than somatic subcomponents of anxiety.

Does meditation reduce anxiety?

To summarize:

(1) It appears that prospective meditators tend to show higher anxiety scores than equivalent population norms.
(2) The regular practice of meditation appears to facilitate a reduction in anxiety for subjects with high or average levels of anxiety. However, there appears to be a 'ceiling effect' at the higher practice frequencies.
(3) Meditation is probably less effective in cases where subjects have a relatively long history of anxiety neurosis. There is evidence that the anxiety scores of prospective meditators could be used to predict their response to meditation, the drop-outs tending to score the highest, and the regulars the lowest, on pre-initiation scores.
(4) Meditation does not appear to be more effective than comparative interventions in reducing anxiety — with the possible exception of progressive relaxation. Nevertheless, meditation does seem to be effective for many subjects in reducing clinically elevated levels of anxiety.

(5) Those who benefit most appear to demonstrate a capacity for autonomous self-absorbed relaxation and/or to be relatively hypnotizable. Intervention credibility and expectancy also appear to play a role in outcome. It thus appears that cognitive set is central to the effects of meditation and that neither the psychodynamic nor the behavioural models of meditation (see Chapter 3) suffice in this respect. Smith (1978) may have been correct when he wrote that 'meditation is quite likely a heterogeneous phenomenon, producing effects ranging from sleep to enlightenment, and incorporating such diverse processes as insight, desensitisation and suggestion' (p. 278).

(6) As all of the reviewed studies — and many of them were well designed — reported significant decrements in anxiety, it must be concluded that meditation practice is associated with anxiety reduction. However, prospective meditators tend to report elevated anxiety. Although practice is associated with decrements in anxiety to a level comparable with that of the norm, there is insufficient evidence to suggest that scores eventually obtained are significantly lower than those of the norm.

(7) Reductions in anxiety associated with the practice of meditation do not always receive convergent validity from behavioural or physiological measures. This finding suggests that the effects of meditation are mode specific, and is in accord with the multiprocess model.

(8) As there is no compelling evidence that meditation is significantly superior to other relaxation procedures in reducing anxiety, the case for unique (state or trait) effects is not supported. Almost all the self-report measures were of trait anxiety and no comment on the relative effectiveness of meditation on state versus trait anxiety can therefore be made.

Self-esteem/self-concept

Van den Berg and Mulder (1976) reported that experienced meditators with an average of 1.5 years of practice had significantly higher self-esteem than a non-meditator comparison group. Similarly, Nystul and Garde (1977) reported that meditators had significantly more positive self-concepts than non-meditators. The above reports are perhaps not surprising in view of the findings that poor self-esteem (Rivers and Spanos 1981) and a negative self-concept (Nystul and Garde 1979) predict attrition from meditation practice. In other words, those with positive self-esteem or self-concept in the first place tend to continue practice.

Spanos *et al.* (1979) compared a group of non-meditators with three groups of meditators with varying degrees of experience (i.e. 6–12 months, 12–24 months, and more than 24 months). They found no significant differences in self-esteem between groups though the meditator groups may have been too small (six per group) for differences to be apparent. On the other hand, much of the attrition from meditation could have occurred during the first 6 months after initiation and hence would not have been revealed. In another study, Spanos *et al.* (1980) randomly assigned people who had no previous experience of meditation to either meditation, non-meditation or 'attention treatment'. 'Attention treatment' was 'almost identical' to meditation and was referred to as 'nonanalytic attending'. After 1 month of practice neither group showed changed self-esteem though it could be argued that twenty 25-minute meditation sessions over 1 month were insufficient to produce change.

In conclusion, there is no compelling evidence that the practice of meditation alters self-image, though research to date has been very limited in scope. More carefully designed longitudinal studies are needed in this area.

Depression

In comparison with drop-outs, those who maintain meditation practice show significantly greater decreases in depression over 1 year (Fehr 1977). Ferguson and Gowan (1976) reported a significant decrease in depression in a group of meditators after 6 weeks of meditation practice, while a comparison group showed no significant change. A group of long-term meditators (with 43 months of TM experience) showed a significantly lower level of depression than the short-term (6 weeks) meditators. However, in this study, the subjects were not randomly assigned to meditation and control groups, and so the long-term meditators may already have had relatively low levels of depression before learning TM.

Carrington *et al.* (1980) randomly assigned 154 telephonists to meditation, progressive relaxation, or control groups. By 5.5 months follow-up the meditation and progressive relaxation subjects showed a significantly greater reduction in neurotic depression than the waiting-list controls. On the other hand, Spanos *et al.* (1980), also allocated subjects randomly to either a meditation or a control group ('attention treatment') but found no significant decreases in depression after 1 month of practice (1 month may well be an inadequate timespan in which to register change). Van den Berg and Mulder (1976) did find a significant decrease in depression after 9 weeks for meditators but not for prospective meditators who formed the control group. Spanos *et al.* (1979) compared a group of non-meditators with three groups of meditators where lengths of practice ranged from 6 months to over 2 years and found no significant differences with respect to depression (though again the meditator groups had only six subjects each). Glueck and Stroebel (1975) reported that an elevated level of clinically assessed depression hinders response to meditation practice, though this was not systematically investigated.

In conclusion, only the Spanos *et al.* studies failed to find an association between meditation and lowered levels of depression—but these studies used either small numbers of subjects or very short follow-ups. Only one study (that by Carrington *et al.* 1980) randomly assigned subjects to treatment and control procedures and followed them up for a reasonable length of time. This well-designed study did provide good evidence of decreased depression but replication is awaited.

Psychosomatic symptomatology

Spanos *et al.* (1979) used Rosenberg's (1965) scale to assess psychosomatic symptomatology in three meditation groups with different amounts of experience and in one control group of non-meditators. No significant differences were found among the (rather small) groups. Similarly, 1 month of meditation practice did not change reported symptomatology (Spanos *et al.* 1980). However, subjects who reported relatively high pretest levels of psychosomatic distress tended to drop out of meditation sooner than those who reported relatively low levels (Rivers and Spanos 1981). The finding that subjects who report relatively high symptomatology tend to drop out is interesting and warrants further investigation, though overall insufficient work has been conducted in this area to allow firm conclusions to be drawn.

Self-actualization

Self-actualization is a concept with its origins in humanistic psychology and refers to the degree to which individuals have actualized their potential for personal growth and development. All measures of self-actualization refer to Shostrom's (1966) Personal Orientation Inventory (POI), except where otherwise stated. Researchers in this area have frequently reported that increases in self-actualization are associated with the regular practice of meditation. In only one study (Kubose 1976) were increases in self-actualization not reported, but here the test–retest interval was only 3 weeks. Stek and Bass (1973) observed that prospective meditators did not differ from controls, whereas Davies (1977) reported that prospective meditators were found to be significantly more self-actualized than control subjects.

Several authors have reported significant changes in some or most of Shostrom's 12 POI subscales after several months of meditation, compared with prior-to-learning meditation levels and compared with controls who showed no significant changes (e.g. Seeman *et al.* 1972; Dick 1973; Nidich *et al.* 1973; Davies 1977). Other researchers have made simple comparisons between meditators and controls and found that meditators were significantly more self-actualized (Hjelle 1974; Van den Berg and Mulder 1976). However, these latter findings could simply represent a self-selection artefact as no pre-meditation scores were recorded. Ferguson and Gowan (1976), using Gowan's Northridge Developmental Scale, also observed significant differences between controls and meditators after only 6 weeks' of meditation. Furthermore, Ferguson and Gowan noted that long-term meditators (with 3.5 years of experience) were significantly more self-actualized than novice meditators (with only 6 weeks experience) though this latter finding could represent a self-selection effect of long-term meditators.

It would be desirable to use prospective meditators as controls — rather than people who are opposed or indifferent to learning meditation — to control for motivation. The pre- to post-test intervals in the above studies were very short (6–10 weeks), and as such one cannot rule out short-term placebo effects. Studies of longer duration will have to be undertaken to control for such effects. Predisposition to, and expectations of, meditation may also explain these findings, since people who take up meditation are probably motivated to 'improve' themselves, and this desire may manifest itself in increased self-actualization scores. Nevertheless, given these cautions, we can conclude that change in the direction of psychological health accompanies the regular practice of meditation among favourably disposed individuals.

Locus of control

Locus of control is the degree to which people feel that either internal factors (e.g. personal values) or external factors (e.g. fate, luck, chance, rules, etc.) influence or control their lives. Hjelle (1974) observed that a group of experienced meditators (2.6 months' experience) were significantly more internally controlled than a group of prospective meditator controls (using Rotter's (1966) Locus of Control Scale). This finding could simply be a sampling effect as the long-term meditators were self-selected, though both Stek and Bass (1973) and Dick (1973) have reported that prospective meditators are not significantly different from control subjects uninterested in meditation.

Goleman *et al.* (1979) found no significant change on a locus of control measure following a 1-week period of practice of meditation. DiNardo and Raymond (1979) found that internally controlled subjects reported significantly fewer thought intrusions during their meditation than 'externals'. Zaichkowski and Kamen (1978) reported that 3 months of meditation practice (unlike an equivalent exposure to EMG biofeedback) did not change locus of control scores. Similarly, Dick (1973) found no change in locus of control following meditation practice.

There is therefore no evidence that the practice of meditation *per se* 'makes' its practitioners more internally controlled. It may be that internally controlled subjects tend to carry on practice and not drop out, but again there is insufficient evidence to allow any firm conclusion.

Introversion–extraversion

A number of authors (West 1980a; Turnbull and Norris 1982) report that those attracted to TM are significantly more introverted than the general population. Similarly, Williams *et al.* (1976) found that (male) prospective TM meditators scored significantly higher on an introversion scale than the published norm (Eysenck's 1968 PEN Inventory), and that 6 months of practice did not bring about any change in their scores. Ross (1972) also found that 3 to 4 months of meditation practice had no effect on extraversion, but Turnbull and Norris report that after 1 month's meditation practice the mean introversion score of the meditation group was almost identical to that of the norm, whereas the comparison group, which was also introverted, showed no such change in the direction of extraversion. In West's study those who dropped out of meditation practice did not differ in extraversion from those who continued.

Tjoa (1975) found that increases in extraversion over 16 months correlated significantly with frequency and regularity of meditation practice. Similarly, Fehr (1977) reported that those who maintained practice over 1 year changed significantly more in the direction of extraversion than drop-outs. Those who maintained practice also had significantly higher extraversion scores than an equivalent population norm.

Overall, there is little compelling evidence to date that meditation practice actually produces change in this dimension of personality. Rather, it appears that those attracted to meditation are relatively introverted. In other words, extraverts may be less inclined to either take up or maintain practice. Those introverts who do take up meditation may, with practice, become somewhat less introverted.

Conclusions

It is noteworthy that negative self-concepts and high levels of reported symptomatology predict attrition from meditation practice. This trend is consistent with reports that high levels of anxiety, neuroticism, and psychological malaise also predict a tendency to drop out of practice (Delmonte 1980, 1981a, 1985b). It appears that those with profiles from the psychological distress end of the continuum tend to respond poorly to meditation and that practice appears to be more rewarding for those who appear to need it least in terms of psychological profile. However, there is evidence that meditation practice increases reported levels of self-actualization and reduces anxiety and depression.

Studies of shorter duration often failed to find significant changes associated with meditation (e.g. Spanos *et al.* 1980). This may indicate that examination of trait (or long-term) effects of meditation requires longitudinal studies of at least three months duration. This is particularly important in the study of personality which does not tend to change rapidly. On the other hand, the state effects of meditation may only be observable once a trainee has become adept in meditation practice. The speed at which this occurs may depend on personality characteristics such as 'absorption' which appears to be positively related to the ability to maintain meditation practice (Spanos *et al.* 1980).

Even though the practice of meditation is associated with decrements in anxiety and depression, and with increments in self-actualization scores we still do not know the mechanism by which this occurs. It may not be any *single* ingredient of, or agent in, meditation that is important here (such as closed eyes, relaxed posture or mantra repetition) but rather the whole experience of meditation together with motivating factors for taking up practice (see Chapter 9). These may be either intrinsic to meditation itself (e.g. phenomenological) or extrinsic to meditation (e.g. increased work productivity, improved health, or other forms of secondary gain). For these reasons, one cannot exclude the importance of expectancy and other 'non-specific' factors known to be of importance in outcome studies. Future research could put to the test some aspects of the theoretical models outlined in Chapter 3, as well as probing further the importance of those factors which are collectively referred to as 'non-specific'.

In conclusion, meditation practice appears to be beneficial in reducing anxiety and depression and in increasing self-actualization. This is particularly so for those individuals who take up meditation for intrinsic reasons, that is, those who are psychologically relatively healthy and are not using meditation to solve serious problems of living. The latter could still benefit from carefully supervised meditation — provided the supervisor is familiar with both meditation and clinical practice. This review therefore suggests that researchers and clinicians alike could profitably direct energies into further exploring the value of meditation, in all its forms, in daily living.

Although practice has been found to be associated with personality changes in the direction of psychological well-being, it may be incorrect to conclude that meditation techniques 'produce' these changes independently of the practitioner's wishes and desires. Meditation is a self-directed and active process in which a technique is used *by* a person (not *on* a person) in the context of particular subjective expectations and objectives. For this reason meditation may not be readily dispensed, like medication, to anxious or depressed patients if they show little motivation to practice. The value of meditation may be greater for those who wish to be involved in directing their own development than for those wanting to be 'cured' passively. This is an exciting area of research which has yet to be explored.

Part III:
Meditation as therapy

Introduction

Is meditation an exercise that clinicians can employ to help people towards greater effectiveness and psychological well-being? Many clinicians believe, on the basis of using meditation in their practices, that the answer is a firm yes. Others await confirmatory research evidence, while others decry it as yet another passing fad in psychotherapy. In Part III we examine the evidence from three different points of view.

First Jonathan Smith reviews the traditional evidence and describes the difficulties of interpeting the results before arguing for a skills-based approach to understanding meditation. He separates out what he believes are the three principal skills involved in meditation practice and urges that we focus on these rather than on the generic notion of meditation. Using this strategy he shows how clinicians can effectively use meditation to help others and how new and possibly more effective research can be conducted.

Patricia Carrington has taught meditation extensively in a clinical setting and relies primarily on this wide experience to offer guidelines on managing meditation in clinical practice. In her chapter she advises clinicians on those most likely to benefit from meditation, how to deal with difficulties which arise, how to avoid such difficulties, and how to teach meditation using Clinically Standardized Meditation (CSM). A feature of Carrington's chapter is the inclusion of three representative case studies from her experience.

David Shapiro is one of the foremost authorities on evaluating psychotherapeutic outcome and he brings this authority to bear in his examination of studies on meditation. The chapter reviews the whole field of psychotherapy research describing the pitfalls, the successes, and the avenues for progress. The chapter effectively describes the problems inherent in evaluating the psychotherapeutic effectiveness of meditation and shows how many researchers have used inappropriate methodologies to answer the wrong question.

8   Meditation as psychotherapy: a new look at the evidence

Jonathan C. Smith

The psychotherapeutic effects of meditation have yet to be demonstrated (Smith 1975, 1976). Meditation is just one of many equally effective approaches to relaxation (Shapiro and Walsh 1984; Woolfolk and Lehrer 1984). These conflicting statements represent two prevailing conclusions concerning meditation's therapeutic potential. With a certain degree of humility, I would like to argue that neither fits the evidence and that it is time to look at meditation in a new way.

The traditional evidence

It has long been argued that meditation has psychotherapeutic potential. Carl Jung (1961), for example, incorporated meditative concepts in his approaches to therapy, though his interest was in symbols such as mandalas rather than techniques. In the 1950s and early 1960s a number of psychotherapists displayed intense interest in meditative practices: Stunkard (1951), Benoit (1955), Kondo (1958), Sato (1958), Fromm (1960), Jung (1961), Fingarette (1963), Assagioli (1965), Boss (1965), Krestschmer (1969), and Hirai (1975). Others, although not psycho-therapists, discussed meditation in psychoanalytic terms (Suzuki 1960; Watts 1961). It was argued that meditation, usually Zen, can be thera-peutic because it facilitates uncovering the unconscious. Also, the Zen view of life, with its emphasis on lessening selfish craving and striving, objective present-centred awareness, spontaneity, and acceptance of the world, was a view of health seen to be consistent with the ends of psychotherapy. Finally, *satori*, an altered state of consciousness characterized by radical diminishing of self-conscious awareness, was seen as having potentially psychotherapeutic effects. Similar arguments are made today. Meditation has been claimed to facilitate uncovering processes central to insight therapy (Carrington 1984; Kutz *et al.* 1985) and is a proposed relaxation tool or reciprocal inhibitor in behaviour therapy (Boudreau 1972; Wolpe in Shapiro 1984, p. 670). Unfortunately, careful clinical research on these ideas is virtually non-existent. Interest instead has turned in another direction.

For the relatively healthy individual, a case has been made for using meditation as a tool for dealing with stress. At one level the claimed meditative relaxation response can be used to minimize or recover from potentially debilitating stressful arousal (Benson 1975). More fundamentally, meditation as an attention-centring technique has been said to facilitate effective coping by enabling one to react with 'curiosity, acceptance, and interest rather than with threat' (Goleman and Schwarz 1976; Lehrer *et al.* 1980, 1983). A large number of studies has produced findings consistent with these claims. Meditation appears to have promise for treating: essential hypertension (Datey *et al.* 1969; Benson and Wallace 1972a; Patel 1973, 1975, 1984; Benson *et al.* 1974b; Patel and North 1975; Stone and DeLeo 1976; Benson 1977; Taylor *et al.* 1977; Frumkin *et al.* 1978; Henry 1978; Seer 1979; and Hafner 1982), type A coronary-prone behaviour (Muskatel *et al.* 1984), bronchial asthma (Honsberger and Wilson 1973; Wilson *et al.* 1975), premature ventricular contractions associated with ischaemic heart disease (Benson *et al.* 1975a), angina pectoris (Tulpule 1971; Zamarra *et al.* 1977), elevated serum cholesterol levels in hypercholesterolaemic patients (Cooper and Aygen 1979), obesity (Weldon and Aron 1977), stuttering (McIntyre *et al.* 1974), sleep-onset insomnia (Woolfolk *et al.* 1976; Miskiman 1977a, b), periodontal inflammation (Klemons 1977), and cancer (Meares 1982).

Finally, meditation has been used to treat various types of addictions and drug abuse. Subjects have reported decreased use of cigarettes, alcohol, amphetamines, barbiturates, marijuana, LSD, and heroin (Benson 1969; Benson and Wallace 1972b; Shafii *et al.* 1974; Shapiro and Zifferblatt 1976b; Brautigam 1977; Lazar *et al.* 1977; Marlatt *et al.* 1984).

Such studies offer the clinician a potentially useful source of ideas to be tried on a case by case basis (Smith 1986). However, they do not constitute substantial support for meditation's clinical impact. At the very least clinical meditation research suffers from methodological flaws I have outlined before (Smith 1975). Few have made an effort to control for the confounding effects of initial group differences, differential attrition, passage of time, repeated test taking, experimenter bias, expectation of relief, and so on. Far too frequently we hear apologies that preliminary studies can be forgiven for their deficiencies, that somehow the process of science permits a fledgling discipline to make a few mistakes, and that a large number of weak results can add up to a strong conclusion. However, meditation research has surely matured beyond its infancy (and is an adult of at least 50 years of age). Indeed, a respectable number of non-meditative treatments have amassed a more impressive record of effectiveness in fewer years. And there is only one way to interpret a growing mass of poorly designed studies: many wrongs still do not make a right.

However, there is a more serious weakness. All too often meditation has been conceptualized primarily as a mechanical self-regulation technique, one that might be applied in drug-like fashion to specific problems. Such an approach has led to two problems. First, if a study appears to show clinical impact, little direction is provided for its interpretation. One has free reign to offer any of a number of unrelated, unrevealing, and potentially contradictory explanations. For example, meditation: induces potentially therapeutic internal rhythms, yet fosters the absence of internal activity; enhances impulse control, yet increases spontaneity; provides an environment of social pressure for change, yet enables a client to rebel against society; provides diversion from sources of anxiety, yet encourages the unearthing of unconscious material; and triggers a physiological relaxation response, yet fosters an altered state of consciousness that may or may not have physiological correlates. Second, any of these claimed processes may operate equally well for other relaxation techniques, tempting one to discount superficially whatever unique potential meditation may possess. To summarize, defining meditation in primarily mechanical terms does little to help us understand its impact and encourages us to equate it with a variety of self-relaxation techniques that may have similar impact.

A skills-focused approach to meditation

Clinical process researchers (Orlinsky and Howard 1978; Parloff *et al.* 1978) have devoted 20 years to looking at two skills that contribute to change in therapy — therapist empathy and client experiential insight (or experiencing level). We can learn much from the direction this work has taken. Put simply, empathy can be seen as the ability to detect and reflect what another is feeling whereas experiencing is the ability to become aware of and share one's own feelings. One line of investigation has examined whether client growth is associated with his or her level of experiential insight as well as the level of therapist empathy. Evidence appears to strongly support both notions. Another path has considered the conditions necessary for the development of insight and empathy. Of particular interest to us is that both lines of research have emphasized skills over techniques. Unlike meditation researchers, those studying empathy and experiential insight have shown little interest in teaching therapists a specific 'empathy technique' or clients a specific 'insight technique'. Empathy and insight are complex skills that call for sophisticated strategies of investigation. I propose that the skills of meditation are no less complex.

To discover the importance of focusing on meditative skills over techniques, all we have to do is turn to traditional meditation texts. For example, Kapleau (1965) has offered a useful and highly quoted description of meditation:

In the broad sense *zazen* embraces more than just correct sitting. To enter fully into every action with total attention and clear awareness is no less *zazen*. The prescription for accomplishing this was given by the Buddha himself in an early sutra: 'In what is seen there must be just the seen; in what is heard there must be just the heard; in what is sensed (as smell, taste or touch) there must be just what is sensed; in what is thought there must be just the thought.'

Note that Kapleau says very little about the mechanics of a specific technique. Instead, he describes one meditative skill, focusing attention. Most traditional meditation texts, whether they be Christian, Buddhist, or Hindu, take a similar approach — considerable attention is devoted to the pyscholical, philosophical, and spiritual aspects of certain meditative skills, and little attention to specific exercises. As we shall see, such an emphasis helps us avoid the pitfalls of technique-focused research and permits a deeper appreciation of meditation's promise.

In two recent books (Smith 1985, 1986) I propose three meditative skills: *focusing*, *letting be*, and *receptivity*. Focusing is the ability to attend to a restricted stimulus for an extended period. Letting be is the ability to put aside unnecessary goal-directed and analytic activity. And receptivity is the willingness to tolerate and accept meditation experiences that may be uncertain, unfamiliar, and paradoxical. These skills may well be displayed in a meditation session. One diverts attention from hectic everyday concerns to, say, the simple flow of breath. One focuses. One puts aside attempts to force a particular pattern of breathing or analyse the breathing process, and so on. One maintains a stance of letting be. And one dispassionately accepts whatever changes may transpire such as images, unexpected feeling states, and the like. One remains receptive.

Meditative skills can be displayed when engaging in any form of relaxation. In progressive/isometric squeeze relaxation attention is focused on tensing up various muscles and then deliberately letting go. In yoga stretching one quietly attends to passively maintaining specific postures. In imagery one lets go of all attempts at physical activity and passively attends to relaxing mental pictures. Meditative skills can be present even in casual relaxation. Consider these examples:

One day I was doing my housework. Everything felt like it had to be done at once. I was wearing myself out. I decided I deserved and needed a rest and thought 'the next few minutes I'm going to set aside for doing just one thing . . . reading my favorite magazine'.

I was getting really tense over my job. Trivial things were getting to me. I finally took a break and relaxed. I said to myself 'Look, take it easy, there's no sense in trying to do everything at once. One task at a time. You can't change the world.'

After studying a few hours I like to rest on my couch and close my eyes. I let a pleasant fantasy of some distant tropical island go through my mind. I used to hesitate relaxing this way because my hands and arms would start feeling really warm and heavy. These sensations were new and strange to me. However, now I let myself feel warm and heavy. These feelings are OK. I even picture images that seem to foster warmth and heaviness.

The person who thinks 'the next new minutes I'm going to set aside for doing just one thing . . . reading my favorite magazine' has decided to focus. In the second example, the statement 'there's no sense trying to do everything at once. One task at a time' represents a decision to let go of unnecessary effortful striving. And the student who realizes 'I let myself feel warm and heavy. These feelings are OK' has learned to be receptive to experiencing the novel and unfamiliar. Focusing, letting be, and receptivity are not static responses, but active ways of dealing with oneself and the world in a more restful and present-centred way. They are the essence of meditation.

In broadest terms, meditative skills can be evoked by a wide range of life experiences. The victim of personal tragedy who learns to transcend cherished attachments; the minority job applicant who challenges an instance of discrimination; and the friend who risks an uncertain reaction by sharing care and love, may well be applauded for their courage and honesty. We can also think of their actions as deeply meditative. Each needless distraction put aside, whether it be to count breaths, accepting life in spite of loss, asserting one's rights, or even to expressing love, is a meditation. Each instance of pointless striving that is let go, whether it be attempting to force a meditative pattern of breathing, maintaining an illusory sense of security by effortfully avoiding confrontation, or trying to achieve the impossible at work, is also a meditation. And every time we risk action without certain reward, or open our eyes to the unspoken mysteries and possibilities of life, we are very much meditating.

Specific meditation instructions, whether they be derived from Zen, yoga, or Christianity, are special in one way. They represent direct requests to apply meditative skills in the simplest way possible. One set of instructions may emphasize quietly attending to a mantra and easily returning attention after every distraction. Another may focus on passively attending to the flow of all present stimuli. Both are essentially direct requests to 'focus your attention, maintain a stance of letting be, and be receptive to whatever may happen'. Such instructions may or may not enhance the acquisition of meditative skills. They may remind us of skills we already have. And they may inspire us to deploy such skills in everyday life. However, we must not be deceived into thinking that such instructions are any more meditative than the lessons of tragedy, love, and honest encounter. The instructions for meditation are found in all of life. And the essence of meditation can be discovered without uttering a single mantra, prayer, or count of breath.

The clinical impact of applying meditative skills: predisposing individual variables

A skills-focused approach to meditation prompts us to take a new look at meditation research, specifically at studies examining individual personality and clinical variables that predict treatment outcome. If a subject who possesses attributes suggesting the presence of meditative skills benefits from meditative treatments, one might argue that the application of meditative skills has clinical impact. Research tends to support this notion.

Absorption

Absorption refers to the disposition to display episodes of total attention 'during which the available representational apparatus seems to be entirely dedicated to experiencing and modeling the attentional object, be it a landscape, a human being, a sound, a remembered incident, or an aspect of one's self' (Tellegen and Atkinson 1974, p. 274). Inspection of the Tellegen Absorption Scale reveals many items that appear to call for specific meditative skills, particularly focusing (example: 'When I listen to music I can get so caught up in it that I don't notice anything else') and receptivity ('I sometimes "step outside" my usual self and experience an entirely different state of being.')

Davidson *et al.* (1976) examined trait anxiety (Spielberger *et al.* 1970) and Tellegen Absorption Scale (Tellegen and Atkinson 1974) scores of beginning, short-term, and long-term (who practised regularly for longer than 24 months) meditators. Most subjects practised TM, Zen, or related techniques. The impact of type of meditation practised was not examined. Advanced meditators displayed lower anxiety and higher absorption scores. This study can be interpreted in two ways. Either meditation reduces anxiety and increases absorption or those initially high in absorption are most likely to stay with meditation (and possibly display reductions in anxiety). The second interpretation seems more likely in light of studies reporting higher absorption scores among those attracted to meditation (Davidson and Goleman 1977). Indeed, my students (Curtis 1984; Siebert 1985) have failed to find any change in absorption among students practising up to 6 months of clinically standardized or mindfulness meditation.

16PF Factors A and M

The Sixteen Personality Factor Questionnaire (Cattell *et al.* 1970) is a popular omnibus inventory of personality. Two of its scales are of particular interest to us: factors A and M. Those scoring high in factor A, or 'sizothymia', are 'reserved, detached, critical, cool, aloof', and 'stiff'. Emotionally they are 'flat' or 'cautious'. They tend to be critical, precise, and sceptical, and like working alone with things or words rather than with people. In interpreting this factor, Cattell (1957) hypothesizes it reflects a 'steadiness in purpose and a high level of interest in symbolic and subjective activity . . . a secondary result of blocking of easy interaction with the changing external world'. Factor A could be argued to reflect a type of focusing ability (steadiness in purpose, blocking easy interaction with external change).

Those scoring high in factor M, or 'autia', tend to be unconventional and interested in 'art, theory, basic beliefs' and 'spiritual matters'. However, their most important characteristic is what Cattell variously describes as a tendency to be 'imaginatively enthralled by inner creations', 'charmed by works of the imagination', and 'completely absorbed' in the momentum of their own thoughts, following them 'wherever they lead, for their intrinsic attractiveness and with neglect of realistic considerations'. Cattell has speculated that fundamental to autia may be a capacity to dissociate and engage in 'autonomous, self-absorbed relaxation'. In sum, factor M contains many characteristics one might associate with focusing (a tendency to be enthralled, absorbed, etc.), letting be (following the momentum of one's own thoughts), and receptivity (neglecting realistic considerations).

In a 6-month double-blind study, Smith (1976) assigned 49 anxious college student volunteers to TM and 51 to a control treatment that involved sitting without meditating. For each treatment 30 demographic and pretest personality variables were correlated with continuation 'in treatment and pre–post test improvements in trait anxiety. The strongest predictors of improvement were factors A and M. Another study (Carrington *et al.* 1980) found factors A and M did not predict outcome for non-anxious subjects receivinng audio-taped training in clinically standardized meditation. If indeed factors A and M indicate the possession of meditative skills, these two studies can be interpreted in different ways. Perhaps those who possess meditative skills are most attracted to the TM rationale (but not Carrington's) and are more likely to apply meditative skills and benefit. Perhaps an initial level of anxiety is necessary to motivate subjects to apply meditative skills. Perhaps audio tapes are inadequate for teaching meditation.

Openness to experience

The Fitzgerald (1966) Experience Inquiry is described as a measure of 'openness to inner and outer experience'. Those who score high are claimed to be 'not bound by the conventional modes of thought, memory and perception; they are sensitive to the possibilities and subtle nuances of experience which elude others; they are at home in the midst of conceptual disorder and complexity' and they 'seek change and novelty'. The test is made up of items derived from the following categories: tolerance for regressive experience, tolerance for logical inconsistencies, constructive use of regression, capacity for regressive experiences, altered states, peak experiences, and tolerance for the irrational. It is a test that appears to reflect meditative receptivity.

In a study involving teaching 4 weeks of Zen breath-counting meditation to 16 Master's level students in counselling, Lesh (1970b) found that subjects scoring highest at pretest on the Experience Inquiry are most likely to report experiences of calm, concentration, alertness, satisfaction, and emotional insight while meditating.

High resting alpha

EEG alpha is a brainwave pattern often associated with reduced anxiety and restful alertness. It is a pattern frequently displayed in meditation and, by inference, may indicate the successful application of meditative skills. Anand *et al.* (1961), researchers who pioneered early EEG meditation studies on yogis, have observed in passing that 'those who had a well marked alpha activity in their normal resting records showed greater aptitude and zeal for maintaining the practice of yoga'.

Low intrusion count in meditation

Distractions are a common experience in meditation. Elsewhere I argue that a high level of distractions may indicate a low level of focusing, letting be, and receptivity (Smith 1985, 1986). In an 8-week study Curtis (1984) taught 43 non-student volunteers CSM. An interesting pattern emerged concerning those who benefited most. Subjects who report the fewest distractions (or 'instrusions') while meditating display the greatest reductions in worry or cognitive stress (but not in somatic symptomatology) over 8 weeks. Distractions were measured directly; in each meditation session subjects pushed a small counter-button every time a distraction was experienced (Van Nuys 1973). Moreover, subjects who display fewest distractions are most likely to practice regularly. These results suggest that those who can deploy meditative skills are more likely to continue meditating and experience reductions in cognitive symptomatology.

However, an additional finding puts this pattern of results in a slightly different perspective. Subjects most likely to display distractions during meditation are, before training begins, more likely to display physical reactions (rather than worry) when under stress. Curtis concluded that somatic stress and anxiety are particularly disruptive during meditation. The meditator with chronic muscle tension, stomach trouble, breathing difficulties, and so on, is likely to be distracted by these symptoms, quit practising, and not benefit. These results suggest another broad pattern of predictive variables: degree of psychopathology, particularly anxiety.

Somatic vs. cognitive anxiety

In a widely cited proposal, Davidson and Schwarz (1976) have suggested that different approaches to self-relaxation can be targeted to somatic or cognitive anxiety. Progressive/isometric squeeze relaxation, a physical approach, should be more effective with somatic symptoms and meditation, a cognitive approach, with cognitive symptoms. Many researchers have presented evidence inconsistent with this proposal (Smith 1976, 1978; Carrington 1984; Lehrer and Woolfolk 1984). However, as mentioned above, initial somatic (but not cognitive) symptomatology may well make application of meditative skills particularly difficult.

Degree of disturbance

A number of studies have found that students who drop out of TM tend to appear highly defensive on the Tennessee Self Concept Scale (Smith 1978) and other measures (Otis 1974a). They also score higher on measures of psychoticism (Smith 1978), have serious problems (Otis 1974a), and are emotionally disturbed (Kanas and Horowitz 1977). Although a variety of interpretations are possible for this pattern, one can speculate that highly disturbed individuals may simply find it difficult to focus, maintain a stance of passivity, or receptively tolerate unusual experiences. They may also experience distracting adverse effects (Davidson and Goleman 1977; Otis 1984).

The Vahia study

Our interpretation of the above studies is, of course, highly speculative. We have no way of knowing for sure whether subjects displaying absorption, 16 PF factors A and M, openness to experience, high resting alpha, fewer intrusions in meditation, and low levels of pathology are indeed deploying meditative skills. Few therapists or researchers have taken a skills-focused approach towards meditation. However, I would like to describe one study that comes close to meeting our notions of how meditation can be applied and studied clinically.

Vahia and his colleagues (Vahia *et al.* 1973) wished to isolate the essential components of 'psychophysiological therapy', a yoga-meditation therapy based on ancient Hindu yoga teachings. Ninety-five neurotic patients who displayed no improvement in response to previous therapy were randomly divided into two groups matched for age, sex, diagnosis, and duration of illness. One group was given total psychophysiological therapy (yoga plus meditation) while the other group was given partial psychophysiological therapy (a control treatment consisting of exercises resembling yoga and no meditation). Both groups practised for 1 hour each day for 4 to 6 weeks and were given support, reassurance, and placebo tablets.

Measurements included: blind clinical assessment before, after, and every week of the project; MMPI and Rorschach tests given before and after the project; the Taylor Manifest Anxiety Scale given before, after, and every week of the project; and daily notebooks written by all subjects on thoughts that came to mind while practising. The results showed treatment with meditation to be more effective than treatment without meditation. Furthermore, those who displayed greater ability to meditate displayed the most clinical improvement.

Two features of this study merit comment. First, meditation was not taught as a mechanical technique. The therapist had 11 years of experience in yoga and took care to teach preparatory stretching and breathing exercises before introducing meditation. Furthermore, meditative exercises were presented in the psychological and philosophical context of Patanjali's yoga system. Secondly, care was taken to score daily notebooks objectively for the degree of meditative concentration each subject displayed. In sum, this project focused primarily on teaching and measuring meditative skills.

Meditative skills and self-relaxation

To appreciate fully the clinical and empirical implications of a skills-focused approach, one needs to step back and examine meditation in the context of popular approaches to self-relaxation. Elsewhere I have proposed that the vast array of relaxation techniques available can be ordered along a nine-level hierarchy (Table 8.1). The meditative skills approach helps us understand their different requirements and effects. Some strategies, such as progressive/isometric squeeze relaxation and yoga stretching, require relatively little skill. For example, progressive/isometric squeeze relaxation makes focusing easy. Each muscle group is relaxed for only a few minutes (at least in revised approaches). Considerable latitude is given concerning the target of attention (muscle sensations, associated images, relaxing internal phrases). Similarly, the required level of letting be is relatively easy to attain through simple isometric action and relaxation. And since with progressive/isometric squeeze relaxation the task is familiar (most people know how to make a fist, cringe, shrug their shoulders, and so on) little receptivity is required.

Imagery approaches require an intermediate level of skill. The focus is more limited. Instead of attending to various body movements,

Table 8.1 Approaches to self-relaxation ranked according to required focus, letting be, and receptivity (Smith 1985)

(1) Isometric squeeze relaxation
   (progressive relaxation)
(2) Yogaform stretching
(3) Breathing exercises
(4) Somatic focusing I
   (beginning autogenic exercises, some hypnosis exercises)
(5) Somatic focusing II
   (advanced autogenic exercises, Kundalini Yoga, some Zen exercises)
(6) Thematic imagery
   (guided imagery, advanced autogenic exercises, some hypnosis exercises)
(7) Contemplation
   ('creativity exercises', some forms of 'prayer' and 'meditation')
(8) Centred-focus meditation
   (TM, CSM, Benson's method)
(9) Open focus meditation
   (Zen, mindfulness, openness techniques)

sensations, and images, one attends only to images. The task is considerably more passive since one ceases all physical activity. Many chronically tense individuals find devoting 15 to 20 minutes to a single set of relaxing images an unfamiliar and even discomforting task. Imagery requires a moderate level of receptivity.

The most difficult approaches to relaxation are contemplation and meditation. For each the focal stimulus is utterly singular: the count of breaths, a mantra, the flow of present stimuli, and so on. It is not easy to restrict attention to such a stimulus for an extended period of time. In addition, considerable skill at letting be is required. Indeed, any effort to direct or control where the session is going would be considered a distraction. One simply attends and passively lets experiences come and go as they will. Finally, meditation can often stir images and sensations that many find unusual and unexpected. To meditate, one must be willing to tolerate and accept such experiences.

Clinical meditation research: new questions

We are now ready to return to our consideration of the clinical investigation of meditation. When careful attention is devoted to ensure that meditative skills are developed, the instruction of meditation becomes a complex challenge. In teaching meditation for research purposes, I have subjects go through the following steps (Smith 1985):

(1) Receive rationale;
(2) Experiment with a variety of premeditation warm-up exercises;
(3) Select a personalized warm-up sequence;
(4) Practise and master a warm-up sequence;
(5) Experiment with a variety of meditation strategies;
(6) Select a personalized meditation strategy;
(7) Practise and master meditation;
(8) Apply meditation in actual life settings; generalize meditative skills outside of the practice session.

Traditionally, meditation researchers teach an abbreviated single technique in a single step. At best, this can be seen as an analogue approach. To elaborate, in psychotherapy analogue research non-clinical volunteers receive shortened versions of therapy. For example, an analogue study of classical desensitization might examine the effects of three sessions of *in vitro* desensitization on fear of spiders. A student might be taught to imagine spiders while remaining relaxed. A complete version of the same treatment would be targeted to a clinical phobia, and might run for 10 sessions involving a full regimen of strategies (presentation of rationale, relaxation training, hierarchy building, graduated *in vitro* desensitization progressing to *in vivo* desensitization in which desensitization is generalized to life outside the therapy session). Analogue studies have their place. They are inexpensive and brief. They enable the researcher to examine the impact of one component of treatment. However, analogues are by definition something less than the real thing. To understand meditation training fully, we will at some time have to examine all of its components.

However, even if studies include complex and sophisticated versions of meditation instruction, important processes may still be missed. It is important actually to state hypotheses in terms of meditative skills. Specifically, one might ask such questions as:

Do subjects who initially possess meditative skills benefit from meditation training more than those who do not?

Do subjects who initially possess meditative skills deploy these skills in everday life, even without formal meditation training? Do they benefit from such deployment?

What is the relative contribution of each component of training — presentation of rationale, warm-up exercises, meditation exercises, and generalization — to the acquisition and deployment of meditative skills?

To what extent do approaches such as isometric squeeze relaxation, yogaform stretching, relaxed breathing, somatic focusing, thematic imagery, and contemplation (Smith 1985) contribute to the development of meditative skills?

Do different meditation techniques require different levels of skill? Do techniques differ in their impact on skills acquisition?

Does the deployment of meditative skills in everyday life have therapeutic potential?

What is the relationship between deployment of meditative skills (both in and out of the meditation session) and somatic arousal or EEG activity?

The clinical use of meditation

It is troubling that more than a few clinicians are content to use meditation analogues with their clients. Although my particular version of full meditation training may or may not be appropriate for others, I would like to share a number of general observations concerning clinical instruction of meditation.

(1) It is a mistake to teach meditation without paying attention to meditative skills and their place in a rewarding and meaningful life. The clinician should be sensitive to manifestations of focusing, letting be, and receptivity in a client's life, variables that contribute to development of such skills, and generalization of meditative skills outside of the meditation session.

(2) Careful attention should be devoted to the rationale for meditation. For spiritually inclined clients, meditation can be described in spiritual terms. For those who are scientifically inclined, a research-derived rationale may be more appropriate. Most important, a rationale can go far towards communicating the nature of focusing, letting be, and receptivity. Indeed, a skilfully presented rationale, sensitively tailored to client needs, can inspire a client to discover and apply meditative skills before first learning a meditation exercise.

(3) The most difficult task in learning to meditate is learning to set time aside on a daily basis. Rather than browbeat clients into compliance, I recommend treating setting time aside as a learnable skill. Before teaching meditation, clients can be instructed to simply sit for 20 to 30 minutes each day while doing a quiet, pleasurable activity. By doing this, the skill of setting time aside is made as easy and rewarding as possible (Smith 1985).

(4) The therapy client may be less prepared for meditation than the average meditation student. Meditation should be preceded with considerable preliminary training designed to enhance skills at generating physical calm, focused attention, letting be, and receptivity. This training might include biofeedback, progressive/isometric squeeze relaxation, yogaform stretching, integrative breathing, or thematic imagery (Smith 1985). Using behavioural shaping, meditation can be taught in easy, rewarding, and interesting steps, that is, through successive approximations. For example, I have clients proceed through the following steps (Smith 1986):

(a) Chart 'meditative' exercises (reflecting focusing, letting be, and receptivity) in everyday life.
(b) Acquire the habit of setting time aside on a daily basis.
(c) Learn a simple, physical relaxation exercise (eventually to be used as a premeditation warm-up).
(d) Learn a simple, basic meditation exercise (concentrative or centred-focus approach).
(e) Learn an advanced meditation exercise (meditative imagery, transcendent imagery, meditative contemplation, open focus meditation)
(f) Apply meditative skills in everyday life.

(5) Care should be taken to tailor meditation and premeditation warm-up exercises to client needs. Since different clients respond to different approaches, it would be unwise to impose the same two or three exercises on all. In my own practice, I introduce clients to six basic and four advanced approaches to meditation (although I make no claim that this exhausts what is available).

(6) Each meditation session should be preceded with a brief warm-up exercise. Five to 10 minutes of stretching and breathing exercises can provide a powerful discriminative cue for meditation

(setting meditation apart from the rest of the day's activities), help focus attention, and reduce potentially distracting sources of physical tension.

Summary

Does meditation have psychotherapeutic potential? Is meditation any different from other relaxation techniques used in therapy? We have seen that such questions have been relatively unproductive and are based on an oversimplified view of meditation as a technique. Meditation is not so much a technique as a set of skills — focusing, letting be, and receptivity. Such an approach reveals significant differences among a wide range of relaxation strategies, including progressive/isometric squeeze relaxation, stretching, breathing, imagery, and contemplation. The technique of meditation represents the simplest application of these skills. The skills-focused approach prompts us to ask a new set of research questions, for example: How are meditative skills acquired and what is the clinical effect of their deployment in everyday life? It is an approach that suggests a comprehensive way of teaching meditation, one that respects the complexity and diversity of meditation and its potential for enriching all of life.

9 Managing meditation in clinical practice

Patricia Carrington

In recent years modern forms of meditation have been developed which possess therapeutic properties. This chapter describes how these new forms, simplified and divested of esoteric trappings and religious overtones, can be applied in clinical practice to achieve specific objectives.

The orientation presented here is based on my supervision of the teaching of approximately 7000 people in clinical settings during the past 14 years. Most of these people were identified by a medical team or through other professional assessment as being under high stress. Some of them were people who had recognized their own symptoms of stress and independently sought clinical assistance from meditation training. In the overwhelming majority of cases, these people benefited from having learned meditation. Often clinical improvement was marked. In the present discussion I will attempt to identify the major clinical benefits that can be expected from the practice of meditation, to outline some of the available training options and to present recommendations for professionals wishing to utilize this form of therapy.

Of all the Westernized forms of meditation, TM is undoubtedly the most widely known and extensively studied. Probably more accurately described as 'transitional' rather than modern, because it retains cultic features such as the *'puja'* (Hindu religious ceremony), TM is taught by an international organization that does not permit mental health practitioners to assume an active role in the clinical management of the technique (unless they are TM teachers). Despite its more general popularity, therefore, the TM method is seldom used in clinical settings.

Among the clinically oriented meditation techniques, CSM (Carrington 1978) and the 'respiratory one method' (ROM—Benson 1975) have been the most widely used to date. These two techniques, devised for clinical purposes and strictly non-cultic, differ from each other in several respects. A trainee learning CSM selects a sound from a standard list of sounds (or creates one according to directions) and then repeats this sound mentally, *without* intentionally linking the sound to the breathing pattern or pacing it in any structured manner. CSM is a relatively permissive meditation technique and may be subjectively experienced as almost 'effortless'. By contrast, when practising ROM, the trainee repeats the word 'one' (or another word or phrase) to himself or herself mentally, while at the same time intentionally linking this word with each exhalation. ROM is thus a relatively disciplined form of meditation with two meditational objects — the chosen word and the breath — which must be synchronized, and requires more mental effort than CSM. Clinical experience suggests (Carrington 1977) that it may thus appeal to a different type of person. Other modern methods of meditation have also been used in some clinical settings, but they are less standardized and depend more heavily on individual expertise and the personality of the instructor. These less commonly used forms will not be discussed here, although their usefulness in the proper hands is not to be negated.

Clinical conditions responding to meditation

Based on both research and clinical reports, a substantial body of knowledge has accumulated concerning the usefulness of meditation in clinical settings. Some of the major findings in this area are as follows:

Reduction in tension–anxiety

Where the effects of meditation on anxiety have been measured, results have shown reduction in anxiety among subjects after they commence the practice of meditation (Carrington 1977 and Chapter 7 this volume). Glueck (1973), in a study conducted with a group of psychiatric in-patients, found that dosages of psychotropic drugs could be greatly reduced after these patients had been meditating for several weeks and that, in a majority of cases, sedatives could also be reduced or eliminated. The quieting effects of meditation differ from the effects brought about by psychotropic drugs; drugs may slow a person down and cause grogginess, while meditative relaxation does not appear to reduce alertness. On the contrary, meditation seems, if anything, to sharpen alertness. Groups of meditators have been shown to have better refinement of auditory perception (Pirot 1977), and to perform more rapidly and accurately on perceptual–motor tasks (Rimol 1978) than non-meditating controls.

Improvement in stress-related illnesses

Many stress-related illnesses have proved responsive to meditation (see Chapter 8). Research has shown meditation to be correlated with improvement in the breathing patterns of patients with bronchial asthma (Honsberger and Wilson 1973), with decreased blood pressure in both pharmacologically treated and untreated hypertensive patients (Patel 1973, 1975; Benson 1977), with reduced premature ventricular contractions in patients with ischaemic heart disease (Benson *et al.* 1975a), with reduced serum cholesterol levels in hypercholesterolaemic patients (Cooper and Aygen 1979), with reduced sleep-onset insomnia (Woolfolk *et al.* 1976; Miskiman 1977a, b), with amelioration of stuttering (McIntyre *et al.* 1974), as well as with reduction of symptoms of psychiatric illness (Glueck and Stroebel 1975).

Increased productivity

Meditation may bring about increased efficiency by eliminating un-necessary expenditures of energy, a beneficial surge of energy often being noted in persons who have commenced the practice. This can manifest itself variously as a lessened need for daytime naps, increased physical stamina, increased productivity at work, increased ideational fluency, the dissolution of writer's or artist's 'block', or the release of hitherto unsuspected creative potentials (Carrington 1977).

Reduced self-blame

A beneficial by-product of meditation may be increased self-acceptance, often evidenced in clients as a lessening of unproductive self-blame. A spontaneous change in the nature of the meditator's 'self-statements' — from self-castigating to self-accepting — suggests that the non-critical state experienced during the meditation session itself often generalizes to daily life. Along with the tendency to be less self-critical, the meditator may show a simultaneous increase in tolerance for the human frailties of others, and accordingly there is often concomitant improvement in interpersonal relationships. Meditation may therefore be indicated when a tendency toward self-blame is excessive or where irrational blame of others is a problem.

Anti-addictive effects

A series of studies (Benson and Wallace 1971; Shafii *et al.* 1974, 1975) has suggested that, at least in persons who continue meditating for long periods of time (usually for a year or more), there may be a marked decrease in the use of non-prescription drugs such as marijuana, amphetamines, barbiturates, and psychedelic substances (e.g. LSD). Many long-term meditators report discontinued use of such drugs entirely. Similar anti-addictive trends have been reported in ordinary cigarette smokers and abusers of alcohol (Shafii *et al.* 1976).

Mood elevation

Some research and clinical evidence indicate that people suffering from mild chronic depression or from reactive depression may experience distinct elevation of mood after commencing meditation (Carrington *et al.* 1980). However, people with acute depressive reactions do not generally respond well to meditation and are likely to discontinue practice (Carrington and Ephron 1975a, b).

Increase in available affect

Those who have commenced meditating frequently report experiencing pleasure, sadness, anger, love, or other emotions more easily than before. Sometimes they experience emotions that have previously been unavailable to them at a conscious level. Release of such emotions may occur during a meditation session or between sessions, and may be associated with the recovery of memories that are highly charged emotionally (Carrington 1977). Meditation may therefore be indicated where affect is flat, where the client tends toward overintellectualization, or where access to memories of an emotional nature is desired for therapeutic purposes.

Increased sense of identity

Clinical experience suggests that meditation may increase 'psychological differentiation', (Carrington 1977). Those with a high degree of psychological differentiation are said to be inner rather than outer directed, better able to use their own selves as reference points when making judgements or decisions, have a clearer sense of their separate identity, and be more aware of needs, feelings, and attributes that they recognize as their own, distinct from those of others. Such persons have been termed 'field independent'. Persons with a less developed sense of separate identity — those who tend to rely on external sources for definition of their attitudes, judgements, sentiments, and views of themselves — have been termed 'field dependent'.

When meditators have been tested for field dependence–independence before learning to meditate, and then retested several months later, studies from several different laboratories have shown changes in the direction of greater field independence (Hines, cited in Carrington 1977; Pelletier 1977). Consistent with this research, meditating clients frequently report that they have become more aware of their own opinions since commencing meditation, are not as easily influenced by others as they were previously, and can arrive at decisions more quickly and easily. By being better able to sense their own needs, they may become more outspoken and assertive. One result of this increased sense of identity may be the improved ability to separate from significant others when appropriate. Meditation can thus be extremely useful in pathological bereavement reactions, or where an impending separation (threatened death of a loved one, contemplated divorce, upcoming separation from growing children, etc.) presents a problem. Since it is particularly useful in bolstering the inner sense of 'self' necessary for effective self-assertion, it may also be helpful as an adjunct to assertiveness training.

Lowered irritability

The meditator may become markedly less irritable in his or her inter-personal relationships within a relatively short time after commencing meditation (Carrington *et al.* 1980), and meditation appears indicated where impulsive outbursts or chronic irritability is a symptom. This recommendation includes cases of organic irritability since preliminary observations have shown meditation to be useful in increasing overall adjustments in several cases of brain injury (Glueck 1973).

Determining when to use meditation

While some attempts have been made to identify personality charac-teristics of the meditation-responsive person, the bulk of studies have used non-clinical populations, and criteria for 'responsiveness to meditation' have often not been relevant to problems involved in clinical assessment. The only area of clinical improvement examined in relation to personality factors is anxiety reduction. Beiman *et al.* (1980) noted that the more internal the locus of control of participants prior to meditation instruction, the greater are the reductions in anxiety. Smith (1978) found that reductions in trait anxiety following meditation training were moderately correlated with two of Cattell's 16PF factors: 'autia' (pre-occupation with inner ideas and emotions) and 'schizothymia' (steadiness of purpose, withdrawal, emotional flatness, and 'coolness'). However, Carrington *et al.* (1980), studying employee stress in a large corporation, found no significant correlations between any of the 16PF factors (including anxiety) measured at pretest, and subsequent drops in symptomatology as measured by the Revised 90-Item Symptom Checklist (SCL-90-R).

The research to date does not therefore enable us to predict, using standard personality tests, which clients will respond positively to meditation. However, there has been at least one attempt to predict successful meditation practice from theory. Davidson and Schwarz (1976) have suggested that relaxation techniques have varied effects, depending on the system (somatic or cognitive) at which they are most directly aimed (see Chapter 3, this volume). They categorize progressive relaxation as a 'somatically oriented technique', because it involves learning to pay close attention to physiological sensations, particularly muscle tension; while they categorize mantra meditations as 'cogni-tively oriented techniques', since repeating a word presumably blocks other ongoing cognitive activity. In support of this, Schwarz *et al.* (1978) report questionnaire data showing that meditation produces greater decreases in cognitive symptoms of anxiety than does physical exercise, while the latter appears to produce greater decreases in somatic anxiety symptoms.

Some clinicians have therefore felt justified in advising meditation for clients who show symptoms of cognitive anxiety, and in advising physiologically oriented techniques such as progressive relaxation or autogenic training for those who show symptoms of somatic anxiety. While this criterion has the advantage of simplicity, present empirical support for cognitive-somatic specialization remains at best insubstantial (Woolfolk and Lehrer 1984).

To assess the suitability of meditation for a particular client therefore, a clinician should check whether the client shows one or more of the following meditation-responsive symptoms or difficulties:

Tension and/or anxiety states;

Psychophysiological disorders;

Chronic fatigue states;

Insomnias or hypersomnias;

Abuse of 'soft' drugs, alcohol, or tobacco;

Excessive self-blame;

Chronic low-grade depressions or subacute reaction depressions;

Irritability, low frustration tolerance;

Strong submissive trends, poorly developed psychological differentiation, difficulties with self-assertion;

Pathological bereavement reactions, separation anxiety;

Blocks to productivity or creativity;

Inadequate contact with affective life;

A need to shift emphasis from client's reliance on therapist to reliance on self (of particular use when terminating psychotherapy).

Clearly other treatment modalities may also be appropriate and the decision to employ meditation therefore becomes largely a practical one. A number of factors may guide this decision:

1. Degree of self-discipline. The degree to which the client has a disciplined lifestyle should be considered since meditation requires less self-discipline than do most other methods currently used for stress control. The technique itself can usually be taught in a single session, with the remainder of the instruction consisting of training in practical management of the method. Unlike some other techniques, meditation does not require the memorization and carrying out of any sequential procedures; it does not even require the mental effort involved in visualizing muscle groups and their relaxation, or in constructing 'calm scenes' or other images. The modern forms of meditation are simple one-step operations that soon become quite automatic.

2. Need for reinforcement. The peaceful, drifting mental state of meditation is experienced as unusually pleasurable by many people and as a 'vacation' from all cares. This self-reinforcing property makes it very appealing to many clients. Clinical experience suggests that, other things being equal, a modern form of meditation is more likely to be continued, once experienced, than are the more focused relaxation

procedures. When motivation to continue with a programme for stress management is minimal, meditation may therefore be a particularly useful strategy.

3.   Clients with an excessive need to control. Clients fearful of losing 'control' may equate meditation with hypnosis or forms of 'mind control' and thus be wary of learning the technique. If they do learn, they may experience the meditation as a form of punishment, a surrender, a loss of dominance, or a threat to a need on their part to manipulate others, and may soon discontinue the practice unless therapeutic intervention brings about a sufficient change in attitude. Such overly controlling clients may prefer a more 'objective' technique that they can manage through conscious effort (e.g. by tensing and relaxing muscles or dealing with biofeedback hardware). The response of a client to a clinician's initial suggestion that he or she learn meditation will often be the clue — those clients who fear loss of control from meditation will usually indicate this and respond very negatively.

Limitations of meditation in clinical settings

Tension-release side effects

Meditation, like all techniques used to bring about personality change, has its limitations. One of these is the stress-release component of meditation, which must be understood if this technique is to be used effectively. Particularly in the new meditator, physiological and/or psychological symptoms of a temporary nature may appear during or following meditation. These have been described elsewhere (Carrington 1977, 1978). They appear to be caused by the release of deep-seated non-verbal tensions. While their occurrence can be therapeutically useful (provided the therapist is trained in handling them properly), too rapid a release of tension during or following meditation can cause difficulties and discouragement in a new meditator and may result in a client's backing off from meditation or even abandoning the practice altogether. For this reason, careful adjustment of meditation time and other key aspects of the technique must be made if this modality is to be used successfully. Such adjustments can usually eliminate problems of tension release in short order.

Too rapid behavioural change

Ironically, a potential problem in the use of meditation stems from the rapidity with which certain alterations in behaviour may occur. Some of these changes may be incompatible with the lifestyle or defensive system of the client. Should positive behavioural change occur before the groundwork for it has been laid (i.e. before the client's value system has readjusted through therapy), an impasse can occur, which must then be resolved in one of two ways: (1) the pathological value system will be altered to incorporate the new attitude brought about by the meditation, or (2) the practice of meditation will be abandoned. If the meditator facing such an impasse has recourse to psychotherapy to work through the difficulties involved, this may allow the individual to continue productively with meditation and make use of it to effect a basic change in lifestyle.

Some of the ways in which meditation-related behavioural changes may threaten a client's pathological lifestyle are:

1. Meditation may foster a form of self-assertion that conflicts with an already established neurotic 'solution' of being overly self-effacing. The tendency toward self-effacement must be modified before meditation can be accepted into the person's life as a permanent and beneficial practice.
2. Meditation tends to bring about feelings of well-being and optimism which may threaten the playing out of a depressive role that has served an important function in the client's psychic economy.
3. The deeply pleasurable feelings that can accompany or follow a meditation session can cause anxiety. For example, clients with masturbation guilt may unconsciously equate meditation (an experience where one is alone and gives oneself pleasure) to masturbation, and thus may characterize it as a 'forbidden' activity.
4. Meditation can result in an easing of life pace which may threaten a fast-paced, high-pressured lifestyle that is used neurotically as a defence, or in the service of drives for power, achievement, or control. Clients sensing this possibility may refuse to start meditating in the first place. If they start they may quickly discontinue the practice unless these personality problems are treated.
5. The client may develop negative reactions to the meditation process, or to a meditational object of focus such as a mantra. Some individuals view meditation initially as being almost 'magical'. When they inevitably recognize that the technique varies in its effectiveness according to external circumstances, or according to their own mood or state of health, they may become outraged and quit the practice unless the clinician can help them modify these irrational demands.

Such complications do not occur in all meditating patients by any means. Often meditation assists the course of therapy in such a straightforward fashion that there is little necessity to be overly concerned with the client's reaction to it.

Representative clinical applications

CASE NO. 1

Adele applied to the guidance clinic for help for her young daughter, who was suffering from severe anxieties which hampered her at school. Although she denied the need for any psychotherapy for herself, she was obviously tense, her voice was high pitched, her breathing rapid, and her speech pressured. She had a chronic heart condition for which she took medication several times a day and she suffered from high blood pressure as well as a thyroid condition. Soon after her daughter began to be seen for psychiatric treatment, Adele complained that she was unable to cope with the child and entered a mothers' guidance group. When she joined the group she was fearful about whether or not she would 'fit in' with the other mothers and it seemed that she was trying extremely hard to be liked by them. Because she was so tense, I recommended meditation as a useful aid to her treatment.

When Adele learned CSM, her initial response was powerful. During her first meditation she felt as though she were a 'bird gliding freely through the skies', experiencing a wonderful sense of freedom as she drifted over the countryside. During this first meditation, too, she spontaneously shifted from using the mantra which she had chosen from the list of CSM mantras, and substituted for it a phrase of her own which suddenly popped into her mind — 'inner peace'. She continued to use this self-made mantra from then on and found it most effective.

The effect of meditation on Adele's life were immediate. Within two days of commencing this practice, her heartbeat became slow and regular and she was able to dispense with her heart medication within the first week of learning to meditate. She has never returned to it.

During the first few weeks, her meditations involved images of floating and drifting in the sky among nature, flowers, and other peaceful symbols. Soon, however, these pleasant 'floating' sensations began to alternate with frightening ones in which she would see atomic explosions or other cataclysmic happenings during her meditation. At this time Adele requested an individual psychotherapy session with me.

Because she seemed unusually tense, I suggested that she and I meditate together. We had been meditating for about 10 minutes when the session was interrupted by loud, almost hysterical laughter. Adele explained that she had had a sudden fantasy during meditation: she had imagined she was on a boat with her mother and she had pushed her mother off into the water. It had given her so much pleasure that she could not restrain herself from bursting out laughing. She confided in me that this fantasy was an 'incredible thought' for her and wanted to know if it was 'normal' for her to have such thoughts. When I assured her it was normal to have many mixed feelings about a parent, a floodgate opened. Up until this point she had insisted that her parents were 'fine and wonderful people — no one could ask for better'. Now she revealed that she had been a battered child living in terror of an apparently psychotic mother. One memory after another came to the surface in this session, and in subsequent meditation sessions. Some of these were memories which she had managed to push out of her mind since childhood.

As she began to discuss her mother's maltreatment of her in individual psychotherapy, her meditations became filled with hostile fantasies towards her mother. At one point she vividly pictured an atomic bomb that killed her parents but spared the rest of the population. So many painful memories were beginning to surface during her meditation sessions that Adele began to dread meditating, while at the same time she did not want to stop because it was obviously benefiting her heart condition. At this point I advised her to reduce her meditation time to 3 to 5 minutes per session to slow up tension release. This worked well and Adele was soon ready to share her painful memories with the mothers' group in which she participated.

Her mother's childhood threats about the terrible punishment that would follow if she told anyone about her maltreatment were still deeply ingrained. When the other women in the group accepted her painful revelations with understanding and support, it was a source of strength for her. She was able to accept the fact that her mother had been mentally ill and probably had not been responsible for her actions. This realization so relieved Adele that she was able to return to meditating for a full 20 minutes twice a day, a schedule she had been able to maintain ever since. Memories now stopped flooding her meditation sessions and the latter were once more filled with largely pleasant fantasies, with only occasionally a momentary violent scene.

From then on Adele found herself less harassed about many things. When her children started yelling at each other around the house, it no longer upset her. Her compulsive nail biting stopped. Lifelong nightmares receded to almost zero. It was instructive to see her lose her need to prove to the world that she was 'self-sacrificing'. She was now easygoing and casual in the mother's group and had stopped trying to solve everyone else's problems for them. As she worked through her painful relationship with her own mother, she also found herself able to play with her little daughter for the first time, and thoroughly enjoyed doing so.

Adele told me that if she had not had individual psychotherapy sessions along with meditation she would have been so frightened by the upsurge of painful memories that she would not have been able to continue meditating. Had she not had my support and later the encouragement of the group to help her handle her anger at her mother, she almost certainly would have had to stop practising meditation. She was initially too fearful of facing the painful areas in her life to have allowed herself to enter individual psychotherapy of the type where free association might have been used to recover repressed memories. Meditation enabled these memories to surface within a remarkably short timespan so they could be constructively dealt with in her therapy.

CASE NO. 2

Meditation was recommended for a middle-aged female client whose chronic tension headaches had consistently resisted all forms of intervention, although her other psychosomatic symptoms (e.g. gastric ulcer and colitis) had abated with therapy. After she commenced meditation, this client's headaches worsened for a period of about a week (temporary symptom acceleration is not unusual following commencement of meditation) and then abruptly disappeared. The patient remained entirely free of headaches for 4 months (for the first time in many years).

During this period, however, she noticed personality changes that disturbed her and that she attributed to meditation. Formerly self-sacrificing and playing the role of a 'martyr' to her children, husband, and parents, she now began to find herself increasingly aware of her own rights and impelled to stand up for them, sometimes so forcefully that it alarmed her. Although she was apparently effective in this new self-assertion (her adolescent sons began to treat her more gently, making far fewer scathing comments), other members of her family commented that she was no longer the 'sweet person' that she used to be, and the client soon complained that 'meditation is making me a hateful person'.

At the same time this client also noticed that she was no longer talking compulsively — a change for which she received favourable comments from others, but which bothered her because she was now able to sense the social uneasiness that had been hidden beneath her compulsive chatter. She related this tendency to remain quieter in social situations directly to meditation, since it was more likely to occur soon after a meditation session. Unable to assimilate the personality changes noted, the client stopped meditating, despite the fact that her tension headaches had returned.

At this point in therapy it was necessary to trace the origins of this client's need to be self-effacing before she could consider reinstating the practice of meditation. In doing so, it was discovered that her competition with an older sister was at the root of much of her difficulty in this respect. This sister had been considered a 'saint' by their parents, while the client had always been considered a troublesome, irritating child. During her childhood she had despaired at this state of affairs; but in her adolescence she developed an intense compulsion to become more 'saintly' than her exalted sister, although this often meant total sacrifice of her own wishes or needs to those of others. Even the simple pleasure of a meditation session seemed to this client to be a self-indulgence out of character for so 'self-sacrificing' a person.

After working on these problems in therapy, and after some role playing with respect to positive forms of self-assertion, the client finally agreed to resume daily meditation. It was soon discovered, however, that the meditative process was once again pushing her toward self-assertion at too rapid a rate for her to handle. The therapist suggested that she reduce her meditation to once weekly. Her meditation session was to take place only at the start of each therapy session, and the therapist was to meditate with the client at these times, giving tacit support to the client's right to independence and self-assertion and serving as a role model in terms of acceptance of a meditation practice in one's life.

These weekly joint meditative sessions proved extremely productive. The client described her sessions with her therapist as being 'deeply restful', pleasurable, and constructive. Her emotional responses to each meditation session were promptly dealt with in the discussion that followed. In this way guilt over self-indulgence was prevented from occurring. With this approach, the client's headaches again disappeared and she began to experience personality changes typical of regular daily meditation, such as an enriched and more enjoyable fantasy life. She repeatedly stated, however, that this weekly meditation session was all she could 'take' of meditation at one time without feeling 'pounded' by it.

In this moderate dose, the client appeared well able to assimilate the changes in self-concept brought about by meditation, and the client–therapist relationship was used to enhance the effectiveness of meditation through the joint meditation sessions.

CASE NO. 3

Richard, a successful professional man who grew up in a home where the family members tended to deny their emotions, rarely showed anger or sadness, always acting 'reasonably'. He had learned to exert a tight control over his own emotions and eventually almost lost awareness of them. Now, more often than not, he could not tell when he was angry or when he was sad, or identify any other strong feeling but could only reason that he 'might have felt a particular way'. One of the few times when genuine feelings were available to him was when he had had some drinks. One of the first tasks of psychotherapy was to help Richard get in touch with his own feelings and, among other therapeutic approaches, I suggested that he learn CSM.

On emerging from his initial meditation, Richard reported that he felt as though he were 'in another world' and would have liked to have stayed there for a long time, in fact indefinitely. When he phoned me the next day to report on his meditation (a routine procedure) he asked me if he might be allowed to meditate more than twice a day, because he found it such a 'pleasant experience'. I suggested that he not increase his meditation time because this might release tensions too fast for him to handle comfortably.

After meditating 1 week, Richard returned for his psychotherapy session already showing changes. He no longer smoked during his session (and has not smoked in a session since) and was more relaxed in his posture. While before he had been businesslike and intellectual, speaking in a highly organized fashion about his relationship with his wife, in this session he talked about himself in a somewhat musing fashion, bringing up thoughts about his childhood and his own inability to enjoy himself or to 'play' in life. He seemed to have a new interest in exploring his own reactions and for the first time expressed a desire to use therapy to enrich his own life rather than just as a tool to improve his marriage.

The following week, while travelling on a plane, he was meditating and had the impression that he heard his own voice saying: 'Empty yourself of your desires!' This rather mysterious statement was followed by an experience of exaltation and the further words: 'I can have a drink or smoke a cigarette if I want to—but I don't have to'. This seemed to him to be a startling revelation, giving him for the first time a feeling that he now had a choice of whether or not to drink.

Richard had always found it extremely difficult to know what his own wishes were. After meditating for about 3 weeks, he reported an 'unusual incident'. His children had asked him to stop at a roadside stand to buy ice cream. His usual response to such a request would have been to buy the same ice cream for himself as for the others, not realizing that he, too, might have preference for a particular flavour. This time, however, he found himself saying, 'Fine, I'll get you what you want—then I'm going to get chocolate ice cream for myself'. This may seem a small thing, but it was important: he had sensed his own need and stayed with it.

The experience of a new and convincing sense of self during meditation often forms a base of self-awareness which can be built upon to advantage in psychotherapy. Certain patients seem unable to move ahead in therapy because they lack a base of self on which to stand in order to produce change. In these cases even deep psychological insights may build on quicksand. Meditation can make an important contribution to therapy by building into the person a new, deeply convincing, largely wordless experience of self.

Precautions

1. An occasional person may be hypersensitive to meditation so that he or she needs much shorter sessions than the average. For example, some people may not be able to tolerate the usual 15 to 20 minute sessions prescribed in forms of meditation such as TM and may require drastic reductions in meditation time before benefiting from a meditation technique. Most problems of this sort can be successfully overcome by simply adjusting the meditation time to suit the individual's needs.

2. Overmeditation can be dangerous. On the theory that 'If one pill makes me feel better, taking the whole bottle should make me feel exceptionally well!', some clients may, on their own, decide to meditate 3 or 4 hours (or more) per day instead of the prescribed 15–20 minutes only once or twice a day. Just as with a tonic or medicine, prolonged meditation may cease to have beneficial effects and become detrimental. Release of emotionally difficult material may occur with prolonged meditation and in those with adverse psychiatric histories the commencement of meditation training has been known to precipitate psychotic episodes (Lazarus 1976; Carrington 1977). Although it is not certain than overmeditation will lead to such serious results in relatively stable people, it is probably unwise for any person to enter into prolonged meditation sessions unless they are in special settings (such as a retreat) where careful supervision is available.

   The fact that meditation may be a tonic and facilitator when used in short well-spaced sessions, but may have an antitherapeutic effect when used in prolonged sessions, is essential to consider when reviewing a psychiatric case history where any form of meditation has previously been practised by a client. Certain forms of meditation currently promoted by 'cults' demand up to 4 hours of daily meditation from their followers — an important factor to note when assessing some of the 'brain-washing' effects frequently reported by ex-members of these cults.

3. Meditation may enhance the action of certain drugs in some clients. Requirements for anti-anxiety and antidepressive drugs, as well as anti-hypertensive and thyroid-regulating medications, should be monitored in patients who are practising meditation. Sometimes the continued practice of meditation may permit a desirable low-dosage treatment with such drugs over more prolonged periods, and occasionally may permit the discontinuance of drug therapy altogether.

Clinical application

Successful use of meditation in a clinical setting depends on teaching the client to manage the technique successfully — a consideration that can easily be overlooked. If the routine problems that arise during the practice of meditation are not handled, the likelihood of obtaining satisfactory compliance is poor. However, if the technique is regulated to meet the needs of a particular client, compliance can be excellent. Since correct learning of meditation relies on the communication of the 'meditative mood' — a subtle atmosphere of tranquillity best transferred through nuances of voice and tonal quality — it is doubtful if meditation can ever be taught effectively through written instructions. It can be taught successfully by means of tape recordings, however, provided the latter effectively convey this elusive meditative mood (i.e. that they are not 'cold' or 'mechanical' in nature) and if the recorded teaching system is sufficiently detailed in terms of the information it conveys that the trainee is instructed in handling minor problems that may arise.

The CSM method (which incorporates the ROM method as an alternative form of meditation) teaches meditation through cassette tapes and a programmed instruction text which comprise a total training programme in the management of meditation. This involves instruction in adjusting the technique to suit individual requirements and in handling problems. Because of these advantages, the following discussion concerning the clinical application of meditation is confined to CSM. Some of the points made, however, can be applied to any of the modern meditation methods.

Introducing meditation to the client

Clinicians are in a uniquely advantageous position to introduce the idea of learning CSM to their clients. This is best done by referring to specific difficulties or symptoms that a client has previously identified. In fact, merely mentioning research that suggests that meditation may be useful for these problems is often all that is needed to motivate the client to learn the technique.

To forestall misunderstandings, several aspects of the CSM method should be mentioned when the subject of meditation is first introduced. The clinician should indicate that this form of meditation is strictly 'non-cultic' in nature. Clients with religious convictions will not want their beliefs violated by competitive belief systems. Often they are relieved to learn that CSM is a 'scientifically developed' form of meditation. Likewise, clients who are uncomfortable with seemingly unconventional interventions may also benefit from being reassured about the non-cultic nature of the method.

The clinician should also emphasize that the technique is easily learned, since one of the most prevalent misconceptions about meditation is the notion that it requires intense mental concentration. People are typically reassured by the knowledge that a modern technique such as CSM does not require forced 'concentration' at all, but actually proceeds automatically once it has been mastered. The clinician should also routinely check on the client's knowledge about and/or previous experience with meditation in order to clear up any further questions.

A brief preliminary discussion between therapist and client may be sufficient in many cases, but certain clients may need to be introduced to meditation in a more detailed manner. 'Type A' clients, for example, can resist learning meditation (or any other relaxation technique) because the idea of 'slowing down' threatens their lifestyle, which is often hectic and high pressured. When recommending CSM to a type A person, a useful strategy may be to indicate that the time that this person will take out of his or her day for meditation practice is likely to result in increased 'efficiency'. Type A or extremely active people can also be helped to accept meditation by being informed that they can break up their practice into a series of what have been termed 'minimeditations' (Carrington 1978). These are short meditations of 2 or 3 minutes (sometimes only 30 seconds) in duration, which can be scattered throughout the day. Frequent minimeditations may be more suitable for an impatient, highly active person than longer periods of meditation (although these can be used too) and they have the advantage of helping the client reduce transient elevations in stress levels as these occur.

A final strategy useful when recommending meditation to type A or exceedingly active persons can be to inform them that they can use CSM while simultaneously engaging in some solitary sport that they may practice and enjoy. Meditation can be successfully combined with solitary, repetitive physical activities such as jogging, walking, bicycling, or swimming (Carrington 1978). Benson *et al.* (1978a) have shown, for example, that repeating a mantra mentally while exercising on a stationary bicycle can lead to increased cardiovascular efficiency.

Setting and equipment for meditation training by tape

CSM is typically taught by means of three cassette recordings and a programmed instruction workbook, but instruction in the technique can also be carried out in person where this seems indicated. With the recorded training, the client is introduced to the principles of meditation by an introductory tape played before instruction *per se* is undertaken. Later (usually on another day), the client listens to the actual instruction recording under quiet conditions in a room set up to certain specifications. During the instruction session, the trainee repeats his or her mantra out loud in imitation of the instructor and meditates silently 'along with' the latter. Subsequently, he or she fills out a postinstruction question-naire and completes the instruction session by listening to the other side of the cassette, which directs their meditation practice for the next 24 hours.

On the following day the trainee listens to still another tape, which discusses potential problems involved in meditation practice, and then he or she plays the final tape of the series 1 week later. The latter prepares the trainee for their permanent practice of meditation. During this 1-week training period, the trainee works with the programmed instruction text to master the details of his or her meditation practice and to adjust the technique to suit personal needs. A supervising clinician may also assist in making clinically relevant adjustments of the technique.

The majority of clients learn CSM in their homes (or hospital rooms) and thus make their own arrangements for a suitable instruction environment. When clients are taught on the premises of the clinician (usually so that the latter can immediately advise readjustment of the technique) the clinician must make available a quiet, uncluttered room where the client can be alone while learning. This room should contain a comfortable straight-backed chair and some visually pleasant object such as a plant or vase upon which the trainee can gaze when entering and exiting from meditation. While the arrangements are simple, they must be carefully observed for maximum effect.

Personal vs. recorded instruction in meditation

When the clinician has selected meditation as the intervention of choice, he or she must decide whether to teach CSM by means of the recordings or in person. Factors influencing this decision usually centre on special requirements of the client. When considering the factors involved, certain advantages of recorded instruction should be noted:

1. Learning the technique at home or in a dormitory room can facilitate the client's generalization of the meditative response to their living situation thus helping to prevent problems that can occur when instruction is given in person in a setting outside the home. In the latter instance, trainees may complain that their subsequent meditation sessions are never 'the same as' or 'as good as' their initial learning session — a factor that may adversely affect compliance.
2. Learning the technique alone, through his or her own efforts, fosters the client's reliance on self as an initiator of the practice.
3. Being able to replay the recordings at intervals can reinforce meditation practice. The recordings may also be used to re-establish a meditation routine after the client has temporarily stopped practising it.
4. The client's family or friends can learn to meditate from the recordings. Their subsequent involvement in the practice (plus the fact that on occasion they may meditate together with the client) can lend substantial support thus improving compliance.
5. Some clients are embarrassed at the idea of speaking the mantra out loud or sitting with eyes closed in anyone else's presence. Such clients find learning by tape preferable.

There are certain situations where tape-recorded instruction is not suitable, however. If a client experiences severe thought disturbances or other clinical symptoms that make it difficult for them to learn from a recording, they will need personal instruction in the technique. Non-English-speaking clients, those who belong to a subculture that uses highly idiomatic speech, clients too physically ill to concentrate on a recording, or those who may have a natural antipathy to learning from recordings, will all need to be instructed in person. There is a standardized procedure for teaching CSM by means of personal instruction.

Since almost all meditation techniques have a number of points in common, people who have successfully used other meditation techniques often make excellent instructors of CSM. However, some personal experience with this particular meditative technique is essential in order that the prospective instructor understands the basic permissiveness of the technique.

Personal instruction

When receiving personal instruction, the trainee first selects a mantra from the list of 16 mantras in the workbook by choosing the one that sounds the most pleasant and soothing to them, or making up a mantra according to simple instructions. The mantras used in this method are resonant sounds (often ending in the nasal consonants 'm' or 'n') that have no meaning in the English language, but that, in pretesting, were shown to have a calming effect on many people. Sounds such as 'ah-nan', 'shi-rim', and 'ra-mah' are among those suggested.

After the trainee has selected the mantra, training is then conducted in a peaceful setting removed from any disturbances that may detract from the 'meditative mood'. The instructor walks quietly, speaks in low tones, and typically conveys by his or her behaviour a respect for the occasion of learning meditation. When teaching meditation, the instructor repeats the trainee's mantra out loud in a rhythmical manner. The trainee then repeats the mantra in unison with the instructor, and finally alone. He or she is next asked to 'whisper it' and then simply to 'think it to yourself silently', with eyes closed. The instructor and trainee then meditate together for a period of 10 minutes, after which the trainee remains seated for 1 or 2 minutes with eyes closed, allowing the mind to return to 'everyday thoughts'. The trainee is then asked to open his or her eyes very slowly.

At this point the instructor answers questions the trainee may have about the technique and corrects any misconceptions, then leaves the room so that the trainee can meditate alone for a stated period of time (usually 20 minutes). A chance to meditate on one's own is included in order to 'wean' the trainee as soon as possible from dependency on the instructor's presence when meditating.

Immediately following the first meditation session, the trainee completes a postinstruction questionnaire and reviews his or her responses with the instructor. Typically there is then a postinstruction interview in which procedures for a home meditation practice are clarified and instructions are given for the trainee's meditation routine for the following week. The trainee is then informed of possible 'tension-release side effects' (Carrington 1978) and taught how to handle these, should they occur. Individual follow-up interviews are later held at intervals, or group meetings may be scheduled where new meditators gather to share meditation experiences, meditate in a group, or pick up pointers on handling any problems that may arise in their practice. By these means, trainees learn to adjust the meditation to suit their own individual needs and lifestyles.

Close clinical supervision of meditation practice is strongly advised. Whatever the method of instruction (recorded or in person), a careful follow-up programme will ensure greater participation in a continued programme of meditation.

Ensuring maximal compliance

Compliance is a problem with any self-management technique and researchers have found that many who learn to meditate will discontinue the practice (Chapters 1 and 7), and an even larger number cut down to once instead of twice a day, or to only occasional use of the practice (Carrington 1977). Some problems emerge when we try to evaluate the existing compliance figures, however. The trend has been to define 'compliance' as 'regular daily practice' of the meditation technique in question, a viewpoint undoubtedly influenced by the TM organization's firm conviction that twice-daily practice is necessary in order to obtain benefits from meditation. However, some recent findings cast doubt on the necessity of daily meditation for all people.

My colleagues and I (Carrington *et al.* 1980) studied the use of two modern techniques (CSM and ROM) in a working population self-selected for symptoms of stress. We found that after 5½ months of practising meditation, these subjects showed highly significant reductions in symptoms of stress in comparison with controls (the SCL-90-R). However, when the groups were broken down into: (1) 'frequent practicers' (subjects who practised their technique several times a week or more), (2) 'occasional practicers' (subjects who practised once a week or less), and (3) 'stopped practicers' (subjects who no longer practised their technique), we obtained some unexpected results. Although SCL-90-R improvement scores for stopped practicers and controls did not differ (as might be expected), no differences in degree of symptom improvement were found between frequent and occasional practicers when the scores for these two groups were compared. This was contrary to our expectation. When frequent and occasional practicers were collapsed into a single 'practicers' group, however, and stopped practicers and controls collapsed into a single 'non-practicers' group, the difference in degree of symptom reduction between these two groups was highly significant. As long as subjects practised at all, then they were likely to show improvement in symptoms of stress. When they did not practise, they were unlikely to improve more than controls.

This finding contradicts the results of several studies using the TM technique, which have reported positive effects of frequent (as opposed to occasional) practice of meditation on neuroticism (Williams *et al.* 1976; Ross 1977; Tjoa 1977), trait anxiety (Davies 1978), autonomic instability (Orme-Johnson *et al.* 1978), intelligence test scores (Tjoa 1975), and measures of self-actualization (Ross 1977). However, the Carrington *et al.* findings are in agreement with research that has reported no differences between frequent and occasional practicers with respect to anxiety reductions (Lazar *et al.* 1977; Ross 1977; Zuroff and Schwarz 1978).

Several differences which may account for this discrepancy exist between the above-mentioned study with the employee group and those studies using the TM technique that did show effects for frequency of practice. All but one of the TM investigations were conducted with subjects who had signed up to learn at TM training centres. These subjects were not selected for high initial stress levels, although in some cases perceived stress may have played a role in their decision to learn meditation. It is therefore possible that they were not under the same degree of stress as the employees in the Carrington *et al.* study, who had been self-selected for this variable and whose initial SCL-90-R scores fell at the edge of the clinical range. When stress symptoms approach clinical levels, even a moderate amount of meditation or the use of meditation when needed may be sufficient to achieve sharp reductions in symptomatology. However, when initial stress levels are close to the norm, it may be necessary to practise meditation more frequently in order to reduce symptoms to a still lower level.

Our study also differs from these others in that teachers of the TM technique prohibit the use of minimeditations, which they consider harmful to proper meditation practice. In our employee study, however, strong emphasis was laid upon the use of minimeditations in addition to full meditation sessions and the effectiveness of this instruction was demonstrated by the fact that at the end of 5½ months 88 per cent of the employees who had learned meditation reported that they were using minimeditations. It may be therefore that minimeditations exerted a levelling effect, causing a blurring of the expected distinctions between frequent and occasional practicers.

Research such as that described above, coupled with clinical reports on the benefits of using meditation on a contingency basis (and/or of using frequent minimeditations), suggests a reconsideration of our present criteria for compliance. For example, in the Carrington *et al.* study, using 'practising at all' (whether frequent or occasional) as the criterion for compliance, 81 per cent of the CSM subjects and 76 per cent of the ROM subjects were still 'practising' their respective techniques at the end of 5 months. However, using 'frequent practice only' as the criterion for compliance, 50 per cent of the CSM subjects and 30 per cent of the ROM subjects were 'practising' their techniques by the end of this time. Which figures are the 'true' ones? Spontaneous comments offered on a postexperimental questionnaire by subjects in the Carrington *et al.* study may offer some clues. When these comments were examined in relation to frequency of practice, analysis revealed that more occasional practicers than frequent practicers were using their techniques for strategic purposes (i.e. as needed), that more frequent practicers than occasional practicers made strong positive statements about the benefit derived from their technique, and that only occasional practicers qualified their statements about their benefits (e.g. 'Under extreme pressure in my department, I don't feel as tensed up, but don't find meditation as beneficial as I had hoped' or 'I think there has been some possible effect'). We might summarize the findings to date by saying that the effects of frequency of practice are not as yet fully known. While frequency may not play a major role in symptom reduction for certain patients, it may be positively related to perceived benefits in other areas such as personal growth, and seems related to the degree of enthusiasm for meditation which subjects report.

For clinical purposes, it is wise to encourage regularity of practice in a client wherever possible, without being unduly alarmed if the client shifts from meditating regularly to using the technique for strategic purposes only, or decides to rely heavily on minimeditations only. The deciding factor should be the degree of benefit that the client is deriving from the practice. If, in the estimation of the clinician, the benefits remain satisfactory, then even if the client meditates only occasionally or uses only minimeditations his or her decision to employ meditation in this manner should be supported.

During the first 3 months of their practice, a more or less permanent stand was taken by trainees in the Carrington *et al.* study with respect to continuation of their meditation practice. Thereafter, while a trainee might shift from frequent to occasional practice (or back again), he or she was extremely unlikely to stop practising entirely. This timetable of attrition strongly suggests that once meditation has been successfully adopted and practised for a period of several months it is likely to become a permanent coping strategy that can then be called upon by a trainee whenever he or she has need of it — in short, that the strategic use of meditation is not likely to be abandoned.

It has also been observed that meditators may stop practising meditation temporarily for a variety of reasons. These 'vacations' from meditation appear to be a normal part of the practice for many people and are not to be taken as evidence of non-compliance. It is important that the clinician not prematurely label a cessation of meditation practice as 'dropping out'. Instead, the client should be helped to understand that such 'vacations' are normal occurrences, and that meditators frequently return to their regular practice later on with renewed enthusiasm. In CSM, I recommend re-use of the meditation instruction recording by the client as a useful means of reinstating meditation practice after having taken a break from it.

The clinician should also recognize that even if a client eventually abandons his or her technique, this is not necessarily a negative sign. Recent reports from a corporate programme using CSM at the New York Telephone Company suggest that after an extended period (e.g. 1 year or more) of successful meditation practice, some people may no longer need to practice meditation on a formal basis, because its benefits have been incorporated into their lifestyle. One telephone company employee reported that he no longer needed to meditate because he had begun to spend his lunch hour eating by the fountain in the courtyard where he worked. 'I just watch the water rise and fall' he said. This he described as so peaceful that afterward he 'felt better for the rest of the day'. He typically spent 20 minutes watching the fountain, but before he learned to meditate (approximately a year earlier) he claims that he 'would never have thought of such a thing, because then I was always in a hurry, even when I had a lunch break'. When we inquired whether his experience of gazing into the fountain had any features in common with meditation, he replied that although this had not occurred to him, actually the two processes were exactly the same, except that he didn't 'think the mantra' when he watched the fountain.

Similar reports from other long-term meditators at New York Telephone suggest that formal meditation may be phased out by some clients, as a 'meditative approach' to life is phased in. Some people appear to have substituted their own meditation equivalents for formal meditation sessions. This is by no means possible for all meditators, however. Many people need to continue with the formal practice of meditation indefinitely in order to maintain the beneficial changes.

Maintaining behavioural change

The maintenance of behavioural change may be closely linked with compliance in some instances. However, cases have been reported where after several years of regular meditation, meditators have suddenly ceased to notice any more benefits accruing from their practice. Since these have been anecdotal reports, it is unclear whether the people involved were actually no longer benefiting from their meditation practice, or whether benefits were still accruing but were no longer perceived because the meditators' tension levels had been reduced for so long a time that the meditators had become habituated to the relaxation. In clinical practice, an empirical test can be applied in the event of reports of diminished benefits. The client can be asked to stop practising meditation for a stated period of time. If this cessation of meditation brings no change in the clinical condition, or if it results in a beneficial change, then meditation (at least as originally learned and practised) has probably outgrown its usefulness for the client. At this point the substitution of another variant of meditation, if this is desired, may result in a revival of the beneficial effects.

Certain meditators experience adverse effects after having practised their techniques for prolonged periods of time. These can usually be brought under control by proper readjustment of the meditation routine, but the practice should be promptly discontinued if they do not cease.

Environmental factors in meditation instruction

The attitude of quiet respect and the peaceful surroundings that have traditionally accompanied the teaching of meditation are important ingredients of the technique. They cannot be lightly discarded without losing something essential to the meditative process (see Chapter 8). Properly taught, meditation can be a compelling subjective experience, but to hand a client a sheet of instructions and tell him or her to 'go home and meditate', is a superficial experience that is likely to result in a serious loss in terms of the importance the client will attach to learning meditation. It also deprives him or her of a role model to demonstrate the subtle meditative mood.

Following the old adage, 'easy come, easy go', those taught meditation quickly and superficially, without attention to the conveying of the delicate mood inherent in this practice, are apt to treat meditation casually and may soon discontinue its practice. When field testing versions of the CSM recorded instructions, I discovered that clients' compliance increased in direct proportion to the inclusion in later versions of informal, 'personal', mood-setting recordings. Similarly, when giving personal instruction in meditation, clinicians do well to give careful attention to the setting and the mood that accompany the teaching of meditation. The instruction need not reflect any belief system, but it should be pleasant, peaceful, and in some sense rather special in nature. Learning meditation is an important moment in an individual's life. If treated as such, the entire practice takes on a deeper meaning.

A related issue is the tendency of some clinicians to view meditation as so 'simple' that it can be taught in one session merely by imparting the technique itself, with the client left to his or her own devices at that point. While the actual technique can indeed be taught in a single session this does not necessarily mean a meditation practice has been successfully established. This requires a number of changes in the trainee's daily routine, individual regulation of the technique, and instruction in handling the problems that may arise in meditation practice. Without this full training in the management of meditation, learning the technique alone can even be detrimental in that encountering problems in meditation practice may lead a trainee to believe that he or she is not a likely candidate for meditation. The clinician who recommends meditation to a client should therefore be careful to supply complete training in all the practical aspects of the technique. Only in this manner can he or she insure that the method will be successful.

Conclusions

In summary, if imparted with full respect for both its inherent ease and for the problems involved in learning it, meditation can be a potent tool for personality change which can greatly enlarge the clinician's repertoire. In addition to the obvious relaxation afforded by it, this state serves to break up prolonged periods of outwardly focused stimulation by short but intense periods during which the 'motor seems to idle' and the meditator is thus enabled to regain a balance between his or her inner and outer self, between the experiencing of the self in action and the experiencing of the self as a state of being.

In modern industrialized society the pace of our lives is determined largely by economic considerations rather than by the rhythms of human life or natural growing things and there is a dearth of spontaneously occurring quiet inner space into which we can retreat for refurbishing. It is well to remember therefore that it is people who live under these conditions of modern society who make up our clinical populations. Outside of the immediate tension-reducing effects of meditation there is another service which the professional performs when introducing this quieting experience into a patient's life. Since a leisurely stroll, a quiet prayer, or listening to the gentle patter of rain as a 'change of pace' are not possible for most people today during their waking hours, and even leisure time is often a time for prolonged sensory bombardment from things such as the ubiquitous television set, the average human being today seems to move from task to task with almost no time to sense his or her own 'self' and to reaffirm the basic tenet 'I exist'.

It should be noted that it is within this context of a vacuum within our society that the modern meditative techniques have gained their popularity, and it is within this context that the need for the therapeutic forms of meditation has been developed. Not only can meditation serve to reduce symptoms of stress, but, perhaps even more importantly, it can reorient and redirect the entire life of the person who practises it by helping him or her to achieve a less hectic, more balanced approach to many different activities. Practised intentionally and systematically over time, meditation can become an important tool for modifying the meditator's essential adjustment both to the society in which he or she lives and to his or her own self.

10 Implications of psychotherapy research for the study of meditation

David A. Shapiro

The argument of this chapter is that efforts to ascertain the effects of meditation on well-being and health are usefully viewed as falling within the larger domain of psychotherapy research. This perspective on meditation studies offers two main advantages. Firstly, methodological advances in psychotherapy research carry enormous potential for the improvement of meditation research. Many methodological problems — and their solutions — are common both to studies of meditation and to studies of any psychosocial intervention designed to enhance well-being or health. Secondly, it opens up new avenues of investigation that promise to be more informative than studies that simply ask 'Does it work?'

To develop this argument, I will outline briefly the history of psychotherapy research, before reviewing in detail key methodological issues bearing upon the validity of studies of any psychosocial treatment, drawing parallels with meditation research at each point. Then I will turn to studies of the mechanisms of change in psychotherapy, exploring their relevance for meditation research, before closing with recommendations for methodological refinements and focal questions that should improve our scientific understanding of the effects of meditation on psychological well-being and health.

Historical overview of psychotherapy research

With the exception of a few isolated precursors, the modern era of psychotherapy research began with Eysenck's (1952) challenging assertion that the efficacy of the psychological treatments of that time, mainly based on psychoanalytic principles, was unsupported by scientific evidence. At about the same time, the controlled trial was being applied to the evaluation of the effectiveness of drugs, including the new psychotropic medications used for controlling psychiatric symptoms. The essential logic of the controlled trial is that the effects of treatment can be ascertained by comparing a group of individuals receiving the treatment with a control group not receiving the treatment (or, in more refined versions of the design, not receiving the purportedly effective ingredients of the treatment). One response to Eysenck's challenge, therefore, was the development of psychotherapy *outcome* research, in the form of corresponding controlled trials of psychological treatments, which began to be reported increasingly during the 1960s and 1970s (Bergin 1971; Bergin and Lambert 1978; Lambert *et al.* 1986).

A simultaneous response was the development of *process* research, the detailed study of what goes on during psychotherapy sessions, based on the argument that it makes no sense to evaluate the outcomes of a treatment without knowing what it is we are attempting to evaluate (Kiesler 1973). A third strand of research activity during the 1960s and 1970s was the development and evaluation of *new treatment methods* grounded in current psychological theories about behaviour change, including learning theory and cognitive psychology (Bandura 1969). A final strand of work in the 1960s was devoted to establishing *links between the processes and outcomes* of psychotherapy, in an effort to identify effective ingredients (e.g. Truax and Carkhuff 1967).

Around 1980, it became clear that these separate strands of research activity were together to provide as positive an answer to the overall question of the effectiveness of psychotherapy as it was reasonable to expect (Van den Bos and Pino 1980). A substantial body of converging evidence suggested that psychological treatments were typically effective; this became particularly apparent with the application of the quantitative approach to literature reviewing known as meta-analysis (Smith *et al.* 1980; Shapiro and Shapiro 1982a; Shapiro 1985).

Consequently, outcome research evaluating treatment against control conditions has given way to comparative outcome research in which different active treatments are compared (Elkin *et al.* 1985; Basham 1986; Kazdin 1986a; Lambert *et al.* 1986; Shapiro and Firth in press). However, it was also abundantly clear that the finding of overall effectiveness begged all questions as to the explanation of this effectiveness. There was no clear consensus within the scientific community as to the relative efficacy of the widely differing treatment methods that had been developed and researched (DeLeon *et al.* 1983; Kiesler 1985). Some argued that the benefits of psychotherapy were largely unrelated to the specific techniques employed (e.g. Frank 1962).

An excellent introduction to current activity in the field of psychotherapy resesarch is given by recent special issues of *American Psychologist* (Van den Bos 1986) and the *Journal of Consulting and Clinical Psychology* (Kazdin 1986b). Research in this field may be framed in terms of different workers' responses to the 'equivalence paradox': despite clear differences demonstrated by process researchers in the contents of diverse psychotherapies, their outcomes have not been convincingly shown to be different. Thus, it would appear that techniques are irrelevant to outcome and it does not matter what the therapist does, the results will be the same (Stiles *et al.* 1986).

Some proposed resolutions of this paradox are based on the claim that the apparent equivalence of outcomes is due to inadequate outcome research, and that better designed studies will indeed yield differential outcomes to match the different treatment contents and rationales; others rest on the argument that the effectiveness of psychotherapy is due to the operation of common features shared by all treatments despite superficial differences of content (Stiles *et al.* 1986).

This historical sketch has striking implications for meditation research. For example, if we view instruction in TM as a psychosocial treatment procedure, then the obvious 'outcome' question to be asked is how effective this is in reducing distress or enhancing well-being, as compared with no treatment or some other supposedly inert control condition. A parallel with process research arises if we ask questions about the precise nature of the teaching procedure (e.g. How is the rationale presented to the novice?; What kinds of group discussion are fostered during follow-up teaching sessions?; How is the technique itself presented during the individual's initiation session?). Just as psychotherapy researchers introduced new treatment methods, so too in meditation researchers developed alleged distillations of the essence of meditation procedures (e.g. Benson *et al.* 1974a).

The attempt to link process to outcome in psychotherapy is paralleled within meditation research by efforts to identify the effective ingredients by relating components of the procedure to its effects. Indeed, the 'equivalence paradox' applies to meditation just as to other psychosocial treatments: demonstration of TM's effectiveness, for example, would not itself entail that the technically specified elements of the procedure thought important by TM teachers are responsible for the benefits experienced; perhaps it makes no difference what the TM initiator does. What are the effects, if any, on the subject's experienced benefits of such elements as the choice of mantra, the kinds of discussion techniques used in 'checking', the persuasiveness of the rationale offered by the initiator, and so on? Indeed, in the context of Herink's (1980) count of over 250 allegedly distinct psychotherapeutic methods, a sceptic could reasonably demand evidence distinguishing any given meditation procedure from other psychosocial treatments in terms of contents, mechanisms, or outcomes.

Validity issues in studies of psychotherapy and meditation

One set of proposed solutions to the 'equivalence paradox' in psychotherapy research argues that the failure to demonstrate different outcomes of diverse therapies is due to methodological weaknesses of the outcome research conducted to date (Stiles *et al.*1986). Many of the methodological problems that must be overcome in designing adequate tests of the effectiveness of psychological treatments (Kazdin 1978, 1986a; Mahoney 1978) may be subsumed within Cook and Campbell's (1979) discussion of validity (Shapiro and Shapiro 1983).

Cook and Campbell (1979) delineate four types of validity. *Statistical conclusion validity* refers to the validity with which a study permits conclusions about covariation between the assumed independent and dependent variables. Threats to statistical conclusion validity typically arise from unsystematic error rather than systematic bias. *Internal validity* refers to the validity with which statements can be made about whether there is a causal relationship from independent to dependent variables, in the form in which they were manipulated or measured. Threats to internal validity typically involve systematic bias. *Construct validity* of putative causes and effects refers to the validity with which we can make generalizations about higher order constructs from research operations. Finally, *external validity* refers to the validity with which conclusions can be drawn about the generalizability of a causal relationship to and across populations of persons, settings, and times. Threats to each of the four types of validity will now be considered in depth. Several of these problems are considered in previous critiques of the meditation literature (Smith 1975; Holmes 1984).

Statistical conclusion validity

A central issue in statistical conclusion validity concerns statistical power, the probability of rejecting the null hypothesis when it is false. This depends primarily upon the size of the effect an experimenter is seeking to detect, and the number of subjects in the groups being compared (Cohen 1962, 1977). Comparing a psychological treatment with no treatment, it is reasonable to expect a large effect around one standard deviation unit (i.e. mean of treated group one standard deviation better than mean of untreated group). To detect such an effect, sample sizes of no more than 10 in each group are necessary (Kraemer 1981). However, if the experiment is seeking to detect a weaker effect, as may be the case when different treatments are compared rather than treatment vs. no treatment, then much larger groups are necessary (Kazdin 1986a). For example, if the effect size is around one-third of a standard deviation unit, samples of around 150 per group are required for the secure detection of the effect. Power problems abound in research on meditation as in research on other psychosocial treatments; they are exacerbated by attrition (missing data), which reduces the available sample size (in addition to introducing possible bias).

Reviewers summarizing data from a series of studies have traditionally tallied the number of positive (i.e. statistically significant) and null (i.e. not statistically significant) findings in a 'box score' total (e.g. Luborsky et al. 1975). This procedure compounds the statistical conclusion validity problems which ensue if each study has inadequate statistical power when considered alone. The 'box score' method misrepresents every study whose results were in the predicted direction, but did not attain significance on account of inadequate statistical power, as evidence against the hypothesized relationship between treatment and outcome. This difficulty is overcome in meta-analysis (Smith *et al.* 1980; Shapiro and Shapiro 1982a, b; Shapiro 1985), in which each finding is represented as an effect size, expressing in standard deviation units the magnitude of the difference between treatment groups, irrespective of the statistical significance of each finding considered alone. The validity of reviews of meditation research (e.g. Holmes 1984) would be improved by the use of meta-analytic techniques.

Uncontrolled variation in the way a treatment is implemented presents a threat to statistical conclusion validity. Shapiro and Shapiro (1983) found that the majority of the outcome studies included in their meta-analysis were deficient in this respect. However, this problem is increasingly being overcome by the preparation of manuals defining the treatment procedures to be followed (Beck *et al.* 1979; Klerman *et al.* 1984; Luborsky 1984). Project therapists are then trained to implement the techniques as specified in the manual, and their adherence to the manual is empirically assessed via process analysis of recorded sessions (DeRubeis *et al.* 1982; Evans *et al.* 1983; Hardy and Shapiro 1985). The importance of this methodological advance is heightened by recent concern with variations in the skilfulness with which therapists are found to deliver a treatment procedure (Schaffer 1982).

A different perspective on statistical conclusion validity derives from the growing concern with *clinical* as opposed to statistical significance of results. From a practitioner's perspective, statistical power may be counterproductive if it enables researchers to report statistically reliable results based upon trivially small differences between groups assigned to alternative treatments. Although there is no agreed standard procedure to ascertain the clinical significance of change, several proposals have been made, such as measurement of the extent to which treatment returns clients to normative levels of functioning, the magnitude of change, and the degree to which change is perceptible by significant others in clients' everyday lives (Hugdahl and Ost 1981; Kazdin and Wilson 1978; Yeaton and Sechrest 1981; Jacobson *et al.* 1984).

Internal validity

Threats to internal validity chiefly concern courses of possible bias in the comparison between experimental conditions. A primary requirement is to ensure that the groups of individuals assigned to different experimental conditions are comparable at the outset. In meditation research, comparisons between people who have chosen to undertake meditation and others who have not so chosen are invalidated by self-selection bias (Smith 1975; Holmes 1984).

The most common solution to this problem is random assignment (Shapiro and Shapiro 1983). However, randomization can often result in non-equivalent groups, especially if the samples are small, with consequent opportunities for the groups to differ by chance. When this happens, investigators can only attempt to 'correct' for the initial differences in some way. One solution is the use of 'residual gain scores' from which the effects of initial differences are statistically partialled out. Instead of raw post-treatment scores, residuals from the regression of post-treatment on pretreatment scores are analysed. This method is only useful if the correlation between pre- and post-treatment scores is large enough for sufficient correction to be obtained (Mintz *et al.* 1979). Another solution is to analyse arithmetic differences between post- and pretreatment scores. However, these difference scores compound the error components in the two scores from which they are derived, with a consequent loss in statistical power. Furthermore, no merely statistical correction can guarantee that the initial difference between the groups under comparison was not responsible for the post-treatment differences observed; such corrections do not address the question of whether the two samples were drawn from the same population and would have changed similarly if given similar treatments. In order to avoid these problems, some investigators have abandoned randomization in favour of prematched groups, but this raises tricky statistical issues.

A related source of bias derives from attrition or loss of subjects from the study (Howard *et al.* 1986). Howard *et al.* point out that this begins before inclusion in the study, as there is a natural filtering process whereby some members of the population deemed to be appropriate for inclusion in a study become unavailable, either through choice or through intervening circumstance, whereas other members have a disproportionately greater chance of inclusion. In meditation research, opportunities for bias from pre-inclusion attrition are legion, as people who seek or are willing to participate in meditation are manifestly not a random sample of any population.

After inclusion in a study, subjects may be lost for a variety of reasons, most of which threaten to bias the study because they cannot be dissociated from the treatment and subjects' reactions to it. People may discontinue treatment, opting to seek alternative treatment or believing that they no longer need help. They may continue treatment but fail or refuse to supply post-treatment data. When the rates of postinclusion attrition differ across groups being compared, the causes of that attrition are like to differ also, so that the groups are no longer comparable. It is difficult to place an upper bound on acceptable attrition rates, as these will vary with the treatment and assessment demands of the study and with the population under investigation. In the light of meta-analytic data presented by Shapiro and Shapiro (1983) on typical postinclusion attrition rates, however, it is reasonable to expect of investigators the loss of no more than the reported mean 10 per cent of participants from any treatment group. Attrition rates in meditation research, however, are often higher than this (Chapter 1, this volume).

Howard *et al.* (1986) review several methods that have been developed to compensate for the effects of attrition, but note that these all rest on the untenable assumption that 'attritors' and 'completers' are equivalent samples of the same population. These authors recommend the elimination from data analyses of all cases missing any independent variable data and the use of only those cases that are not missing data on a dependent variable in any analysis involving that particular dependent variable.

More radically, however, Howard *et al.* (1986) propose a reorientation of research strategy away from the pretence of control for what cannot be controlled, towards a new perspective in which the basic unit of study is the individual case, described with as much dependent and independent variable information as is required at the present state of development of psychotherapy research. In this new strategy, it is the knowledge of which points in the independent variable space are associated with the best average outcomes that is ultimately of clinical importance. Thus, if dependent variable data are missing from a point in the independent variable space represented by the combination of two independent variable values each of which is associated with better than average outcomes, it becomes important to design a study that will capture data at this point.

Construct validity

Representativeness of treatments.   Cook and Campbell (1979) consider the adequacy with which the independent variable is represented within a study as an important aspect of construct validity. It is important that the treatments incorporated within a study be designed to represent the techniques of interest, both with respect to such obvious structural features as the number and duration of sessions, and more subtle aspects such as the specific interventions or general interpersonal style of the therapist. Kazdin (1986a) presents a careful discussion of 'treatment integrity', noting that in some comparative studies it may be appropriate to allow some features of the treatments to vary to represent the treatments more faithfully, even though the variations may also be looked upon as confounds. This arises, for example, when different treatments are expected to require differing numbers of sessions to attain their optimal effectiveness.

In relation to meditation studies, the number, duration and format (group vs. individual) of teaching sessions, together with the frequency and duration of recommended practice of meditation, should correspond to the patterns typical of the meditation practice under investigation. In addition, the lesson of psychotherapy research is that teaching procedures and instructions to subjects concerning meditation practice should also conform to relevant, standard practice. However, meditation research suffers from the problem that practice varies so much that such a standard does not exist and so representativeness cannot in this respect be assured.

Control for non-specific effects.   A major issue in psychotherapy research has been the extent to which treatment effects are attributable to the specific techniques under investigation, rather than to so-called 'non-specific' factors such as the arousal of expectations on the part of clients that the treatment will be beneficial. In the 1960s and 1970s, increasingly sophisticated controls for such effects were incorporated into research designs, on the basis of an explicit analogy with the use of pharmacologically inert placebos in drug research (Shapiro and Morris 1978). An early example of this was Paul's (1966) incorporation into his comparative outcome study of an 'attention placebo' condition.

Subsequently, however, the adequacy of such controls was questioned (Borkovec and Nau 1972; Kazdin and Wilcoxon 1976; Shapiro 1981). Specifically, it was suggested that optimal control for non-specific effects required empirical demonstration that the control condition was as credible as the active treatments with which it was to be compared. Failing that, Kazdin and Wilcoxon (1976) advocated a *treatment-element control* strategy, in which the control procedure resembles the active treatment as closely as possible. For example, Holroyd *et al.* (1984) found that tension headache sufferers improved as much with EMG feedback increasing muscle activity as with feedback reducing it. Shapiro and Shapiro (1983) report that only a small minority of comparative outcome studies incorporated such controls.

More recently, however, it has been argued that the predominant conceptualization of non-specific effects in psychotherapy as analogous with the placebo effect in drug therapy (Shapiro and Morris 1978) is misguided (Wilkins 1984; Parloff 1986).

For example, Parloff (1986) argues that under the necessarily non-blind experimental conditions of psychotherapy research it is well-nigh impossible to ensure that therapists and their patients will view the experimental and placebo treatments as equally credible. The neat medical distinction between core somatic pathology and symptoms cannot be sustained with respect to psychological disorder. The effectiveness of all psychological treatments is likely to be based in part upon common factors arousing hope and expectation of benefit. Thus it is misguided to seek a true placebo, controlling for the actual active ingredients of a treatment, whether such ingredients are characteristic or incidental, unique or common. These considerations led Parloff (1986) to recommend research designs comparing known alternate treatment forms and modalities, which can serve as natural placebo controls for each other (Rosenthal and Frank 1956).

The implication of this debate for meditation research is that the effects of meditation on psychological well-being are almost certain to reflect, at least in part, the action of factors common to a wide variety of psychological treatments as well as to placebo treatments. An early study taking up this issue was carried out by Smith (1976), whose treatment-element control conditions matched TM's effectiveness. Holmes *et al.* (1983) found similar effects to be associated with meditation and with a resting condition, and Holmes (Chapter 5) argues that the effects of meditation on somatic arousal are no greater than those of simply resting. The construct validation of meditation as a psychological treatment requires some demonstration of factors specific to meditation that are effective over and above the effects of factors it shares in common with other procedures not grounded in the rationale and philosophy of meditation.

Investigator bias. Closely linked with the question of non-specific effects is the likely impact of experimenter bias upon psychotherapy studies. Reasons for suspecting the influence of subtle, unwitting demands by investigators upon the responses made by subjects include the substantial evidence for experimenter effects in psychological research (Rosenthal and Rubin 1978). These effects are the social influences at work in a situation defined as one in which one person is professionally engaged in the task of helping another, the strong and enthusiastic allegiances of psychotherapists to their preferred orientations and treatment methods, and the above-noted impossibility of double-blind conditions in psychotherapy research.

Smith *et al.* (1980) found a substantial correlation between the allegiance of investigators (inferred from analysis of their published reports) and the results they obtained for a given treatment. There is a tendency for new psychotherapeutic methods to show outstandingly good results in early studies published by their originators, followed by more modest findings characteristic of the field as a whole when studied by less committed workers. For example, Berman *et al.* (1985) attribute the failure of recent studies to confirm earlier reports of the superiority of cognitive therapy over other methods (Shapiro and Shapiro 1982a) to the greater allegiance of earlier investigators to cognitive therapy. A striking parallel in meditation research is the contrast, for example, between the positive results of Wallace *et al.* (1971) and the more cautious conclusions suggested by Holmes (1984).

The implications for meditation research are clear. Studies from individuals or institutions with a strong and explicit commitment to a particular method are vulnerable to the charge of experimenter bias, not necessarily for ideological, philosophical, or economic reasons unique to meditation, but simply on the grounds that no investigator is immune to the risks of unwitting experimenter bias. Independent replication in several institutions is required for the true importance of any psychosocial treatment to be established.

Assessment of outcome. A further, related construct validity issue concerns the vulnerability of outcome measures to the biasing effects discussed above. For example, measures administered 'blind' by individuals unaware of the treatment condition to which subjects have been assigned tend to yield smaller treatment effects (Shapiro and Shapiro 1983). This is despite the fact that the impact of the blind is in reality reduced by unavoidable disclosures to experimenters of the subject's treatment assignment. For example, during interviews subjects often refer, directly or indirectly, to their treatment experiences; if the interviewer knows which treatments are under comparison, it is often impossible to avoid matching these incidental remarks to the treatment conditions.

Different outcome measures vary in the extent to which they are vulnerable to bias. Thus, therapist ratings or self-report measures of the severity of the problem for which the person is seeking help are highly reactive to demand characteristics, whereas a physiological index is much less so. There is meta-analytic evidence that more reactive measures yield more favourable results (Shapiro and Shapiro 1983; Smith *et al.* 1980). Meditation studies in which self-report data yield more favourable results than behavioural data (e.g. Zuroff and Schwarz 1978) may be interpreted in these terms.

An important construct validity issue arises in respect of the specificity and relevance of the outcome measures used. Some investigators (e.g. Rachman and Wilson 1980) attribute the apparent equivalence of treatment outcomes to excessively general, crude outcome measures based upon simplistic models of such constructs as anxiety. Shapiro and Shapiro (1983) found more powerful effects with measures that were more specific to the goals of treatment. In relation to meditation, it may be questioned whether such constructs as trait or state anxiety are indeed appropriate indices of its effects, given the origin of these constructs in Western formulations of personality processes and symptomatology.

It is a commonplace observation in psychotherapy research that different outcome measures applied to the same clients in the same treatments may yield quite different results. For this and other reasons, there is general agreement (Lambert *et al.* 1983; Kazdin 1986a; Lambert *et al.* 1986) that outcome assessment needs to be multifaceted, involving different perspectives (the treated individual, significant others, professional observers), different aspects of the individual (e.g. behaviour, affect, and cognition), and different modalities of assessment (e.g. self-report, direct observation, and clinician ratings). However, Shapiro and Shapiro (1983) found that most investigators confined themselves to only one or two out of five assessment modalities. Within any one meditation study, it is exceptional (Zuroff and Schwarz 1978; Holmes *et al.* 1983) to find a wider range than this of assessment methods.

A possible resolution of the 'equivalence paradox' distinguishes psychotherapeutic effects from their value, arguing that different psychotherapies may have different and potent effects that are valued directly by different people (Strupp and Hadley 1977; Stiles 1983). Projecting multiple dimensions on to a single dimension of 'improvement' or 'change' by using averaged scales makes therapies comparable but at a cost of masking their diversity and potency of effect (Stiles *et al.* 1986).

A final aspect of measurement that bears on construct validity relates to the timing of outcome assessment. In principle, outcome research should demonstrate the maintenance of treatment effects over time. Although Nicholson and Berman (1983) have provided persuasive meta-analytic evidence that follow-up data are typically very similar to data obtained immediately after the completion of treatment, there are striking exceptions to this generalization for particular problems and treatments (Kazdin 1986a). For example, Kingsley and Wilson (1977) found that individual behaviour therapy was more effective in achieving weight reduction at post-treatment when compared with a group treatment based on social pressure; 1 year later, however, weight loss data favoured the social pressure treatment. In the Shapiro and Shapiro (1983) meta-analysis, 77 per cent of outcome data were obtained immediately after treatment, and only 6 per cent were obtained 4 or more months after the end of treatment. Investigators' reluctance to present long-term follow-up data is readily explicable: such data are costly to obtain, and are often compromised by attrition or by participation in additional treatment. Meditation research similarly tends to lack long-term follow-up data (West 1986).

External validity

External validity is defined by Cook and Campbell (1979) in relation to problems of generalizing to particular target persons, settings, and times, and of generalizing across types of persons, settings, and times. For psychotherapy research, the central problem is the extent to which the persons and settings studied in the literature represent those of clinical practice. In meditation research, the corresponding issue concerns the extent to which the persons and settings studied represent those of meditation as practised by people in their daily lives.

Much psychotherapy research has taken the form of 'analogue' studies in which undergraduate students are solicited to participate in brief treatments designed to help them overcome circumscribed and relatively minor problems such as public-speaking anxiety or specific phobias (Kazdin 1978; Mathews 1978; Borkovec and Rachman 1979). There is some evidence that such studies may show larger gains in treatment than are found in settings and with populations more representative of clinical practice (Smith *et al.* 1980; Shapiro and Shapiro 1983). Krupnick *et al.* (1986) reviewed 14 studies presenting direct comparisons between solicited and non-solicited patients receiving treatment in clinically representative settings. These authors concluded that results of studies using solicited patients alone must be interpreted with caution. Not only may such studies over- or underestimate response to treatment, but they may also yield conclusions concerning the relative efficacy of different treatments that do not hold up when tested with non-solicited patients.

Subject selection issues for meditation research are complex, depending on the population to which the investigator wishes to generalize. Studies of highly trained and experienced meditators (e.g. Holmes *et al.* 1983) might be thought to give the technique the best chance to demonstrate its effects, but do not provide a secure basis for generalizing to novices, whose likely experience of meditation is better represented by studies of undergraduate volunteers (e.g. Zuroff and Schwarz 1978).

Change mechanisms in psychotherapy and meditation

As already noted, the 'equivalence paradox' (Stiles *et al.* 1986) results from the fact that process researchers have demonstrated large differences in the contents of different psychotherapies, despite the absence of corresponding differences in their apparent effectiveness. In the previous section, methodological issues, many of which may be invoked to impugn the validity of findings of equivalent outcomes, were reviewed. We turn now to consider substantive issues relating to the mechanisms of psychotherapeutic change, which can also be invoked to resolve the 'equivalence paradox', and which carry implications for the study of the effects of meditation.

Specificity of effectiveness

One solution to the equivalence paradox that challenges the apparent equivalence of outcomes became orthodox during the 1970s. In a seminal article, Kiesler (1966) argued that psychotherapy research was hampered by 'uniformity myths' — implicit assumptions that therapists, clients, and methods were all interchangeable. 'The question towards which all outcome research should ultimately be directed is the following: *What* treatment, by *whom*, is most effective for *this* individual with *that* specific problem, and under *which* set of circumstances' (Paul 1967, p. 111; italics in original).

If outcome research has failed to identify each method's narrow range of maximal effectiveness, and compares methods in an unduly coarse, blunderbuss fashion, then apparently equivalent results will follow. Some well-known studies (e.g. Gilbreath 1967, 1968; DiLoreto 1971; see review by Shapiro 1975) have found the comparative effectiveness of different therapies to vary with client personality variables. This line of reasoning could equally be applied to meditation research. The effects of a given meditation procedure may be expected to vary with the personality and attitudes of the subject and of those introducing the subject to the procedure, and with the philosophical, social, cultural, and physical setting in which the procedure is learned. In addition, the intended effects of meditation, as of psychotherapy, need to be framed with considerable precision. Thus, it is preferable to define a target problem (such as anxiety, depression, or academic underachievement) rather than try to evaluate the effects of meditation on well-being as an undifferentiated construct. These implications of psychotherapy research have yet to be taken up on any scale by meditation researchers.

Going beyond the level of the individual investigation, meta-analytic reviews (Shapiro 1985) permit quantitative estimates of the differential efficacy of given techniques with given populations and target problems and in different settings. Meditation research is probably at the threshold of readiness for such 'disaggregation' of findings, which requires a sufficient body of data addressing a common question under sufficiently and systematically varied circumstances (Glass *et al.* 1981; Shapiro and Shapiro 1982b).

Common factors in treatment effectiveness

Another approach to resolving the equivalence paradox argues that, despite superficial diversity of content, the core processes or mechanisms are the same across therapies. This idea has already arisen in our discussion of non-specific effects, which may be viewed as reflecting just such common core processes. These core processes could reside with the therapist or the client, or reflect features of the relationship between them.

Therapist factors. Broadly defined attitudes, qualities, or conditions provided by therapists in their relationships with clients—qualities that cut across different therapy schools' variations in specific technical contents, have been widely studied. Over 30 years ago, Fiedler (1951) reported that therapists and clients of different schools rated the ideal treatment similarly with respect to such global aspects as warmth and overall quality of the therapeutic relationship. Most of the proposed general therapist factors fall into two groups: (1) warm involvement with the client, and (2) communication of a new perspective on the client's person and situation (Stiles *et al.* 1986).

Client factors. Similarly, other workers have proposed that client behaviour or attitudes are the key to therapeutic change, and that therapists' diverse techniques represent alternative approaches to facilitating these core processes. For example, Gendlin's (1970, 1978) work on 'focusing' and 'experiencing' describes a contemplative process that may be common to meditation and other psychotherapies.

Another candidate is the formation of positive expectancies, commonly invoked to explain the effectiveness of so-called placebo treatments, and a likely contributor to change in any psychological therapy. As already noted, this idea was examined in relation to meditation by Smith (1976). A related construct is Bandura's (1977) concept of self-efficacy, the client's belief that he or she can successfully execute a specific behaviour. Numerous studies have shown that changes in phobic behaviour correspond closely to changes in self-efficacy associated with diverse treatments (Stiles *et al.* 1986).

Self-efficacy may be invoked to explain seemingly anomolous findings such as the above-reviewed results of Holroyd *et al.* (1984) suggesting that biofeedback remains effective despite reserving the direction of physiological change. Many of those seeking therapy experience help-lessness, the belief that they cannot influence what happens to them (Abramson *et al.* 1975). Thus, a procedure that leads them to believe that they have gained mastery over their own physiology may achieve therapeutic benefits, irrespective of the precise nature of the physiological changes achieved, by enhancing self-efficacy and dispelling helplessness. This analysis could well apply to the experience of mastering the skills of meditation.

Therapeutic alliance.   A current line of work seeks to unify client and therapist general factors under the integrative rubric of 'therapeutic alliance', the emotional bond and mutual involvement between therapist and client (Luborsky 1976, 1984; Bordin 1979; Marziali 1984). Proponents of this view suggest that competent therapists of all per-suasions are able to establish a positive emotional bond and a sense of mutual collaboration with receptive clients, and that this relationship carries most of the therapeutic weight. According to this view, the specific tasks, techniques, and theories attached to particular therapies are relatively unimportant except as vehicles for enacting the therapeutic alliance. Research reviewed by Stiles *et al.* (1986) suggests that the client's contribution to and perception of the therapeutic alliance best predicts successful outcome. The implication for meditation would be that the relationship with the meditation teacher is the crucial vehicle of change; the central role of the religious leader or 'guru', and of the individual initiator as an empowered representative of a cultish, religious movement, may be subsumed within such an analysis.

Recommendations

1. Comparisons of meditation with no-treatment conditions are likely to be uninformative, because any procedure offered as helpful by a credible expert will show apparent benefits that cannot be attributed on the basis of such data to any specific element of the procedure. It is therefore better to compare different forms of meditation, or meditation with some other procedure that is likely to be beneficial.
2. Such comparisons between putatively beneficial procedures require relatively large samples. Outcome differences among active procedures are unlikely to be revealed with fewer than 30 subjects per group. On the other hand, it is unwise to interpret outcome findings resting on similar improvements with meditation and other established

procedures, partly because of the limitations inherent in confirming the null hypothesis, and partly because such findings may merely reflect common factors unrelated to specific procedural elements of meditation or of the comparison treatment.

3. Comparative outcome studies require highly differentiated outcome measures, targeted upon the goals of each treatment, that are likely to be sensitive to the differential effects of the procedures being compared. In meditation research, this entails more careful specification of the expected benefits of a given procedure, and how these should differ from those of other procedures to be compared in a given study.

4. The procedures to be followed in teaching meditation should be more closely defined and monitored in meditation research, because uncontrolled variations in the teaching approach will reduce the replicability of findings and obscure the true impact of the meditation technique.

5. Meditation researchers should pay as much attention to the magnitude of effects observed as to their statistical reliability.

6. Particular care is required in meditation research to avoid the biases flowing from individuals' chosen self-selection into meditation groups, and from differential attrition due to participants choosing to cease meditation practice. Random allocation should be accompanied by thorough comparisons between groups, and between those remaining in and those quitting the study, with a view to discarding subjects whose data could introduce bias.

7. In principle, meditation as taught and practised in research should resemble as closely as possible the activities of meditators outside the research context. However, this goal is made problematic by the unstandardized nature of meditation practice.

8. A central problem in meditation research is the difficulty in establishing that the effects of meditation are due to the specific procedures and rationales espoused by meditators and their trainers, rather than to factors common to meditation and other procedures ranging from conversational psychotherapy to simple rest. Much more work needs to be done on this problem, and the research methods and conceptualizations developed in studies of psychological treatments more generally will help in this endeavour. As in psychotherapy generally, the search for 'effective ingredients' should take in a wide range of individual differences, and procedural, interpersonal, and contextual factors.

9. More confidence could be placed in the results of meditation research if there were more examples of convergent findings from different investigators holding different views and hence with different potentials for unwitting bias.

10. The effects of meditation need to be assessed using a variety of measures tailored to the changes anticipated in each condition under comparison.

11. Participants must be selected for meditation research who will adequately represent the population(s) to which the findings are to be generalized.
12. There is good reason to suspect that the effects of a given meditation technique will not be uniform across meditators, teachers, and settings. Accordingly research should specify and/or systematically compare types of participant and setting.

Conclusion

The aim of this chapter is to highlight the gains from viewing the study of meditation within the broader domain of research on psychological treatments of all kinds. Several specific advantages are summarized in the foregoing recommendations. However, there remains an additional, more abstract and possibly more fundamental gain. The challenge of psychotherapy research is the attempt to capture the sometimes elusive and yet far-reaching benefits of psychotherapy, traditionally felt to be beyond the reach of science, within the net of critical scientific enquiry. This effort has yielded findings ranging from the mundane to the intensely illuminating and provocative. Involvement in such research, however, invariably refines and sharpens up the way psychotherapists think about their work. Similarly, meditation may seem beyond the grasp of Western science. However, comparable advances to those made in psychotherapy await exponents of meditation prepared to take up the research challenge.

Part IV:
Conclusions

Introduction

In the final chapter the lack of consensus between meditators and researchers over the effects of meditation is presented as a personal *koan* for the meditator–researcher. The results of the research are overviewed and a variety of unexplored research areas are identified. It is argued that much of value can be gained from a careful reading of Eastern psychology and from self-concept theory in Western psychology. Illustrations of the power of such theory for hypothesis derivation are presented. Self-awareness theory, reversal theory, and social psychology are also discussed as fruitful generators of predictions about the effects of meditation. Finally, it is argued that research on meditation presents a particular challenge to psychologists. Consciousness is emerging within theoretical physics as a concept of considerable importance, and meditation is a precisely devised research tool for investigating consciousness, and Western psychologists are challenged to adopt meditation as a vehicle for research in order to explore the nature of human consciousness.

11 Meditation: magic, myth, and mystery
Michael A. West

In Rinzai Zen students are given a riddle or paradox called a 'koan' upon which they are instructed to meditate diligently. The *koan* is not a rational problem that can be solved in the usual manner by thinking logically through rational alternatives and computing an answer. This chapter represents some of my struggles with a *koan*. It begins with a brief description of my experience with meditation before presenting this *koan*. The research evidence described in previous chapters is then considered and alternative research directions are proposed. In response to what is considered to be a predominantly atheoretical approach to the psychology of meditation, the chapter then describes a number of apposite theoretical orientations which can be integrated with Eastern approaches to psychology. Finally, and on the basis of the contents of the chapter, an answer to the *koan* is offered. The reader will be in the position of the Zen teacher who can accept the answer as evidence of real progress or reject it urging the student to go away and work more diligently.

Many times I have sat alone in meditation over the years and have experienced a profound sensation which seemed to me the essence of meditation. As recognition of the experience dawns I wave it goodbye but, once or twice before it has disappeared, I have succeeded in capturing the words to describe it as they drifted by. Once I promptly lost them again, but the second time I managed to hold on to a new set. They are not quite right, I am sure of that, but they do communicate to me something of that experience: *'the still completeness'*.

Recently one evening as I walked back from the hills above the city where I live, I looked across the distant fields and old stone walls as the sun neared the horizon. The gently curving green hills were bathed in a soft yellow light and there was a slight summer haze in the air. In the distance I could see, but not hear, a tractor ranging methodically backwards and forwards across a field. The whole scene engendered in me a recognition of the deep peace of its continuity — a stillness that endures and endures and endures. I thought then how far from that deep peace, that stillness I am — despite my hundreds of hours of doing meditation and my thousands of hours of thinking about it. Later that night, just before midnight I sat facing a table upon which were a lighted candle, a plant, and a Buddha figure. My son Thomas lay sleeping deeply and peacefully beside me as I practised breathing meditation followed by traditional *zazen* (which involves sitting and maintaining a quiet awareness, without comment, of all that is here and now). And in a moment I had a clear realization that I did indeed experience the peace and stillness of the evening's scene. That stillness is there so often in meditation. It's just that as soon as I get up — or at least shortly after — my world goes haywire again!

But some trace of the quality of that still completeness is left lingering if only for a short time, or at least as a memory later in the day. Sometimes it is just an intellectual perspective from which I can view events and arguments. Some might argue that this is a justification and that I meditate now because I can't back out and admit to myself I've been investing in a lost cause all this time. I feel sure though of the importance and reward of meditation for me. Its primary reward is in helping me to deal with that most fundamental of human experiences — knowledge of one's being. Knowing that I am is truly awe-ful, in both senses of the word. Both wonder and fear are potential responses to the experiential (as opposed to intellectual) reality and meditation confronts me with the reality at an experiential level. But it does so in a step by step way like 'drips of water on a stone'. By becoming aware of the contents of consciousness through meditation and seeing the chatter and dreaminess of my mind I have become more aware of the silence and continuity of my being behind it all. This too has become integrated, ever so slightly, into my daily experience . . . but ever so slightly!

Let me also assert that it has not been some gentle progression, producing increasing sensations of peace and bliss. On the contrary, I think meditation has had something of a good press and that the pains, the boredom, and the frustration of meditation itself are underplayed. Moreover, it is my experience that one can have sudden confrontations with painful or even frightening realities as a result of meditation practice. Becoming painfully aware of the enormity of my own 'isness' as I prepare to talk to a large audience about some subject which suddenly seems not quite so important after all, creates its own tortures. Nevertheless my overall experience of meditation is of a benign influence which leads to 'disillusionment' and a broadening of understanding about my being.

A *koan*

For those readers who have not yet abandoned this leaky vessel of introspection I will now present the *koan* with which I grappled for a number of years. It is a question many reading this book will confront. My study of meditation has been both through my own experience and through psychological research. I found the first vastly more fruitful and the second vastly more frustrating and have described some of the reasons for this in Chapter 1. The *koan* lay in resolving the discrepancy between my fruitful meditation experience and the thin validating research evidence. Looking back through the chapters of this book there is little evidence to suggest that meditation is an easy path to either happiness or truth. Indeed, one author even compares it with blood-letting as a method of helping. Psychological research tells us that meditation produces decreases in arousal no greater than those observed during simple rest. EEG patterns during meditation seem to be unusual but putting electrodes on people's scalps to discover more about human consciousness has been likened to putting electrodes on a television set to discover what programme is on! The research on personality suggests that meditation practice is associated with decreases in neuroticism, anxiety, and depression but the causal mechanisms have not been identified. Phenomenologically the experience of meditation does not seem to be unique and most of the research is methodologically unsound. Finally, there are many questions still to be answered in order to satisfy the researcher about the therapeutic potential of meditation, even though many clinicians are already convinced.

In spite of the discrepancy between my experience and the research evidence, I keep on meditating and wait for the research to catch up. Why have I kept on meditating? The simple answer would be to say that I trust my experience more than my science. But the more complex answer is that my reading of the research and theoretical literature in this area has not given me reason to discontinue my practice and has offered some reason for sustaining it (if any more reason beyond my subjective experience were needed). Let us look again at the research evidence presented in previous chapters and examine briefly both the questions asked, the answers achieved, and the questions still to be asked.

An overview

The phenomenology of meditation

Pekala's chapter represents the first careful analysis of the research evidence in this area and provides at the same time an overview of the nature of reported experience of meditation (e.g. 'intensification and change in consciousness', 'transcendence of space and time', 'ineffability', 'deeply felt positive mood'). Many of the descriptions resonate with personal experience of meditation and meditators will acknowledge the face validity of the results of some of these studies. At the same time, however, Pekala points out that much of this research is methodologically inadequate and goes on to offer some methodological innovations to meet the design requirements of validity and reliability.

New ways forward might also be found in the use of repertory grid techniques (Bannister and Fransella 1971) both to examine the changes in experience during and outside of meditation and to compare meditation with other significant experiences. Thus the experience of meditation might be compared with experiences such as making love, prayer, sitting on a hillside on a summer's day, and gazing out of a window in reverie. Research is needed too to explore significant experiences associated with meditation, and the emerging psychology of peak experiences (Privette 1983) points one way forward. Privette has described peak experiences as characterized by absorption, valuing, joy, spontaneity, a sense of power, personal identity and involvement, and mystic and transpersonal sensations, and distinguishes these from 'flow' and 'peak performance'. The utility of her topology for the study of meditators and their daily lives is apparent.

Future research could also usefully examine phenomenological differences in meditation experience over time. Cross-sectional research comparing reports of those with short- and long-term experience of meditation practice (i.e. 1 or 2 years' versus 10 or 20 years' experience) would be of value, but the field desperately needs to be sown with new longitudinal studies following meditators over time. Such research is difficult, expensive and time consuming, but the pay-offs are generally greater than those from quick and easy cross-sectional studies characteristic of research to date on the phenomenology of meditation.

Phenomenological research has not examined the question of whether different meditation methods produce dissimilar experiences. Repertory grid techniques or 'laddering' provide means of comparing phenomenological accounts of both the content and processes of different types of meditation (Hinkle 1965). Another way in which the phenomenological research might be extended is by exploration of advanced states of consciousness (e.g. Fenwick 1986), given that the traditional aims of meditation are to effect dramatic qualitative improvement in the functioning of consciousness. Though the idea of advanced states of consciousness is one which few psychologists are currently exploring, it is fundamental to Eastern psychological approaches to understanding consciousness (Hall and Lindzey 1978).

Perhaps the most glaring inadequacy in this research is the exclusive focus on the phenomenology of the meditation state itself, rather than an examination of experience outside of meditation or careful comparisons of meditation with other states. The traditional aims of meditation are to prepare the mind 'for the immediate non-conceptual awareness of reality' (Capra 1983), the implication being that meditation is the preparation period and that it is outside meditation that the fruits of its practice are to be picked.

Perhaps this bias in the research is another consequence of the fact that it is easier to conduct research on the state of meditation than it is to examine change outside meditation but associated with its practice. Thus, although the research in this area has not shown meditation to be unique or unusual in its effects upon subjective experience, it is clear that many of the most important research questions are still to be asked.

They include: How does meditation compare with other subjective experiences? What is the content of peak experiences during and outside meditation? How does the experience of meditation change with practice? How does experience outside meditation, but associated with practice, change over time? Do different meditation techniques differ phenomenologically?

Physiological studies of meditation

Probably more attention has been paid to physiological changes associated with meditation than almost any other area. In Chapter 1, I discussed the reasons for the research emphasis on physiological changes occurring during meditation practice. Briefly they seem to be a consequence of the ease of such research and a concern amongst researchers to demonstrate change on respectable measures (and what can be more respectable than heart rate!). Unfortunately, as Holmes shows in Chapter 5, much research effort has produced very little reward. His chapter cuts through the myths of somatic arousal reduction during meditation and challenges proponents of meditation to substantiate their claims in other areas of meditation research.

However, the focus of the physiological studies is primarily on short-term change in physiological arousal and few studies have examined physiological change associated with meditation practice outside of the meditation state itself. Perhaps the concern with physiology is misplaced anyway since reduction of arousal has never been a traditional aim of meditation. The stress-reducing function of meditation is one which has been claimed by movements such as the TM organization and, while the sell has worked well, the evidence has not been supportive, as Holmes so clearly demonstrates.

Fenwick's chapter is iconoclastic in cutting through the mythology and mysticism surrounding the use of the EEG; he reminds us that it is simply a gross measure of the summed electrical activity of the brain and that phenomena such as EEG coherence and symmetry do not in themselves imply anything dramatic about the nature of consciousness during meditation. At the same time he presents a powerful and simple argument against equating meditation with rest and sleep. Even though physiologically they appear indistinct, people are doing different things when they meditate, rest, and sleep. Moreover they say these activities *feel* different from each other. On what basis therefore can we then deny their psychological distinctiveness?

Research on physiological effects of meditation has not fulfilled its early promise and proponents of meditation will not find the security they may seek in the use of measures of blood chemicals or heart rate. Despite this qualification, this line of research should not yet be abandoned. Studies of advanced practitioners might well be worthwhile and the careful plotting of long-term changes in physiological patterning both during meditation over time and outside of meditation over time are still needed. Nevertheless, the existing research evidence is clear: meditation is not characterized by dramatic decreases in arousal and arguments about its therapeutic potential based on such a supposition are built on shifting sand. The value of Holmes' and Fenwick's reviews is that they may channel the efforts of those researchers interested in meditation in new directions. In particular they may encourage researchers to discard methodologies which focus on what is happening during meditation in favour of longer term research examining changes occurring outside meditation. This admittedly is much more difficult but it focuses on areas that Eastern psychologies imply are the more deserving of investigation.

Meditation, personality and therapeutic applications

Delmonte's review of personality research supports the argument presented above for longitudinal studies of experience outside meditation since the evidence he describes suggests consistent and beneficial effects of meditation practice. The difficulty lies in ascribing causal mechanisms between meditation itself and personality change. Jonathan Smith poses one creative solution, in arguing for a skills-based approach to understanding meditation, and researchers seeking guidance will find a number of new directions signposted in his chapter. The idea of viewing meditation not as a unidimensional behaviour but as a combination of focusing, letting go, and receptivity is something of a paradigm shift which promises progress. It also draws our attention to the fact that meditation is a generic term referencing a multiplicity of behavioural patterns from Tai Chi to *zazen* to *kinhin* (walking meditation) to the day-long practice of *vipassana* (awareness of all that is happening here and now). Too little research has acknowledged that there is no representative meditation practice (see Shapiro's comments on this in Chapter 10).

The variation in types demands appropriately tailored research designs. It also demands the development of research which acknowledges and responds to the different aims and processes of these different types of meditation practice.

The fact that many meditation researchers are themselves meditators is advantageous since it gives them clues about appropriate research directions. Its disadvantage is that it reproduces my *koan*—how to resolve the discrepancy between personal experience and research evidence. Carrington does this by relying primarily on her vast experience of practising and teaching meditation. She succeeds in avoiding the careful ambivalence of the meditator–researcher and unashamedly presents a rich account of her experience of the successful use of meditation in therapy. But how appropriate is the use of meditation in clinical settings?

Guy Claxton (1986) has explored the parallels between meditation and psychotherapy in his book *Beyond therapy*. He argues that clients come to therapy seeking greater happiness or less pain and that there are limits to the purposes of such therapy. For example, dealing with a specific phobia of public speaking would usually not involve exploration of the client's spiritual poverty. Such areas of experience are likely to be 'out of bounds' in the therapeutic relationship. On the spiritual path however there are no such limits:

> The quest is for Truth not Happiness, and if happiness or security or social acceptability must be sacrificed in the pursuit of this ruthless enquiry then so be it. The spiritual seeker's task is not problem-solving but problem-seeking. Whatever experiences are upsetting must be mounted and ridden in any direction they choose to go, so that the fear that underlies them can be confronted and scrutinised. No thought or feeling or behaviour is 'righter' than any other. It is all grist to the mill — the mill that puts experience to the test, and that relentlessly separates out and discards any belief, however cherished, that turn out to be unjustified. (Claxton 1986) (pp. 316–17).

Claxton goes on to warn that meditation practice may stimulate 'dangerous' or 'bad' feelings into consciousness which the person in therapy is happier to keep buried since their defences have worked well in the past in keeping them at bay. Meditation would then involve risk for many clients because it will tend to push them further than they are ready to go. Claxton challenges therapists themselves to begin the path of exploration of the boundaries of self through meditation, as a necessary part of their training in order to 'appraise their value to their clients in terms of qualities of *being*, rather than the skills and techniques of *doing* or the conceptual understanding of *knowing*'.

These cautions about the use of meditation in clinical settings are worthy of note. However, as many clinicians are already teaching meditation to clients, what can research tell us about which techniques are most appropriate, for whom, with what difficulties and with what outcomes? David Shapiro traces a path through the maze of psychotherapy outcome research and shows how meditation research faces all the same sorts of barriers. He signals a need to look more at the process by which change is effected in meditation and questions the appropriateness of state and trait anxiety as outcome measures in meditation research, given the origins of these constructs in Western psychology. There is a case too for arguing that each individual might react in her own unique way to the experience of meditation and that aggregated data would fail to capture such change. Furthermore, as Shapiro suggests, experimental studies of the effects of meditation may be unrepresentative of the kinds of effects that meditation has when practised by people in their ordinary daily lives. It may not be anxiety reduction which is salient for meditators but such things as more harmonious social relationships, or a more accepting attitude towards the inevitability of death (see subjective reports of meditators in West 1986). These outcomes are amenable to psychological measurement—perhaps at greater cost in terms of energy and difficulty—but probably with greater reward in terms of understanding. Indeed, it is precisely such outcomes reported by some meditators which are venerated by the Eastern traditions and which meditation is supposed to develop. Perhaps our cultural and methodological hegemony has determined our tendency to focus on heart rate, skin conductance, stress reactivity, and standardized personality measures.

But probably the major drawback to our understanding of the psychology of meditation has been the atheoretical orientation of the research. Below a number of directly relevant theories are described and predictions about the processes and effects of meditation are derived from them.

Putting practice into theory

Those who become involved in researching or writing about the psychology of meditation have usually been practising meditators themselves. Often they begin with practice, move on to conducting research, and then write about their results. This process often ends in the frustration of research results which do not live up to personal expectations or of methodological difficulties which render interpretation of results impossible. The research energy dissipates soon despite the enthusiasm the subject matter engenders, for pay-offs are exceeded overall by the losses. What is lacking in the psychology of meditation is the effective utilization of existing psychological theory to generate intelligent methodologies, explain results, and develop theory further.

Eastern psychological theory

Guy Claxton (Chapter 2) has shown how Eastern psychologies provide us with sophisticated theories which make explicit predictions about the effects of meditation. The notion of the self is central to these theories, for it is argued that the practice of meditation will undermine a belief in the self as a separate, persistent, and autonomous entity. Furthermore it is argued that as a consequence resistance, resentment, and frustration lessen, and that simplicity, spontaneity, kindliness, and humour increase. These are predictions which can be tested. But of even more value might be a focus on those elements of the traditional theories which specify the causal processes producing such change. Mere correlational and outcome studies repeat the errors of previous research but drawing upon these theories for explanations of process enables much more precise predictions to be made. Thus, Claxton's exposition of Buddhist theory suggests that the individual through meditation will come to have a clearer insight into the workings of her own mind and the presuppositional framework on which experience is built; this also leads to the abandonment of aspects of one's own identity as contradictory experiential information surfaces during meditation. The use of repertory grids (Bannister and Fransella 1971) would enable researchers to examine such processes and to chart their effects over time of meditation practice.

Research drawing upon traditional theory could also focus on changing attitudes and values, since the Eastern traditions predict that meditation itself will engender revolutions in belief and value systems. It is true that responses are likely to be affected also by the conceptual system within which meditation is taught and espoused, but appropriate research designs can control for such influences. Standardized scales already exist in the literature which are perhaps more apposite to traditional Eastern psychologies than scales such as the Eysenck Personality Questionnaire or Cattell's personality measure, the 16PF (for examples of such scales see Robinson and Shaver 1973). There is also a case for arguing that measures of belief systems of meditators should be incorporated into some research designs since such systems as well as rationales for meditation practice may be important in influencing the outcomes of meditation practice (Wilson 1986). Those from Buddhist traditions which emphasize compassion, love, and equality may be more likely to experience change in the quality of their social interactions. Thus we might predict different outcomes from the meditation practice of the Mahayana Buddhist and the prison officer practising TM to relieve work stress. One excellent example of such research is a study of the personal change experienced by members of a newly established community of Western Theravadan Buddhist monks and nuns in England (Goswell 1986). The study, using 'cooperative enquiry' methods examined how the experience of the inner life of the participants changed over a period of time through meditation and living by the monastic rule within a community.

Identity theory and the self

The history of research, writing, and theorizing about the self in psychology is as long as the discipline itself (see Burns 1979). Wrangles over the extent to which the self is socially determined and whether there is, in observable behaviour, such a phenomenon or whether it is merely an inferred homunculus have continued unabated over many years (e.g. Mischel 1977; Rosenberg and Turner 1981). This area of psychology is rich in theory and empirical research. However, surprisingly few studying the psychology of meditation have taken advantage of the smooth pathways that have been created by writers in this area. Instead, many have set out with no clear theoretical guidance and ended up struggling through briars of uncertainty and confusion.

The self-concept is the outcome of the reflexive capacity of the person to distinguish between the self as knower ('I') and the self as known ('me'), a distinction that Mead (1934) has argued develops as a consequence of the emergence of language. Gecas and Mortimer (1987) argue that the self-concept is a multidimensional phenomenon encompassing two broad dimensions — identity and self-evaluation:

The concept of identity focuses on the meanings constituting the self as an object, gives content, structure and continuity to self-conceptions, and anchors the self to social systems. Self-evaluation refers to the value placed on the self-concept as a whole or on its particular components . . . 'Identity' and 'self-evaluation' correspond to the meaning and value aspects of self-concept — the two basic components of symbols in general. (p. 2)

Gecas and Mortimer go on to distinguish between three aspects of identity. First is role identity or the structural features of group membership which people internalize and become committed to (e.g. lecturer, feminist, parent) and social categories (gender, race, age, etc.). Second is 'character', which refers to the qualities which individuals and others attribute to the self, for example honest, brave, resourceful, religious. These attributions are typically expressed in terms of values, beliefs, and character traits. Finally there is existential identity which refers

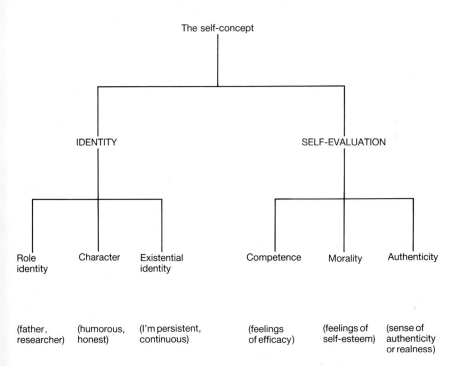

Figure 11.1 The self-concept (after Gecas and Mortimer 1987)

to the person's sense of uniqueness and continuity (Figure 11.1). Gecas and Mortimer describe this as being similar to Erikson's (1959) concept of ego identity — 'the awareness of the fact that there is a self-sameness and continuity' of the self.

How can such an analysis help those concerned with the psychology of meditation? Take for example the notion of existential identity. There are clear similarities between the descriptions of self offered by Gecas and Mortimer and Buddhist psychology (see Chapter 2). Buddhism proposes that through meditation the sense of self as separate and continuous diminishes. Thus while we might be tempted to suppose that meditation would strengthen a sense of existential identity in the short term, traditional Eastern psychology would predict a long-term weakening of feelings of persistence and separateness (or to use Gecas and Mortimer's terms 'continuity' and 'uniqueness').

Let us look briefly at the second component of the self-concept in Gecas and Mortimer's model to show how this too enables predictions about the psychology of meditation to be derived. This second component, evaluation, comprises assessments of one's competence, morality, and significance (Figure 11.1). Positive self-evaluations along these three dimensions lead to feelings of self-efficacy (Bandura 1977; Gecas 1982), self-esteem (Rosenberg 1965), and 'authenticity'. This last concept according to Gecas and Mortimer 'addresses the question of whether the various identities constituting the self-concept are meaningful and "real" to the individual'. Thus Turner (1976) distinguishes between people who locate their sense of authenticity or their 'real self' in the performance of institutional roles and those whose sense of 'real self' is located in the expression of impulse. This concept of authenticity is similar to Stryker's (1968) notion of identity salience and Rosenberg's (1979) concept of psychological centrality in that all three are concerned with the relative importance, salience, and centrality of different identities in the person's self-concept.

Research on the self-concept in the psychology of meditation has focused almost exclusively on the evaluative dimension and within this on the effects of meditation on self-esteem (e.g. changes in real versus ideal self — Seeman *et al.* 1972; Nidich *et al.* 1973). But the other dimensions of the self-concept and of identity have been largely ignored. On the evaluative dimension (to use Gecas and Mortimer's model) the effects of meditation on self-efficacy and authenticity have not been examined. Eastern psychology might lead us to predict that meditation practice would lead to shifts in authenticity in the self-concept. Thus, with the blurring of the boundaries of the self and a greater awareness of internal processes, the meditator may invest institutional roles (such as university lecturer, psychologist, husband) with less authenticity, centrality, or salience. At the same time other less socially sharply defined aspects of identity (e.g. conservationist, member of the wider, human race, entity in a universe) would become invested with more.

Support for such speculations can be found in the work of Cheek and Briggs (1982) who found a reliable correlation between private self-consciousness (a tendency to attend to the elements of the self that are personal in focus and not accessible to the scrutiny of others) and importance ratings for personal aspects of identity.

This is not to argue that the best way forward for meditation research is necessarily to focus on the self-concept or even to claim that the Gecas and Mortimer model is the most useful. The point is that existing psychological theories already provide an excellent conceptual basis for developing hypotheses and designing research. Nevertheless, it is clear that the self is a central notion in both Eastern and Western psychology and that drawing upon the well-developed ideas and arguments of both traditions is likely to further understanding of meditation and of the concept of self. Let us take another example to illustrate the power of theory in this area.

Zurcher (1977) has distinguished between four central components of reported self-concept — physical, social, reflective, and oceanic. The physical component has to do with factors such as weight and height; the social component indicates the individual as a social entity identified with specific roles and statuses in society (I am a father, I am a researcher); the reflective component indicates the individual's feeling states, evaluations of statuses occupied, and assessments of role performances (I am a good father, I am a worried researcher); the oceanic component refers to orientations towards belief systems, ideologies, and 'other world' views abstracted from social networks (I am one with the universe, I am part of existence). How are these ideas of use to those concerned with the psychology of meditation? A quick reading of Zurcher's ideas might lead the researcher to predict that meditation would lead to a development of the oceanic component of the self-concept and that we would expect meditators to become more philosophically or theologically detached from their social worlds.

But this would be leaping too hastily to prediction. Buddhist texts argue that meditation will lead to a blurring of the boundaries of self and not-self. This is important when we consider the next stage in Zurcher's arguments. He proposes (Zurcher 1984) that his concept of self is useful when predicting which individuals are likely to act as agents for change in society — people who intentionally attempt to modify values, norms, statuses, or roles at the societal, organizational, group, or individual level. The theory predicts that those who rigidly adhere to the physical self-concept would be too withdrawn to be helpful in confronting social problems, being likely to react only if their physical safety were threatened. People who rigidly adhere to perception of the self as a social person with self-concepts largely based upon their role identities would serve the status quo of social structures. Thus they would be unlikely to accommodate easily to, or be pro-active in effecting, socio-cultural change. Zurcher goes on to argue that the reflective person would:

maintain a self-serving alienation, probably criticising the flaws in society
. . . but the strategies they elected (to achieve social change) might be limited
more to symbolic protest than to instrumental change. (p. 4)

Finally, those adhering rigidly to the oceanic mode would be detached
from society abstracting away from social structure and ignoring its
attendant problems. This last rigidity is interesting in light of a common
criticism of the meditative traditions that they encourage passivity in the
face of social injustice and human suffering (see, for example, Schur 1976).
   The final step in Zurcher's theory proposes that some people are more
'mutable' than others, that is, they have a more flexible perception of
themselves as physical, social, reflective, and oceanic individuals, and
are more able to see themselves in one mode or another depending upon
the social setting. Such people, the theory predicts, are more likely to
be optimally adaptive to, and controlling of, the social change impinging
on them and more effective social-change agents than those who are
less mutable. Through the physical mode, persons with mutable selves
would be able to consider themselves as, and thus use, their physical
resources. Through their social selves they would have a facility to deal
with the social world — able to change the system partly because of their
good knowledge of it. The reflective self-perspective would give them
the detachment from (but not the abandonment of) the social structures
perceived to be in need of change. This perspective would also give them
the ability to evaluate their own roles as change agents. Through the
oceanic mode mutable-self change agents would derive value
orientations to guide their interventions.
   What would we predict to be an outcome of meditation practice — a
more rigid oceanic self and less salience of the social, physical, and reflective selves or Zurcher's mutable self? Clear alternative predictions can be
derived from this theory. Using measurement techniques such as the
Twenty Statements Test (Kuhn and McPartland 1954) or more reliable
instruments (Kinch *et al.* 1983) researchers could discover whether those
who practise meditation (or even whether those learning different meditation types) become more or less active as agents of social change.
   Drawing upon just two examples of the many theoretical orientations
in the literature on the self-concept illustrates how recourse to existing
theory, in conjunction with an understanding of the traditional aims
and claims for meditation, can lead to a rich trove of testable predictions.
It also illustrates how this can lead to hypothesis testing which is of
potentially greater value, both to a psychology of meditation and to
psychology more generally, than the adherence to studying outcomes
of meditation on mainstream personality tests or physiological
parameters. But areas of theoretical relevance go beyond a consideration
of self-concept. The aims of meditation are to effect change in awareness
and self-awareness and there is a rich body of theorizing in this area
of Western psychology.

Awareness and self-awareness

Mindfulness, self-focus, self-observation, awareness, and attention are words which appear frequently in subjective accounts of the experience of meditation (West 1986). There is a well-developed theoretical literature within psychology exploring notions of awareness and self-awareness (Underwood 1982), and elsewhere the usefulness of these theories for a psychology of meditation has been discussed (West 1982). Here these ideas will therefore be only briefly outlined.

Duval and Wicklund (1972) and Wicklund (1975) proposed a theory of objective self-awareness which stimulated the development of ideas about self-consciousness and public and private self-awareness. They argued that attention is either directed towards external events or towards the self. When attention is directed towards the self, the initial reaction is self-evaluation. The theory proposes that no matter what self-related dimension becomes the focus of attention, there will be discrepancies between aspiration and attainment—between one's current condition and one's goals. Wicklund argues that 'it is a reasonable assumption that virtually all naturally occurring discrepancies are negative'. The reaction will be one of attempted discrepancy reduction, either by avoiding the conditions producing the self-aware state or, if that is not possible, by trying to change behaviour to bring it into line with the standards or goals with which it is discrepant. Experimental manipulations inducing states of objective self-awareness, using tape-recordings of subjects' own voices or mirrors, generally support the theory's predictions. What does this theory predict about meditation?

There is a strong case for claiming that, according to the Duval and Wicklund dichotomy of awareness, meditation is quintessentially a state of self-focused attention. Consequently three predictions about meditation and objective self-awareness can be derived:

(1) Meditation will cause the individual to evaluate herself;
(2) This evaluation will almost always reveal a negative discrepancy between behaviours and goals or standards, creating in turn negative affect;
(3) To achieve self-consistency, behaviour will be altered to reduce the discrepancy.

These predictions can be partially evaluated by reference to phenomenological studies and studies of those who persist with and drop out of meditation, but the existing evidence is still inadequate to test the predictions satisfactorily. It seems unlikely that these predictions would be borne out, since many meditators report positive rather than negative affect and a tendency to view experience objectively rather than evaluatively during meditation (see Chapter 4). Nevertheless testing them would tell more about meditation and about the limits of the theory of objective self-awareness.

Contemporary research in this area is focusing on the concept of self-consciousness, which is defined as the tendency to focus attention on the private aspects of the self. Fenigstein *et al.* .(1975) developed an instrument called the Self-Consciousness Scale (SCS) which distinguishes between the tendencies to attend to the private and public aspects of the self. A person who scores high on the private self-consciousness scale is one who, '. . . introspects, examines moods and motives, is aware of mental processes, spins fantasies and, in general, is self-reflective' (Buss 1980). Those who score highly on the public self-consciousness scale attend to more overtly displayed aspects of the self such as qualities that other people respond to as social stimuli (e.g. humour, aggressiveness). Behavioural differences between those scoring high on the separate subscales of the SCS have been found (Froming and Carver 1981). Where subjects encountered erroneous judgements on the part of other group members, the dispositional tendency to focus on private self-aspects was a significant predictor of the tendency to ignore the group in giving one's own judgements. The dispositional tendency to focus on public self-aspects was a significant predictor of going along with the group's erroneous judgements.

It can be argued that the practice of meditation will increase private self-consciousness, since meditation inevitably increases the attention paid to the private aspects of the self. From this presupposition a number of predictions can be made in relation to the effects of meditation (for more details of the derivation of these predictions see West 1982):

(1) Those taking up and regularly practising meditation will experience greater awareness of themselves and will show greater resistance to false suggestions about their experience;
(2) Their self-reports will become more elaborated and will correspond more accurately to their behaviour;
(3) New meditators will experience more intense affect and practising meditators will exhibit stronger responses to affect-laden stimuli.

Some very limited and indirect evidence is available to support these predictions but further research specifically designed to test them would be valuable both in extending our understanding of the psychology of meditation and in exploring further the theories of self-awareness and private self-consciousness. Again the concern here is not simply to urge particular lines of research but to draw to the attention of those concerned with the psychology of meditation the value of existing theories about human behaviour for helping to increase understanding of meditation.

Alternative theoretical contexts

Crook (1980) has argued that although meditation is used as an aid to self-understanding we need to be aware that the expression of this understanding is realised only in a social context. This suggests the importance of research examining the interaction between the individual and his or her social environment. Crook has also suggested that the use of practices such as Zen meditation leads people to break free from highly ritualized habits of thinking about themselves, about other people, and the world around them. Such changes 'may amount to a disidentification of the self process from assumptions about its own character and provide an opening to a less filtered experience of relations with others' (Crook 1983). Watts (1979), in a review of research on meditation and perception, also talks of the possibility that meditative perception may have a profound effect on social perception, social prejudice, and interpersonal sensitivity.

The practice of an exercise with the implicit or explicit aims of altering consciousness, self-awareness, and self-understanding may well affect social relationships. Furthermore it has been argued that changes in individual consciousness may have an impact on social systems (Borland and Landrith 1977). Given the need for new approaches and the suggestions that our understanding of meditation may be deepened by discussion of its impact on identity, self-concepts, interpersonal relations, and relationships between individuals and social systems, then social psychology may well be the discipline from which new and fruitful research approaches may emanate.

To take this further, the study of organizations which teach meditation, especially those which are evangelical in nature, e.g. the TM organization, the School of Meditation, would also be of interest to social psychologists (see Zurcher and Snow 1981; Llewelyn and Fielding 1984). Some research on the Divine Light Mission has been reported (Buckley and Galanter 1979) and anecdotal reports about Rajneesh International have also been published (e.g. Milne 1986). More focused efforts, perhaps exploring the relationships between meditation systems and organizational cultures, would be instructive.

Brown (1977) has argued that the classical texts of the meditative traditions describe the effects of meditation in terms of perceptual and attentional processes and make empirically testable claims. According to such texts, the purpose of mindfulness meditation is to cultivate a finely attuned non-reactive awareness of the succession of passing events in the stream of consciousness. This suggests the possibility of measuring changes in sensitivity to perceptual stimuli. Brown *et al.* (1984a, b) have conducted such studies and though the results are not entirely convincing they do suggest useful avenues for further effort. Their methods included using subjects on an intensive mindfulness meditation course, who were practising meditation for 16 hours a day over a 3-month period. The study of such intensive meditation experiences may well provide an alternative to more difficult longitudinal studies.

While much effort has been expended in examining outcomes little attention has been paid to the processes of meditation. One theoretical context which offers explanations for the processes of meditation is reversal theory (Apter *et al.* 1985). Reversal theory calls into question the notion of homeostasis which underlies most theories of motivation and offers instead a notion of bistability. The theory proposes that people switch (or reverse) between states, for example 'telic' and 'paratelic' states. The defining feature of the telic state is that the individual in that state sees herself as pursuing an end or goal whereas in the paratelic state it is the behaviour which is the focus of enjoyment. Thus, we might contrast adding up a column of figures with sunbathing to illustrate the differences between the two states. In adding up the focus is on the end result, whereas sunbathing is something enjoyed for its own sake with the added bonus of a healthy looking body at the end (unless of course one ends up burned!). The process of meditation may be studied in the context of reversal theory for, one might argue, the switching between a focus on a mantra and drifting away on trains of thought may be conceptualized as representing psychological reversals in the theory's terms. The theory further postulates dispositional tendencies for people to be 'telic dominant' or 'paratelic dominant'. This suggests a framework for understanding such things as who is attracted to which meditation types, who is likely to persist with practice, and why the aims of meditators differ. The great advantage of this theory for the study of meditation is that it focuses concurrently on both the physiology and phenomenology of behaviour.

It is the thesis of this chapter that theories such as reversal theory, self-awareness theory, mutable-self theory, and identity theory place the subject of meditation on firmer theoretical bases. Or, to mix metaphors, the chapter proposes that there are many fertile fields, already well ploughed, upon which meditation research can be sown and that it is a waste of effort to scatter such seed on hard and potentially barren ground.

An answer to the *koan*

The psychology of meditation is multifaceted, spanning physiological psychology, personality theory, phenomenological psychology, social psychology, clinical psychology, and cognitive psychology. Though each of these areas has been represented in previous chapters, it has been argued that theoretical orientations specific to them have not been used to guide research. In many instances the questions that have been asked by researchers about meditation have been irrelevant to both Western and Eastern theories of human behaviour. Consequently the harvest has been poor and has told us little about meditation and less about our theories. The former is understandable when a new area of research is opening up; the latter indicates faulty hypothesis development.

However, new directions for exploration by researchers and theoreticians alike are suggested by the contributors to this volume. The study of altered states of consciousness and peak experiences associated with meditation, a focus on intensive meditation practice and advanced practitioners of meditation, and a sensitivity to the differences between meditation types are all strategies likely to advance our understanding in psychology more generally. Helen Graham (1986), in an examination of the parallels between modern physics and psychology, argues that a focus on altered states of consciousness, mystical experience, psychic phenomena, and psychedelic experience, in the light of developments in theoretical physics, can no longer be dismissed as trivial:

They have to be admitted within any scientific framework which purports to be a complete understanding of reality . . . the emergent paradigm offered by quantum theory and the new physics admits consciousness in a previously unconceived way, implying, in contradistinction to common sense views of reality, that it may not be the brain that produces consciousness, but rather consciousness that creates the appearance of the brain, matter, space, time and everything that is taken as constituting the physical universe. (pp. 125–6).

And what of the answer to the *koan*? How does one resolve personal experience and research evidence? The answer I have come to is that the questions I asked about my meditation were very different to the questions research psychologists asked about meditation. I meditated and examined such things as the nature of shifts in awareness, profound experiences, subtle shifts in the quality of my moment to moment experiencing outside meditation. These are very different questions from those researchers have asked and it is not surprising therefore that we arrive at different answers. But this answer to the *koan* leads to a new question: 'How can the research evidence and personal experience be resolved in the future?'

Conducting research on meditation involves conducting research on a method of research, since meditation is the methodology of Eastern psychology. Recognizing this involves 'breaking set' away from seeing meditation as simply a therapeutic tool and viewing it as a vehicle for the exploration of consciousness. Change resulting from meditation according to this view is likely to be subtle, demanding sensitivity of measures beyond personality tests and electrodes. Examples of such measures have been described above but paradigm shifts are also required to meet the challenge. It is easy to fall into the trap of believing that existing methodologies and paradigms are appropriate for the study of previously unexplored phenomena, and the pattern of research in this area implies just such a fall. And yet the study of meditation promises so much because it is a research method precisely adapted for the study of consciousness. The challenge lies in incorporating and combining meditation with existing methodologies in psychological research to penetrate more deeply the mysteries of the human experiences of awareness, consciousness, and being. As psychologists eager to chart and understand such complexities of human behaviour we can perhaps best benefit from the advice of the Zen teacher who urges students — 'Keep don't know mind, only keep don't know mind'.

REFERENCES

Abdullah, S. and Schucman, H. (1976). Cerebral lateralisation, biomodal consciousness and related developments in psychiatry. *Research and Communications in Psychology, Psychiatry and Behaviour,* 1, 671-9.

Abramson, L. Y., Seligman, M. E. P. and Teasdale, J. D. (1978). Learned helplessness in humans: Critique and reformulation. *Journal of Abnormal Psychology,* 87, 49-74.

Akishige, Y. (1968). Psychological studies on Zen. *Bulletin of Faculty of Literature,* 11, 1, Kyushu University.

Alexander, F. (1931). Buddhist training as an artificial catatonia (the biological meaning of psychic occurrences). *Psychoanalytic Review,* 18, 129-45.

Anand, B., Chhina, G. and Singh, B. (1961). Some aspects of electroencephalographic studies in Yogis. *Electroencephalography and Clinical Neurophysiology,* 13, 452-6.

Anderson, J. R. (1980). *Cognitive psychology and its implications.* W. H. Freeman, San Francisco.

Angell, J. (1907). The province of functional psychology. *Psychological Review,* 14, 61-91.

Apter, M.J., Fontana, D. and Murgatroyd, S. (1985). *Reversal theory: applications and developments.* University College Cardiff Press, Cardiff.

Ashworth, P. (1976). Some notes on phenomenological approaches in psychology. *Bulletin of the British Psychological Society,* 29, 363-9.

Assagioli, R. (1965). *Psychosynthesis: a manual of principles and techniques.* Hobbs and Dorman, New York.

Avila, D. and Nummela, R. (1977). Transcendental meditation: a psychological interpretation. *Journal of Clinical Psychology,* 33 (3), 842-4.

Bagchi, B. and Wenger, M. (1957a). Simultaneous EEG and other recordings during some yogic practices. *Electroencephalography and Clinical Neurophysiology,* 10, 193.

Bagchi, B. and Wenger, M. (1957b). Electrophysiological correlates of some yogic exercises. *Electroencephalography and Clinical Neurophysiology,* Supplement 7, 132-49.

Bagchi, B. K. and Wenger M. A. (1959). Electrophysiological correlates of some yogi exercises. In *First international congress of neurological sciences* (eds. L. van Bogaert and J. Radermacker) Vol. 3, pp. 132-49. Pergamon Press, London.

Bahrke, M. S. and Morgan, W. P. (1978). Anxiety reduction following exercise and meditation. *Cognitive Therapy and Research,* 2, 323-33.

Baker, R. (1981). Quoted in *Buddhism: a way of life and thought* (ed. N. W. Ross). Collins, London.

Bakker, R. (1977). Decreased respiratory rate during the transcendental meditation technique: a replication. In *Scientific research on the transcendental meditation program* (eds. D. W. Orme-Johnson and J. T. Farrow), Vol. 1, pp. 140-1. Maharishi European Research University Press, Los Angeles.

Bali, L. R. (1979). Long-term effects of relaxation on blood pressure and anxiety levels of essential hypertensive males: a controlled study. *Psychosomatic Medicine*, **41**, 637–46.

Bandura, A. (1969). *Principles of behavior modification*. Holt, Rinehart and Winston, New York.

Bandura, A. (1977). Self-efficacy: toward a unifying theory of behavioral change. *Psychological Review*, **84**, 191–215.

Bannister, D. and Fransella, F. (1971). *Inquiring man: the theory of personal constructs*. Penguin Books, Harmondsworth.

Banquet, J. P. (1972). EEG in meditation. *Electroencephalography and Clinical Neurophysiology*, **33**, 454.

Banquet, J. P. (1973). Spectral analysis of the EEG in meditation. *Electroencephalography and Clinical Neurophysiology*, **35**, 143–51.

Banquet, J. P. and Sailhan, M. (1974). Analysee d'état de conscience induits et spontanes. *Revue d'EEG et de Neurophysiologie Clinique*, **4**, 445–53.

Bärmark, S. M. and Gaunitz, S. C. B. (1979). Transcendental meditation and heterohypnosis as altered states of consciousness. *International Journal of Clinical and Experimental Hypnosis*, **27**, 227–39.

Basham, R. B. (1986). Scientific and practical advantages of comparative design in psychotherapy research. *Journal of Consulting and Clinical Psychology*, **54**, 88–94.

Bateson, G. (1980). *Mind and nature: a necessary unity*. Fontana, Glasgow.

Battista, J. R. (1978). The science of consciousness. In *The stream of consciousness: scientific investigations into the flow of human experience* (eds. K. S. Pope and J. L. Singer) pp. 55–87. Plenum, New York.

Bear, D. (1979). Temporal lobe epilepsy — a syndrome of sensory–limbic hyperconnection. *Cortex*, **15**, 357–84.

Bear, D. (1986). Hemispheric assymetries in emotional function: a reflection of lateral specialisation in cortical–limbic connections. In *The limbic system: functional organization and clinical disorders* (eds. B. K. Doane and K. E. Livingstone) pp. 29–42. Raven Press, New York.

Bear, D. and Fedio, P. (1977). Quantitative analysis of interictal behaviour in temporal lobe epilsepy. *Archives of Neurology*, **34**, 454–67.

Beary, J. F. and Benson, H. (1974). A simple psychophysiologic technique which elicits the hypometabolic changes of the relaxation response. *Psychosomatic Medicine*, **36**, 115–20.

Beck, A. T., Rush, A. J., Shaw, B. F. and Emery, G. (1979). *Cognitive therapy of depression*. Guildford Press, New York.

Becker, D. and Shapiro, D. (1981). Physiological responses to clicks during Zen, yoga and TM meditation. *Psychophysiology*, **18**, 694–9.

Beiman, I. H., Johnson, S. A., Puente, A. E., Majestic, H. W. and Graham, L. B. (1980). Client characteristics and success in TM. In *The science of meditation* (eds. D. H. Shapiro and R. N. Walsh). Aldine, Chicago.

Benjamin, l. (1967). Facts and artifacts in using analysis of covariance to 'undo' the law of initial values. *Psychophysiology*, **4**, 187–206.

Bennett, J. and Trinder, J. (1977). Hemispheric laterality and cognitive style associated with transcendental meditation. *Psychophysiology*, **14**, 293–6.

Benoit, H. (1955). *The supreme doctrine*. Pantheon Books, New York.

Benson, H. (1969). Yoga for drug abuse. *New England Journal of Medicine*, **281**, 1133.

Benson, H. (1975). *The relaxation response*. Morrow & Co., New York.

Benson, H. (1977). Systemic hypertension and the relaxation response. *New England Journal of Medicine*, **296**, 1152–6.

Benson, H. and Friedman, R. (1985). A rebuttal to the conclusions of David S. Holme's article: Meditation and somatic arousal reduction. *American Psychologist*, **40**, 725–8.

Benson, H. and Wallace, R. K. (1971). Decreased drug abuse with transcendental meditation: A study of 1,862 subjects. Congressional Record, 92nd Congress, 1st Session, Serial No. 92-1. US Government Printing Office, Washington DC.

Benson, H. and Wallace, R. K. (1972a). Decreased blood pressure in hypertensive subjects who practice meditation. *Circulation*, Supplement 2, **45**, 516.

Benson, H. and Wallace, R. K. (1972b). Decreased drug abuse with transcendental meditation: A study of 1,862 subjects. In *Drug abuse: proceedings of the international conference* (ed. C. Zarafonetis), pp. 369–76. Lea and Febiger, Philadelphia.

Benson, H., Alexander, S. and Feldman, C. L. (1975a). Decreased premature ventricular contractions through the use of the relaxation response in patients with stable ischaemic heart disease. *Lancet*, **2**, 380–2.

Benson, H., Beary, J. F. and Carol, M. P. (1974a). The relaxation response. *Psychiatry*, **37**, 37–46.

Benson, H., Dryer, T. and Hartley, H. L. (1978a). Decreased CO_2 consumption with elicitation of relaxation response. *Journal of Human Stress*, **4**, 38–42.

Benson, H., Greenwood, M. and Klemchuk, H. P. (1975b). The relaxation response: psychophysiologic aspects and clinical implications. *International Journal of Psychiatry and Medicine*, **6**, 87–98.

Benson, H., Rosner, B. A. and Marzetta, B. R. (1973). Decreased blood pressure in hypertensive subjects who practiced meditation. *Journal of Clinical Investigation*, **52**, 8a–11a.

Benson, H., Rosner, B. A., Marzetta, B. R. and Klemchuk, H. P. (1974b). Decreased blood pressure in pharmacologically treated hypertensive patients who regularly elicited the relaxation response. *Lancet*, **1**, 289–91.

Benson, H., Steinart, R. F., Greenwood, M. M., Klemchuk, H. M. and Peterson, N. H. (1975c). Continuous measurement of O_2 consumption and CO_2 elimination during a wakeful hypometabolic state. *Journal of Human Stress*, **1**, 37–44.

Benson, H., Frankel, F., Apfel, R., Daniels, M., Schniewind, H., Nemiah, J., Sifneos, P., Crassweller, K., Greenwood, J., Kotch, J., Arns, P. and Rosner, B. (1978b). Treatment of anxiety: a comparison of the usefulness of self-hypnosis and a meditational relaxation technique. *Psychotherapy and Psychosomatics*, **30**, 229–42.

Bergin, A. E. (1971). The evaluation of therapeutic outcomes. In *Handbook of psychotherapy and behavior change: an empirical analysis* (eds. A. E. Bergin and S. L. Garfield) pp. 139–89. John Wiley, New York.

Bergin, A. E. and Lambert, M. J. (1978). The evaluation of therapeutic outcomes. In *Handbook of psychotherapy and behavior change: an empirical analysis* (eds. S. L. Garfield and A. E. Bergin), 2nd edn., pp. 139–89. John Wiley, New York.

Berman, J. S., Miller, R. C. and Massman, P. J. (1985). Cognitive therapy versus systematic desensitization: Is one treatment superior? *Psychological Bulletin*, **97**, 451–61.

Berwick, P. and Oziel, L. J. (1973). The use of meditation as a behavioural technique. *Behaviour Therapy*, **4**, 743–5.

Blackwell, B., Hanenson, I. B., Bloomfield, S. S., Magenheim, H. G., Nidich, S. I., and Gartside, P. (1975). Effects of transcendental meditation on blood pressure: a controlled pilot experiment. *Psychosomatic Medicine*, **37**, 86.

Blackwell, B. Hanenson, I., Bloomfield, S., Magenheim, H., Gartside, P., Nidich, S., Robinson, A. and Zigler, R. (1976). Transcendental meditation in hypertension: individual response patterns. *Lancet*, **1**, 223–6.

Block, B. (1977). Transcendental meditation as a reciprocal inhibitor in psychotherapy. *Journal of Pychotherapy*, **9**(1), 78–82.

Bloomfield, H. H., Cain, M. P., Jaffee, D. T. and Kory, R. B. (1975). *TM:discovering inner energy and overcoming stress*. Dell Publishing Co., New York.

Boals, G. F. (1978). Towards a cognitive reconceptualisation of meditation. *Journal of Transpersonal Psychology*, **10**(2), 143–82.

Bordin, E. S. (1979). The generalizability of the psychoanalytic concept of working alliance. *Psychotherapy: Theory, Research and Practice*, **16**, 252–60.

Boring, E. G. (1953). A history of introspection. *Psychological Bulletin*, **50**, 176–89.

Borkovec, T. D. and Bernstein, D. A. (1985). Foreword to relaxation dynamics. In *Relaxation dynamics: nine world approaches to self-relaxation* (ed. J. C. Smith pp. 1–5. Research Press, Champaign, Ill.

Borkovec, T. D., and Nau, S. D. (1972). Credibility of analogue therapy rationales. *Journal of Behaviour Therapy and Experimental Psychiatry*, **3**, 257–60.

Borkovec, T. D. and Rachman, S. (1979). The utility of analogue research. *Behaviour Research and Therapy*, **17**, 253–61.

Borland, C. and Landrith, G. (1977). Improved quality of city life through the transcendental meditation program: decreased crime rate. In *Scientific research on the transcendental meditation program* (ed. D. W. Orme-Johnson and J. T. Farrow). Vol. 1, pp. 639–48. Maharishi European Research University Press, Los Angeles.

Boss, M. (1965). *A psychiatrist discovers India*. Oswald Wolff, London.

Boswell, P. C. and Murray, E. J. (1979). Effects of meditation on psychological and physiological measures of anxiety. *Journal of Consulting and Clinical Psychology*, **47**, 606–7.

Boudreau, L. (1972). Transcendental meditation and yoga as reciprocal inhibitors. *Journal of Behavior Therapy and Experimental Psychiatry*, **3**, 97–8.

Bradley, B. W. and McCanne, T. R. (1981). Autonomic responses to stress: the effects of progressive relaxation, the relaxation response, and expectancy of relief. *Biofeedback and Self-Regulation*, **6**, 235–51.

Brautigam, E. (1977). Effects of the transcendental meditation program on drug abusers: a prospective study. In *Scientific research on the transcendental meditation program* (eds. D. W. Orme-Johnson and J. T. Farrow), Vol. 1, pp. 506–14. Maharishi European Research University Press, Los Angeles.

Brown, D. P. (1977). A model for the levels of concentrative meditation. *International Journal of Clinical and Experimental Hypnosis*, **25**, 236–73.

Brown D. P. and Engler, J. (1980). The stages of mindfulness meditation: a validation study. *Journal of Transpersonal Psychology*, **12**(2), 143–92.

Brown, D. P., Forte, M. and Dysart, M. (1984a). Differences in visual sensitivity among mindfulness meditators and non-meditators. *Perceptual and Motor Skills*, **58**, 3, 727–33.

Brown, D. P., Forte, M. and Dysart, M. (1984b). Visual sensitivity and mindfulness meditation. *Perceptual and Motor Skills*, **58**, 775–84.

Brown, D. P., Fischer, R., Wagman, A. and Horrom, H. (1977). The EEG in meditation and therapeutic touch healing. *Journal of Altered States of Consciousness*, **3**, 169–80.

Brown, D. P., Forte, M., Rich, P. and Epstein, G. (1982). Phenomenological differences among self-hypnosis, mindfulness meditation, and imaging. *Imagination, Cognition, and Personality*, **2**, 291–309.

Bruner, J. (1956). You are your constructs. *Contemporary Psychology*, **1**, 355–6.

Buckley, P. and Galanter, M. (1979). Mystical experience, spiritual knowledge and a contemporary ecstatic religion. *British Journal of Medical Psychology*, **52**, 281–9.

Bumgartner, J. and Epstein, C. (1982). Voluntary alteration of visual evoked potentials. *Annals of Neurology*, **12**, 475–8.

Burns, R. B. (1979). *The self concept: theory, measurement and behaviour*. Longman, London.

Busby, K. and DeKoninck, J. (1980). Short-term effects of strategies for self-regulation on personality dimensions and dream content. *Perceptual and Motor Skills*, **50**, 751–65.

Buss, A. H. (1962). Two anxiety factors in anxiety patients. *Journal of Abnormal and Social Psychology*, **65**, 426–7.

Buss, A. H. (1980). *Self consciousness and social anxiety*. Freeman, San Francisco.

Butler, C. (1922). *Western mysticism*. Constable, London.

Candelent, T. and Candelent, G. (1975). Teaching transcendental meditation in a psychiatric setting. *Hospital and Community Psychiatry*, **26**, 156–9.

Cannon, W. B. (1914). The emergency function of the adrenal medulla in pain and the major emotions. *American Journal of Physiology*, 356–72.

Capra, F. (1983). *The tao of physics*. Fontana, London.

Carpenter, J. T. (1977). Meditation, esoteric traditions—contributions to psychotherapy. *American Journal of Psychotherapy*, **31**(3), 394–404.

Carrington, P. (1978). *Clinically standardized meditation (CSM) instructor's kit*. Pace Educational Systems, Kendall Park, NJ.

Carrington, P. (1979). *Clinically standardized meditation (CSM); instructor's manual*. Pace Educational Systems, Kendall Park, NJ.

Carrington, P. (1977). *Freedom in meditation*. Anchor Press/Doubleday, New York.

Carrington, P. (1984). *Releasing*. William Morrow, New York.

Carrington, P. (1984). Modern forms of meditation. In *Principles and practice of stress management* (eds. R. L. Woolfolk and P. M. Lehrer) pp. 108–41. Guildford Press, New York.

Carrington, P. and Ephron, H. S. (1975a). Meditation as an adjunct to psychotherapy. In *New dimensions in psychiatry: a world view* (eds. S. Ariety and G. Chrzanowski). John Wiley, New York.

Carrington, P. and Ephron, H. S. (1975b). Meditation and psychoanalysis. *Journal of the American Academy of Psychoanalysis*, **3**, 43–57.

Carrington, P., Collings, G., Benson, H., Robinson, H., Wood, L., Lehrer, P., Woolfolk, R. and Cole, W. (1980). The use of meditation–relaxation techniques for the management of stress in a working population. *Journal of Occupational Medicine*, **22**, 221–31.

Carroll, L. (1960). *The annotated Alice: Alice's adventures in Wonderland and through the looking glass*. Clarkson N. Potter, New York.

Cattell, R. B. (1957). *Personality and motivation: structure and measurement.* World Book Co., New York.

Cattell, R. B., Eber, H. W. and Tatsuoka, M. M. (1970). *Handbook for the sixteen personality factor questionnaire.* Institute for Personality and Ability Testing, Champaign, Ill.

Cauthen, N. R. and Prymak, C. A. (1977). Meditation versus relaxation: An examination of the physiological effects of relaxation training and different levels of experience with transcendental meditation. *Journal of Consulting and Clinical Psychology*, **45**, 496–7.

Cheek, J. M. and Briggs, S. R. (1982). Self consciousness and aspects of identity. *Journal of Research in Personality*, **16**, 401–8.

Cirignotta, F., Todesco, C. and Lugaresi, E. (1980). Dostoivskian epilepsy. *Epilepsia*, **21**, 705–10.

Claxton, G. L. (1981). *Wholly human: Western and Eastern visions of the self and its perfection.* Routledge and Kegan Paul, London.

Claxton, G. L. (ed.) (1986). *Beyond therapy: the impact of Eastern religions on psychological theory and practice.* Wisdom Publications, London.

Cohen, J. (1962). The statistical power of abnormal-social psychological research: a review. *Journal of Abnormal and Social Psychology*, **65**, 145–53.

Cohen, J. (1977). *Statistical power analysis for the behavioral sciences*, 2nd edn. Academic Press, New York.

Coleman, J. E. (1971). *The quiet mind.* Rider and Co, London.

Collins, A. M. and Quillian, M. R. (1969). Retrieval time from semantic memory. *Journal of Verbal Learning and Verbal Behaviour*, **8**, 240–8.

Conze, E. (1975). *Buddhist wisdom books*, 2nd edn. George Allen and Unwin, London.

Cook, T. D. and Campbell, D. T. (1979). *Quasi-experimentation:* design and analysis for field settings. Rand McNally, Chicago.

Cooper, M. J. and Aygen, M. M. (1979). A relaxation technique in the management of hypercholesterolemia. *Journal of Human Stress*, **5**, 24–7.

Cooper, R., Winter, A. L., Crow, H. J. and Walter, W. G. (1965). Comparison of subcortical and scalp activity using chronically indwelling electrodes in man. *Electroencephalography and Clinical Neurophysiology*, **18**, 217–28.

Corby, J. C., Roth, W. T., Zarcone, V. P. and Kopell, B. S. (1978). Psychophysiological correlates of the practice of Tantric yoga meditation. *Archives of General Psychiatry*, **35**, 571–7.

Corey, P. W. (1977). Airway conductance and oxygen consumption changes associated with practice of the transcendental meditation technique. In *Scientific research on the transcendental meditation program* (eds. D. W. Orme-Johnson and J. T. Farrow), Vol. 1, pp. 94–107. Maharishi European Research University Press, Los Angeles.

Credidio, S. G. (1982). Comparative effectiveness of patterned biofeedback versus meditation training on EMG and skin temperature changes. *Behavior Research and Therapy*, **20**, 233–41.

Creutzfeldt, O. D., Watanabe, S., and Lask, H. D. (1966). Relations between EEG phenomena and potentials of single cortical cells. *Electroencephalography and Clinical Neurophysiology*, **20**, 19–36.

Cronbach, L. and Furby, L. (1970). How we should measure change — or should we? *Psychological Bulletin*, **74**, 68–80.

Crook, J. H. (1980). *The evolution of human consciousness*. Clarendon Press, Oxford.

Crook, J. H. (1983). Meditation. *Update*, 48–54.

Curtin, T. G. (1973). The relationship between transcendental meditation and adaptive regression. *Dissertation Abstracts International*, **34**,(4-A), 1969.

Curtis, J. W. (1984). Motivation to continue meditation and the ability to sustain nonanalytic attention. Unpublished Master's thesis, Roosevelt University.

Curtis, W. D. and Wessberg, H. W. (1975-6). A comparison of heart rate, respiration, and galvanic skin response among meditators, relaxers, and controls. *Journal of Altered States of Consciousness*, **2**, 319–24.

Daniels, L. K. (1975). The treatment of psychophysiological disorders and severe anxiety by behavior therapy, hypnosis and transcendental meditation. *American Journal of Clinical Hypnosis*, **17**, 267–9.

Das, N. N. and Gastaut, H. (1955). Variations de l'activité électrique du cerveau, du coeur et des muscles squelettiques au cours de la méditation et de l'extase yogique. *Electroencephalography and Clinical Neurophysiology*, Supplement 6, 211–19.

Datey, K. K., Deshmukh, S. N., Dalvi, C. P. and Vinekar, S. L. (1969). 'Shavasan': A yogic exercise in the management of hypertension. *Angiology*, **20**, 325–33.

Davidson, J. M. (1976). The physiology of meditation and mystical states of consciousness. *Perspectives in Biology and Medicine*, **19**, 345–80.

Davidson, R. and Goleman, D. (1977). The role of attention in meditation and hypnosis: a psychobiological perspective on transformation of consciousness. *International Journal of Clinical and Experimental Hypnosis*, **25**, 291–308.

Davidson, R. and Schwarz, G. E. (1976). The psychobiology of relaxation and related states: a multiprocess theory. In *Behavior control and modification of physiological activity* (ed. D. Mostofsky) pp. 339–442. Prentice Hall, New Jersey.

Davidson, R., Goleman, D. and Schwartz, G. (1976). Attentional and affective concomitants of meditation: a cross-sectional study. *Journal of Abnormal Psychology*, **85**, 235–8.

Davies, J. (1977). The transcendental meditation program and progressive relaxation: comparative effects on trait anxiety and self-actualisation. In *Scientific research on the transcendental meditation program* (eds. D. W. Orme-Johnson and J. T. Farrow), Vol. 1, pp. 449–52. Maharishi European Research University Press, Los Angeles.

Deatherage, G. (1975). The clinical use of mindfulness meditation techniques in short-term psychotherapy. *Journal of Transpersonal Psychology*, **7**(2), 133–43.

Deikman, A. J. (1963). Experimental meditation. *Journal of Nervous and Mental Disorders*, **136**, 329–73.

Deikman, A. J. (1966). Deautomatisation and the mystic experience. *Psychiatry*, **29**, 324–38.

Deikman, A. J. (1971). Bimodal consciousness. *Archives of General Psychiatry*, **25**, 481–9.

DeLeon, P. H., Van den Bos, G. R. and Cummings, N. A. (1983). Psychotherapy—is it safe, effective and appropriate? The beginning of an evolutionary dialogue. *American Psychologist*, **38**, 907–11.

Delmonte, M. M. (1979). Pilot study of conditioned relaxation during simulated meditation. *Psychological Reports*, **45**, 169–70.

Delmonte, M. M. (1980). Personality characteristics and regularity of meditation. *Psychological Reports*, **46**, 703–12.

Delmonte, M. M. (1981a). Expectation and meditation. *Psychological Reports*, **49**, 699–709.

Delmonte, M. M. (1981b). Suggestibility and meditation. *Psychological Reports*, **48**, 727–37.

Delmonte, M. M. (1984a). Meditation: some similarities with hypnoidal states and hypnosis. *International Journal of Psychosomatics*, **31**(3), 24–34.

Delmonte, M. M. (1984b). Physiological concomitants of meditation practice: a literature review. *International Journal of Psychosomatics*, **31**, 23–36.

Delmonte, M. M. (1984c). Electrocortical activity and related phenomena associated with meditation practice: a literature review. *International Journal of Neuroscience*, **24**, 217–31.

Delmonte, M. M. (1985a). Biochemical indices associated with meditation practice: a literature review. *Neuroscience and Biobehavioral Reviews*, **9**, 557–61.

Delmonte, M. M. (1985b). Meditation and anxiety reduction: a literature review. *Clinical Psychology Review*, **5**, 91–102.

DeRubeis, R., Hollon, S., Evans, M. and Bemis, K. (1982). Can psychotherapies for depression be discriminated? A systematic investigation of cognitive therapy and interpersonal therapy. *Journal of Consulting and Clinical Psychology*, **50**, 744–56.

Dhanaraj, V. J. and Singh, M. (1977). Reduction in metabolic rate during the practice of the transcendental meditation technique. In *Scientific research on the transcendental meditation program* (eds. D. W. Orme-Johnson and J. T. Farrow), Vol. 1, pp. 137–9. Maharishi European Research University Press, Los Angeles.

Dick, L. (1973). A study of meditation in the service of counseling. Unpublished PhD thesis, University of Oklahoma, Norman, Oklahoma.

Dillbeck, M. (1977). The effect of the transcendental meditation technique on anxiety level. *Journal of Clinical Psychology*, **33**, 1076–8.

Dillbeck, M. and Bronson, E. (1981). Short-term longitudinal effects of the transcendental meditation technique on EEG power and coherence. *International Journal of Neuroscience*, **14**, 147–51.

DiLoreto, A. O. (1971). *Comparative psychotherapy: an experimental analysis*. Aldine-Atherton, Chicago.

DiNardo, P. and Raymond, J. (1979). Locus of control and attention during meditation. *Journal of Consulting and Clinical Psychology*, **47**, 1136–7.

Duval, S. and Wicklund, R. A. (1972). *A theory of objective self-awareness*. Academic Press, New York.

Earle, J. B. (1977). Hemispheric specialisation and the hypnogogic process in meditation: an EEG study. Unpublished Master's thesis, Tufts University.

Earle, J. B. (1981). Cerebral laterality and meditation: a review of the literature. *Journal of Transpersonal Psychology*, **13**, 155–73.

Earle, J. B. (1984). Cerebral laterality and meditation: a review of the literature. In *Meditation: classic and contemporary perspectives* (eds. D. Shapiro and R. Walsh), pp. 155–73. Aldine Publishing Co., New York.

Ehrlichman, H. and Wiener, M. (1980). EEG asymmetry during covert mental activity. *Psychophysiology*, **17**, 228–35.

Elkin, I., Parloff, M. B. Hadley, S. W. and Autry, J. H. (1985). NIMH treatment of depression collaborative research program: background and research plan. *Archives of General Psychiatry*, **42**, 305–16.

Eliot, T. S. (1939). *The family reunion*. Faber and Faber, London.

Ellis, A. (1975). Rational–emotive psychotherapy. In *Issues and approaches in the psychological therapies* (ed. D. Bannister) pp. 163–86. John Wiley, London.

Elson, B. D., Hauri, P. and Cunis, D. (1977). Physiological changes in yoga meditation. *Psychophysiology*, **14**, 52–7.

Ericsson, K. A. and Simon, H. A. (1980). Verbal reports as data. *Psychological Review*, **87**, 215–51.

Erikson, E. H. (1959). The problem of ego identity. *Psychological Issues*, **1**, 101–64.

Evans, M., Hollon, S., DeRubeis, R., Tuason, V. B. Weimer, M. and Auerbach, A. (1983). Development of a system for rating psychotherapies for depression. Paper presented at the 14th Annual Meeting of the Society for Psychotherapy Research, Sheffield, England.

Eysenck, H. J. (1952). The effects of psychotherapy. An evaluation. *Journal of Consulting Psychology*, **16**, 319–24.

Eysenck, S. B. G. and Eysenck, H. J. (1968). The measurement of psychoticism. *British Journal of Social and Clinical Psychology*, 286–94.

Farrow, J. T. and Hebert, J. R. (1982). Breath suspension during the trans-cendental meditation technique. *Psychosomatic Medicine*, **44**(2), 133–53.

Fedio, P. and Mirsky, A. F. (1969). Selective intellectual deficits in children with temporal lobe or centrencephalic epilepsy. *Neuropsychologica*, **7**, 287–300.

Fehr, T. (1977). A longitudinal study of the effect of transcendental meditation program on changes in personality. In *Scientific research on the transcendental meditation program* (eds. D. W. Orme-Johnson and J. T. Farrow), Vol. 1, pp. 476–83. Maharishi European Research University Press, Los Angeles.

Fenigstein, A., Scheier, M. F. and Buss, A. H. (1975). Public and private self-consciousness: assessment and theory. *Journal of Consulting and Clinical Psychology*, **43**, 522–7.

Fenwick, P. (1969). Computer analysis of the EEG during mantra meditation. Paper presented at a conference on the effects of meditation, concentration and attention on the EEG. University of Marseilles.

Fenwick, P. (1974). Metabolic and EEG changes during transcendental meditation. *Psychophysiology Group Newsletter*, **1**, 24–5.

Fenwick, P. (1983). Some aspects of the physiology of the mystical experience. In *Psychology Survey* (eds. J. Nicholson and B. Foss), Number 4, pp. 203–23. British Psychological Society, Leicester.

Fenwick, P. (1986). The EEG in meditation: right temporal lobe functioning, enlightenment and the 'Zen Master'. Paper presented at the International Conference on Eastern Approaches to Mind and Self, July. University College Cardiff, Wales.

Fenwick, P., Donaldson, S., Gillies, L., Bushman, J., Fenton, G., Perry, I., Tilsley, C. and Serafinowicz, H. (1977). Metabolic and EEG changes during transcendental meditation. *Biological Psychology*, **5**, 101–18.

Fenwick, P., Galliano, S., Coate, M., Ripere, V. and Brown, D. (1985). 'Psychic sensitivity', mystical experience, head injury and brain pathology. *Journal of Medical Psychology*, **58**, 35–44.

Ferguson, P. and Gowan, J. (1976). TM: Some preliminary psychological findings. *Journal of Humanistic Psychology*, **16**, 51–60.

Fiedler, F. E. (1951). Factor analysis of psychoanalytic, nondirective and Adlerian therapeutic relationships. *Journal of Consulting Psychology*, **15**, 32–8.

Fingarette, H. (1963). *The self in transformation:psychoanalysis, philosophy, and the life of the spirit*. Basic Books, New York.

Finkelstein, S., Benowitz, L. I., Badessarini, R. J., Arana, D. W., Levine, E., Woo, E., Bear, D., Moya, K. and Stoll, A. L. (1982). Mood, vegetative disturbance, dexamethosone suppression test after stroke. *Annals of Neurology*, **12**, 463–8.

Fitzgerald, E. T. (1966). The measurement of openness to experience: a study of regression in the service of the ego. *Journal of Personality and Social Psychology*, **4**, 655–63.

Fling, S., Thomas, A. and Gallagher, M. (1981). Participant characteristics and the effect of two types of meditation vs. quiet sitting. *Journal of Clinical Psychology*, **37**, 784–90.

Forte, M., Brown, D. and Dysart, M. (1984). Through the looking glass: phenomenological reports of advanced meditators at visual threshold. *Imagination, Cognition, and Personality*, **4**, 323–38.

Frank, J. D. (1961). *Persuasion and healing: a comparative study of psychotherapy*. Johns Hopkins University Press, Baltimore.

Frank, J. D. (1982). Therapeutic components shared by all psychotherapies. In *Psychotherapy research and behaviour change* (eds. J. H. Harvey and M. M. Parks), Vol. 1. The Master Lecture Series pp. 5–37. American Psychological Association, Washington DC.

French, R. (1968). *The way of a pilgrim*. Seabury Press, New York.

Freuchen, P. (1959). *The book of the Eskimoes*. Fawcett, New York.

Freud, S. (1958). *The interpretation of dreams* (1900). Basic Books Inc., New York.

Froming, W. J. and Carver, C. S. (1981). Divergent influences of private and public self consciousness in a compliance paradigm. *Journal of Research in Personality*, **15**, 159–71.

Fromm, E. (1960) Psychoanalysis and Zen Buddhism. In *Zen Buddhism and psychoanalysis* (ed. E. Fromm) pp. 77–141. Grove Press, New York.

Fromm, E. (1977. An ego psychological theory for altered states of consciousness. *International Journal of Clinical and Experimental Hypnosis*, **25**, 372–87.

Fromm, E. (1981). Primary and secondary process in waking and in altered states of consciousness. *Academic Psychology Bulletin*, **3**, 29–45.

Frumkin, K., Nathan, R. J., Prout, M. F. and Cohen, M. C. (1978). Non-pharmacological control of essential hypertension in man: a critical review of the experimental literature. *Psychosomatic Medicine*, **40**, 294–320.

Gainotti, G. (1972). Emotional behaviour and hemispheric side of the lesion. *Cortex*, **8**, 41.

Galin, D. (1974). Implications for psychiatry of left and right cerebral specialisation. *Archives of General Psychiatry*, **31**, 572–83.

Gasparini, W. G., Satz, P., Heilman, K. and Coolidge, F. L. (1978) Hemispheric asymmetrics of affective processing as determined by the Minnesota Multiphasic Personality Inventory. *Journal of Neurology, Neurosurgery and Psychiatry*, **41**, 470.

Gecas, V. (1982). The self concept. *Annual Review of Sociology*, **8**, 1–33.

Gecas, V. and Mortimer, J. T. (1987). Stability and change in the self-concept from adolescence to adulthood. In *Self and identity: perspectives across the lifespan* (eds. T. Honess and K. Yardley). Routledge and Kegan Paul, London.

Gellhorn, E. and Kiely, W. F. (1972). Mystical states of consciousness: neuro-physiological and clinical aspects. *Journal of Nervous and Mental Disease*, **154**, 399–405.

Gendlin, E. T. (1970). A theory of personality change. In *New directions in client-centred therapy* (eds. J. T. Hart and T. M. Tomlinson) pp. 129–72. Houghton-Mifflin, Boston.

Gendlin, E. T. (1978). *Focusing*. Bantam Books, New York.

Gilbreath, S. H. (1967). Group counseling, dependence, and college male underachievement. *Journal of Counseling Psychology*, **14**, 449–53.

Gilbreath, S. H. (1968). Appropriate and inappropriate group counseling with academic underachievers. *Journal of Counseling Psychology*, **15**, 506–11.

Girodo, M. (1974). Yoga meditation and flooding in the treatment of anxiety neurosis. *Journal of Behavior Therapy and Experimental Psychiatry*, **5**, 157–60.

Glass, G. V., McGaw, B. and Smith, M. L. (1981). *Meta-analysis in social research*. Sage Publications, Beverly Hills, Calif.

Glueck, B.C. (1973). Current research on transcendental meditation. Paper presented at Rensselear Polytechnic Institute, March 1973. Hartford Graduate Center, Conn.

Glueck, B. C. and Stroebel, C. (1975). Biofeedback and meditation in the treatment of psychiatric illness. *Comprehensive Psychiatry*, **16**, 303–21.

Goleman, B. L., Domitor, P. J. and Murray, E. J. (1979). Effects of Zen meditation on anxiety reduction and perceptual functioning. *Journal of Consulting and Clinical Psychology*, **47**, 551–6.

Goleman, D. (1971). Meditation as meta-therapy: hypothesis towards a proposed fifth state of consciousness. *Journal of Transpersonal Psychology*, **3**, 1–25.

Goleman, D. (1977). *The varieties of the meditative experience*. E. P. Dutton, New York.

Goleman, D. J. and Schwarz, G. E. (1976). Meditation as an intervention in stress reactivity. *Journal of Consulting and Clinical Psychology*, **44**, 456–66.

Goswell, L. (1986). Psycho-social aspects of Theravadan Buddhist monasticism in the West. Paper presented at the International Conference on Eastern Approaches to Mind and Self, July. University College Cardiff, Cardiff.

Graham, H. (1986). *The human face of psychology: humanistic psychology in its social and cultural context*. Open University Press, Milton Keynes.

Greenfield, T. K. (1977). Individual differences and mystical experience in response to three forms of meditation. Unpublished doctoral dissertation, University of Michigan.

Greenwood, M. and Benson, H. (1977). The efficacy of progressive relaxation in systematic desensitisation and a proposal for an alternative competitive response—the relaxation response. *Behavior Research and Therapy*, **15**, 337–43.

Gregory, R. (1966). *Eye and brain*. Weidenfeld & Nicholson, London.

Grof, S. (1975). *Realms of the human unconscious*. Souvenir Press, London.

Hafner, R. J. (1982). Psychological treatment of essential hypertension: a controlled comparison of meditation and meditation plus biofeedback. *Biofeedback and Self-Regulation*, **7**, 305–16.

Halevi, Z'ev Ben Shimon (1976). *The way of Kabbalah*. Samuel Weiser, New York.

Hall, C. S. and Lindzey, G. (1978). *Theories of personality*. John Wiley, New York.

Hamilton, M. (1959). The assessment of anxiety states by rating. *British Journal of Medical Psychology*, **32**, 50–5.

Hardy, G. E. and Shapiro, D. A. (1985). Therapist verbal response modes in prescriptive versus exploratory psychotherapy. *British Journal of Clinical Psychology*, **24**, 235–45.

Hartmann, H. (1958). *Ego psychology and the problem of adaptation*. International University Press, New York.

Haynes, C. T., Hebert, J. R., Reber, W. and Orme-Johnson, D. W. (1977). The psychophysiology of advanced participants in the transcendental meditation programme: correlations of EEG coherence, creativity, H-reflex recovery, and experience of transcendental consciousness. In *Scientific research on the transcendental meditation program* (eds. D. W. Orme-Johnson and J. T. Farrow), Vol. 1, pp. 208–12. Maharishi European Research University Press, Los Angeles.

Hebb, D. O. (1949). *The organisation of behaviour*. John Wiley, New York.

Hebert, J. R. (1977). Periodic suspension of respiration during the transcendental meditation technique. In *Scientific research on the transcendental meditation program* (eds. D. W. Orme-Johnson and J. T. Farrow), Vol. 1, pp. 134–5. Maharishi European Research University Press, Los Angeles.

Hebert, R., and Lehmann, D. (1977). Theta bursts: an EEG pattern in normal subjects practising the transcendental meditation technique. *Electroencephalography and Clinical Neurophysiology*, **42**, 397–405.

Heide, F., Wadlington, W. and Lundy, R. (1980). Hypnotic responsitivity as a predictor of outcome in meditation. *International Journal of Clinical and Experimental Hypnosis*, **28**, 358–66.

Hendlin, S. J. (1979). Initial Zen intensive (*Sesshin*): a subjective account. *Journal of Pastoral Counseling*, **14**, 27–43.

Hendricks, C. C. (1975). Meditation as discrimination training: a theoretical note. *Journal of Transpersonal Psychology*, 7(2), 144–6.

Henry, J. P. (1978). Relaxation methods and the control of blood pressure. *Psychosomatic Medicine*, **40**, 273–5.

Herink, R. (ed.) (1980). *The psychotherapy handbook*. New American Library, New York.

Herman, B. P. and Riel, P. (1981). Interictal personality and behavioural traits in temporal lobe and generalised epilepsy. *Cortex*, **17**, 125–8.

Hewitt, J. (1978). *Meditation*. Hodder and Stoughton, London.

Hilgard, E. R. (1980). Consciousness in contemporary psychology. *Annual Review of Psychology*, **31**, 1–26.

Hinkle, D. N. (1965). The change of personal constructs from the viewpoint of a theory of implications. Unpublished PhD thesis. Ohio State University.

Hirai, T. (1975). *Zen meditation therapy*. Japan Publications, Tokyo.

Hjelle, L. A. (1974). Transcendental meditation and psychological health. *Perceptual and Motor Skills*, **39**, 623–8.

Hoffman, J. W., Benson, H., Arns, P. A., Stainbrook, G. L., Landsberg, L., Young, F. B. and Gill, A. (1982). Reduced sympathetic nervous system responsivity associated with the relaxation response. *Science*, **215**, 190–2.

Holmes, D. S. (1984). Meditation and somatic arousal reduction: a review of the experimental evidence. *American Psychologist*, **39**, 1–10.

Holmes, D. S. (1985a). To meditate or to simply rest, that is the question: a response to the comments of Shapiro. *American Psychologist*, **40**, 722–5.

Holmes, D. S. (1985b). To meditate or rest? The answer is rest. *American Psychologist*, **40**, 728–31.

Holmes, D. S., Solomon, S., Cappo, B. M. and Greenberg, J. L. (1983). Effects of transcendental meditation versus resting on physiological and subjective arousal. *Journal of Personality and Social Psychology*, **44**, 1245–52.

Holroyd, K. A., Penzien, D. B., Hursey, K. G., Tobin, D. L., Rogers, L., Holm, J. E., Marcille, P. J., Hall, J. R. and Chila, A. G. (1984). Change mechanisms in EMG biofeedback training: cognitive changes underlying improvements in tension headache. *Journal of Consulting and Clinical Psychology*, **52**, 1039–53.

Honsberger, R. W. and Wilson, A. F. (1973). Transcendental meditation in treating asthma. *Respiratory Therapy: Journal of Inhalation Technology*, **3**, 79–81.

Howard, K. I. Krause, M. S. and Orlinsky, D. E. (1986). The attrition dilemma: toward a new strategy for psychotherapy research. *Journal of Consulting and Clinical Psychology*, **54**, 106–10.

Hugdahl, K. and Ost, L. (1981). On the difference between statistical and clinical significance. *Behavioral Assessment*, **3**, 289–95.

Hume, D. (1888). *A treatise on human nature*. Clarendon Press, Oxford.

Hunt, H. T. and Chefurka, C. M. (1976). A test of the psychedelic model of altered states of consciousness. *Archives of General Psychiatry*, **33**, 867–76.

Hurlburt, R. T. (1980). Validation and correlation of thought sampling with retrospective measures. *Cognitive Therapy and Research*, **4**, 235–8.

Husserl, E. (1913/77). *Ideas: general introduction to pure phenomenology*. Collier Books, New York.

Jacobson, N. S., Follette, W. C. and Revenstorf, D. (1984). Psychotherapy outcome research: methods for reporting variability and evaluating clinical significance. *Behavior Therapy*, **15**, 336–52.

James, W. (1890/1950). *The principles of psychology*. Vol. 1. Dover Press, New York.

Janby, J. (1977). Immediate effects of the transcendental meditation technique: increased skin resistance during first meditation after instruction. In *Scientific research on the transcendental meditation program* (eds. D. W. Orme-Johnson and J. T. Farrow), Vol. 1, pp. 213–15. Maharishi European Research University Press, Los Angeles.

Jarrell, H. R. (1985). *International meditation bibliography*, 1950–1982. Scarecrow Press, London.

Jevning, R., Pirkle, H. C. and Wilson, A. F. (1977). Behavioral alteration of plasma phenylalanine concentration. *Physiology and Behavior*, **19**, 611–14.

Jevning, R., Wilson, A. F. and Davidson, J. M. (1978a). Adrenocortical activity during meditation. *Hormones and Behavior*, **10**, 54–60.

Jevning, R., Wilson, A. F. and VanderLann, E. F. (1978b). Plasma prolactin and growth hormone during meditation. *Psychosomatic Medicine*, **40**, 329–33.

Jevning, R., Wilson, A. F., Smith, W. R. and Morton, M. E. (1978c). Redistribution of blood flow in acute hypometabolic behavior. *American Journal of Physiology*, **235**, R89–92.

Jung, C. (1958). Psychological commentary on the *Tibetan Book of Great Liberation*. In *Psychology and religion* (translated by R. F. Hull), Vol. 2, collected works, pp. 457–508. Pantheon Books, New York.

Jung, C. (1961). *Memories, dreams, reflections*. Vintage Books, New York.

Kadloubovsky, E. and Palmber, G. E. H. (1969). *Early fathers from the Philokalia*. Faber and Faber, London.

Kanas, N. and Horowitz, M. J. (1977). Reactions of transcendental meditators and non-meditators to stress films: a comparative study. *Archives of General Psychiatry*, **34**, 1431–6.

Kanellakos, D. and Lukas, J. (1974). *The psychobiology of transcendental meditation*. Benjamin, Menlo Park.

Kapleau, P. (1965). *The three pillars of Zen*. Beacon Press, Boston.

Kapleau, P. Roshi. (1980). *The three pillars of Zen*, 2nd edn. Rider, London.

Kasamatsu, A. and Hirai, T. (1966). An electroencephalographic study on the Zen meditation (*zazen*). *Folia Psychiatrica et Neurologica Japonica*, **20**, 315–36.

Kasamatsu, A., Okuma, T., Takenaka, S., Koga, E. Ikeda, K. and Sugiojama H. (1957). The EEG of 'Zen' and 'Yoga' practitioners. *Electroencephalography and Clinical Neurophysiology*, Supplement **9**, 51–2.

Katz, R. (1973). *Preludes to growth: an experiential approach*. Free Press, New York.

Kazdin, A. E. (1978). Evaluating the generality of findings in analogue therapy research. *Journal of Consulting and Clinical Psychology*, **46**, 673–86.

Kazdin, A. E. (1986a). Editor's introduction to the special issue. *Journal of Consulting and Clinical Psychology*, **54**, 3.

Kazdin, A. E. (1986b). Comparative outcome studies of psychotherapy: methodological issues and strategies. *Journal of Consulting and Clinical Psychology*, **54**, 95–105.

Kazdin, A. E. and Wilcoxon, L. A. (1976). Systematic desensitization and non-specific treatment effects: a methodological evaluation. *Psychological Bulletin*, **83**, 729–58.

Kazdin, A. E. and Wilson, G. T. (1978). *Evaluation of behavior therapy: issues evidence, and research strategies*. Ballinger, Cambridge, Mass.

Kelly, G. A. (1955). *The psychology of personal constructs*. Norton, New York.

Kendall, P. C. and Korgeski, G. P. (1979). Assessment and cognitive–behavioral interventions. *Cognitive Therapy and Research*, **3**, 1–21.

Kiesler, C. A. (1985). Meta-analysis, clinical psychology, and social policy. *Clinical Psychology Review*, **5**, 3–12.

Kiesler, D. J. (1966). Some myths of psychotherapy research and the search for a paradigm. *Psychological Bulletin*, **65**, 110–36.

Kiesler, D. J. (1973). *The process of psychotherapy: empirical foundations and methods of analysis*. Aldine Publishing, Chicago.

Kinch, J. R., Falk, F. and Anderson, D. (1983). A self-image inventory: its theoretical background, reliability, and validity. *Symbolic Interaction*, **6**, 229–42.

Kingsley, R. G. and Wilson, G. T. (1977). Behavior therapy for obesity: a comparative investigation of long-term efficacy. *Journal of Consulting and Clinical Psychology*, **45**, 288–98.

Kinsman, R. A. and Staudenmayer, H. (1978). Baseline levels in muscle relaxation training. *Biofeedback and Self-Regulation*, **3**, 97–104.

Kirsch, I. and Henry, D. (1979). Self-desensitization and meditation in the reduction of public speaking anxiety. *Journal of Consulting and Clinical Psychology*, **47**, 536–41.

Klemons, I. M. (1977). Changes in inflammation in persons practicing the transcendental meditation technique. In *Scientific research on the transcendental meditation program* (eds. D. W. Orme-Johnson and J. T. Farrow), Vol. 1, pp. 287–91. Maharishi European Research University Press, Los Angeles.

Klerman, G., Rounsaville, B., Chevron, E., Neu, C. and Weissman, M. (1984). *Manual for short-term interpersonal therapy for depression*. Basic Books, New York.

Klinger, E. (1978) Modes of normal conscious flow. In *The stream of consciousness: scientific investigations into the flow of human experience* (eds K. S. Pope and J. L. Singer), pp. 225–58. Plenum Press, New York.

Kohr, R. L. (1977). Dimensionality of meditative experience: a replication. *Journal of Transpersonal Psychology*, **9**(2), 193–203.

Kohr, R. L. (1978). Changes in subjective meditation experience during a short-term project. *Journal of Altered States of Consciousness*, **3**(3), 221–34.

Kohr, R. L. (1984). Dimensionality in meditative experiences: a replication. In *Meditation: classic and contemporary perspectives* (eds. D. H. Shapiro and R. H. Walsh), pp. 271–280. Aldine Publishing Co., New York.

Kondo, A. (1958). Zen in psychotherapy. *Chicago Review*, **12**, 57–64.

Kornfield, J. (1979). Intensive insight meditation: a phenomenological study. *Journal of Transpersonal Psychology*, **11**, 41–58.

Kraemer, H. C. (1981). Coping strategies in psychiatric clinical research. *Journal of Consulting and Clinical Psychology*, **49**, 309–19.

Kretschmer, W. (1962). Meditation techniques in psychotherapy. *Psychologia*, **5**, 76–83.

Kretschmer, W. (1969). Meditative techniques in psychotherapy. In *Altered states of consciousness* (ed. C. Tart), pp. 219–28. John Wiley, New York.

Krishnamurti, J. (1973). *The awakening of intelligence*. Victor Gollancz, London.

Krupnick, J., Shea, T. and Elkin, I. (1986). Generalizability of treatment studies using solicited patients. *Journal of Consulting and Clinical Psychology*, **54**, 68–78.

Kubose, S. K. (1976). An experimental investigation of psychological aspects of meditation. *Psychologia*, **19**, 1–10.

Kuhn, M. H. and McPartland, T. A. (1954). An empirical investigation of self-attitudes. *American Sociological Review*, **19**, 68–76.

Kuhn, T. (1970). *The structure of scientific revolutions*. University of Chicago Press, Chicago.

Kumar, V. K. and Pekala, R. J. (1986a). Hypnotizability, absorption, and individual differences in phenomenological experience. Unpublished manuscript, Jefferson Medical College, Pennsylvania.

Kumar, V. K. and Pekala, R. J. (1986b). Variations in phenomenological experience as a function of low, medium, and high susceptibility: a replication. Unpublished manuscript, Jefferson Medical College, Pennsylvania.

Kutz, I., Borysenko, J. Z. and Benson, H. (1985). Meditation and psychotherapy: a rationale for the integration of dynamic psychotherapy, the relaxation response, and mindfulness meditation. *The American Journal of Psychiatry*, **142**, 1–8.

Lacey, J. (1956). The evaluation of autonomic responses: toward a general solution. *Annals of New York Academy of Science*, **67**, 123–64.

Lambert, M. J., Christensen, E. R. and DeJulio, S. S. (eds.) (1983). *The assessment of psychotherapy outcome*. John Wiley, New York.

Lambert, M. J., Shapiro, D. A. and Bergin, A. E. (1986). The effectiveness of psychotherapy. In *Handbook of psychotherapy and behavior change* (eds. S. L. Garfield and A. E. Bergin), 3rd edn., pp. 157–211. John Wiley, New York.

Lang, R., Dehob, K., Meurer, K. and Kaufman, W. (1979). Sympathetic activity and transcendental meditation. *Journal of Neural Transmission*, **44**, 117–35.

Laurie, G. (1977). An investigation into the changes in skin resistance during the transcendental meditation technique. In *Scientific research on the transcendental meditation program* (eds. D. W. Orme-Johnson and J. T. Farrow), Vol. 1, pp. 216–23. Maharishi European Research University Press, Los Angeles.

Lazar, Z., Farwell, L. and Farrow, J. (1977). Effects of transcendental meditation program on anxiety, drug abuse, cigarette smoking and alcohol consumption. In *Scientific research on the transcendental meditation program* (eds. D. W. Orme-Johnson and J. T. Farrow), Vol. 1, pp. 524–35. Maharishi European Research University Press, Los Angeles.

Lazarus, A. (1976). Psychiatric problems precipitated by transcendental meditation. *Psychological Reports*, **39**, 601–2.

Lehrer, P. M. and Woolfolk, R. L. (1984). Are stress reduction techniques interchangeable, or do they have specific effects? A review of the comparative empirical literature. In *Principles and practice of stress management* (eds. R. L. Woolfolk and P. M. Lehrer), pp. 404–77. Guilford Press, New York.

Lehrer, P. M., Schoicket, S., Carrington, P. and Woolfolk, R. L. (1980). Psychophysiological and cognitive responses to stressful stimuli in subjects practicing progressive relaxation and clinically standardized meditation. *Behavior Research and Therapy*, **18**, 293–303.

Lehrer, P. M., Woolfolk, R. L., Rooney, A. J., McCann, B. and Carrington, P. (1983). Progressive relaxation and meditation: a study of psychophysiological and therapeutic differences between two techniques. *Behavior Research and Therapy*, **21**, 651–62.

Lesh, T. V. (1970a). Zen and psychotherapy: a partially annotated bibliography. *Journal of Humanistic Psychology*, **10**, 75–85.

Lesh, T. V. (1970b). Zen meditation and the development of empathy in counselors. *Journal of Humanistic Psychology*, **10**, 39–74.

LeShan, L. (1983). *How to meditate*. Turnstone, Wellingborough.

Levine, P. H. (1976). The coherence spectral array (COSPAR) and its application to the study of spatial ordering in the EEG. *Proceedings of San Diego Biomedical Symposium*, **15**, 237–47.

Levine, P. H., Hebert, J. R., Haynes, C. T. and Stroebel, U. (1977). EEG coherence during the transcendental meditation technique. In *Scientific research on the transcendental meditation program*, (eds. D. W. Orme-Johnson and J. T. Farrow), collected papers, Vol. 1, pp. 187–207. Maharishi European Research University Press, Los Angeles.

Levine, S. (1979). *A gradual awakening*. Hutchinson, London.

Lieberman, D. A. (1979). Behaviorism and the mind: A (limited) call for a return to introspection. *American Psychologist*, **34**, 319–33.

Linden, W. (1971). Practicing of meditation by school children and their levels of field dependence–independence, test anxiety and reading achievement. *Journal of Consulting and Clinical Psychology*, **41**, 139–43.

Lintel, A. G. (1980). Physiological anxiety responses in transcendental meditators and nonmeditators. *Perceptual and Motor Skills*, **50**, 295–300.

Llewelyn, S. and Fielding, G. (1984). Destructive cults — a view from the inside. *Changes*, **3**, 1, 8–11.

Long, B. (1982). *Meditation: a foundation course*. Barry Long Centre, London.

Luborsky, L. (1976). Helping alliances in psychotherapy. In *Successful psychotherapy* (ed. J. L. Claghorn). Brunner/Mazel, New York.

Luborsky, L. (1984). *Principles of psychoanalytic psychotherapy: a manual for supportive-expressive treatment.* Basic Books, New York.

Luborsky, L., Singer, B. and Luborsky, L. (1975). Comparative studies of psychotherapies: Is it true that 'Everyone has won and all must have prizes?' *Archives of General Psychiatry,* **32,** 995-1008.

Ludwig, A. H. (1972). Altered states of consciousness. In *Altered states of consciousness* (ed. C. T. Tart), pp. 11-24. John Wiley, New York.

Lukas, J. (1973). The effects of TM on concurrent heart rate, peripheral blood pulse volume and the alpha wave frequency. Paper presented at the APA Conference, Montreal.

McCuaig, L. (1974). Salivary electrolytes, protein, and pH during transcendental meditation. *Experimentia,* **30,** 988-9.

McIntyre, M. E., Silverman, F. H. and Trotter, W. D. (1974). Transcendental meditation and stuttering: a preliminary report. *Perceptual and Motor Skills,* **39,** 294.

McWilliams, S. A. (1984). Construing and Buddhist psychology. *Constructs,* **3**(1), 1-2.

Maharishi Mahesh Yogi (1963). *The science of being and art of living.* Unwin, London.

Mahoney, M. J. (1978). Experimental methods and outcome evaluation. *Journal of Consulting and Clinical Psychology,* **46,** 660-72.

Malec, J. and Sipprelle, C. H. (1977). Physiological and subjective effects of Zen meditation and demand characteristics. *Journal of Consulting and Clinical Psychology,* **45,** 339-40.

Maliszewski, M. Twemlow, S. W., Brown, D. P. and Engler, J. M. (1981). A phenomenological typology of intensive meditation. *ReVision,* **4,** 3-27.

Marlatt, C. A., Pagano, R. R., Rose, R. M. and Marques, J. K. (1984). Effects of meditation and relaxation training upon alcohol use in male social drinkers. In *Meditation: classic and contemporary perspectives* (eds. D. H. Shapiro and R. N. Walsh), pp. 105-20. Aldine Publishing, New York.

Marziali, E. A. (1984). Three viewpoints on the therapeutic alliance: similarities, differences and associations with psychotherapy outcome. *Journal of Nervous and Mental Disease,* **172,** 417-23.

Mathews, A. M. (1978). Fear reduction research and clinical phobias. *Psychological Bulletin,* **85,** 390-404.

Maupin, E. W. (1962). Zen Buddhism: a psychological review. *Journal of Consulting Psychology,* **26**(4), 362-78.

Maupin, E. W. (1965). Individual differences in response to a Zen meditation exercise. *Journal of Consulting Psychology,* **29,** 139-45.

Maupin, E. W. (1969). On meditation. In *Altered states of consciousness* (ed. C. Tart), pp. 177-86. John Wiley, New York.

Mead, G. H. (1934). *Mind, self and society.* Chicago University Press, Chicago.

Meares, A. (1982). A form of intensive meditation associated with the regression of cancer. *American Journal of Clinical Hypnosis,* **25,** 114-21.

Merton, T. (1960). *The wisdom of the desert.* New Directions, New York.

Mesulam, M. and Geschwind, N. (1978). On the possible role of neocortex and its limbic connections in the process of attention and schizophrenia: critical cases of inattention in man and experimental anatomy in monkey. *Journal of Psychiatric Research,* **14,** 249-59.

Michaels, R. R., Huber, M. J. and McCann, D. S. (1976). Evaluation of transcendental meditation as a method of reducing stress. *Science*, **192**,
1242–4.

Michaels, R. R., Parra, J., McCann, D. S. and Vander, A. J. (1979). Renin, cortisol,
and aldosterone during transcendental meditation. *Psychosomatic Medicine*,
41, 50–4.

Mikulas, W. L. (1978). Four Noble Truths of Buddhism related to behaviour
therapy. *Psychological Record*, **28**, 59–67.

Mikulas, W. L. (1981). Buddhism and behaviour modification. *Psychological
Record*, **31**, 331–42.

Miller, L. S. and Cross, H. J. (1985). Hypnotic susceptibility, hypnosis and EMG
biofeedback in the reduction of frontalis muscle tension. *International Journal
of Clinical and Experimental Hypnosis*, **33**, 258–72.

Milne, H. (1986). *Bhagwan: the God that failed*. Caliban Books, London.

Mintz, J., Luborsky, L. and Christolph, P. (1979). Measuring the outcomes of
psychotherapy: findings of the Penn Psychotherapy Project. *Journal of
Consulting and Clinical Psychology*, **47**, 319–34.

Mischel, T. (1977). *The self: psychological and philosophical issues*. Basil
Blackwell, Oxford.

Miskiman, D. E. (1977a). The treatment of insomnia by the transcendental
meditation program. In *Scientific research on the transcendental meditation
program* (eds. D. W. Orme-Johnson and J. T. Farrow), Vol. 1, pp. 296–8.
Maharishi European Research University Press, Los Angeles.

Miskiman, D. E. (1977b). Long-term effects of the transcendental meditation
program in the treatment of insomnia. In *Scientific research on the transcendental meditation program* (eds. D. W. Orme-Johnson and J. T. Farrow),
Vol. 1. pp. 299–300. Maharishi European Research University Press, Los
Angeles.

Morse, D. R., Martin, J. S., Furst, M. L. and Dubin, L. L. (1977). A physiological
and subjective evaluation of meditation, hypnosis, and relaxation.
Psychosomatic Medicine, **39**, 304–24.

Mungus, D. (1982). Interictal behaviour abnormality in temporal lobe epilepsy:
a specific syndrome of non-specific psychopathology. *Archives of General
Psychiatry*, **39**, 108–11.

Muskatel, N., Woolfolk, R. L., Carrington, P., Lehrer, P. M. and McCann, B. S.
(1984). Effect of meditation training on aspects of coronary-prone behavior.
Perceptual and Motor Skills, **58**, 515–18.

Naranjo, C. (1974). The domain of meditation. In *What is meditation?* (ed.
J. White). Anchor Books, New York.

Naranjo, C. and Ornstein, R. E. (1971). *On the psychology of meditation*. Viking
Press, New York.

Neisser, U. (1976). *Cognition and reality*. W. H. Freeman, San Francisco.

Nicholson, R. A. and Berman, J. S. (1983). Is follow-up necessary in evaluating
psychotherapy? *Psychological Bulletin*, **93**, 261–78.

Nidich, S., Seeman, W. and Dreskin, T. (1973). Influence of transcendental
meditation: a replication. *Journal of Counseling Psychology*, **20**, 565–6.

Nisbett, R. E. and Wilson, T. D. (1977). Telling more than we can know: verbal
reports on mental processes. *Psychological Review*, **84**, 231–359.

Nystul, M. S. and Garde, M. (1977). The self-concepts of transcendental
meditators and nonmeditators. *Psychological Reports*, **41**, 303–6.

Nystul, M. S. and Garde, M. (1979). The self-concepts of regular transcendental meditators, dropout meditators and nonmeditators. *Journal of Psychology*, **103**, 15–18.

Orlinksy, D. E. and Howard, K. I. (1978). The relation of process to outcome in psychotherapy. In *Handbook of psychotherapy and behavior change: an empirical analysis* (eds. S. L. Garfield and A. E. Bergin), 2nd edn., pp. 283–329. John Wiley, New York.

Orme-Johnson, D. W. (1973). Autonomic stability and transcendental meditation. *Psychosomatic Medicine*, **35**, 341–9.

Orme-Johnson, D. W., Dillbeck, M. C., Wallace, R. K. and Landrith III, G. S. (1982). Intersubject EEG coherence: is consciousness a field? *International Journal of Neuroscience*, **16**, 203–9.

Orme-Johnson, D. W., Kiehlbauch, J., Moore, R. and Bristol, J. (1978). Personality and autonomic changes in prisoners practising the transcendental meditation technique. In *Scientific research on the transcendental meditation program* (eds. D. W. Orme-Johnson and J. T. Farrow), Vol. 1, pp. 556–61. Maharishi European Research University Press, Los Angeles.

Orne, M. (1962). On the social psychology of the psychological experiment: with particular reference to demand characteristics and their implications. *American Psychologist*, **17**, 776–83.

Ornstein, R. (1971). The techniques of meditation and their implications for modern psychology. In *On the psychology of meditation* (eds. C. Naranjo and R. Ornstein), pp. 137–232. Viking, New York.

Ornstein, R. E. (1972). *The psychology of consciousness*. W. H. Freeman and Co. Ltd., San Francisco.

Osis, K., Bokert, E. and Carlson, M. L. (1973). Dimensions of the meditative experience. *Journal of Transpersonal Psychology*, **2**, 109–35.

Osuna, Fray F. De (1931). *The third spiritual alphabet*. Benziger, London.

Otis, L. (1973). The psychobiology of meditation: some psychological changes. Paper presented at the APA Convention, Montreal, Canada.

Otis, L. (1974a). The facts on transcendental meditation: if well-integrated but anxious, try TM. *Psychology Today,* 7(4), 45–6.

Otis, L. (1974b). TM and sleep. Paper presented at the APA Convention, New Orleans.

Otis, L. (1984). Adverse effects of transcendental meditation. In *Meditation: classic and contemporary perspectives* (eds. D. H. Shapiro and R. N. Walsh), pp. 201–8. Aldine, New York.

Pagano, R. and Frumkin, L. (1977). Effects of TM in right hemisphere functioning. *Biofeedback and Self-regulation*, **2**, 407–15.

Pagano, R. R. and Warrenburg, S. (1983). Meditation: in search of a unique effect. In *Consciousness and self regulation* (eds. R. J. Davidson, G. E. Schwarz and D. Shapiro), pp. 153–205. Plenum Press, New York.

Pagano, R., Rose, R., Strivers, R. and Warrenburg, S. (1976). Sleep during transcendental meditation. *Science*, **191**, 308–10.

Parker, J. C., Gilbert, G. S. and Thoreson, R. W. (1978). Reduction of autonomic arousal in alcoholics: a comparison of relaxation and meditation techniques. *Journal of Consulting and Clinical Psychology*, **46**, 879–86.

Parloff, M. B. (1986). Placebo controls in psychotherapy research: a *sine qua non* or a placebo for research problems? *Journal of Consulting and Clinical Psychology*, **54**, 79–87.

Parloff, M. B., Waskow, I. E. and Wolfe, B. E. (1978). Research on therapist variables in relation to process and outcome. In *Handbook of psychotherapy and behavior change: an empirical analysis* (eds. S. L. Garfield and A. E. Bergin), 2nd edn., pp. 233–82. John Wiley, New York.

Patel, C. H. (1973). Yoga and biofeedback in the management of hypertension. *Lancet*, **2**, 1053–5.

Patel, C. H. (1975). 12-month follow-up of yoga and biofeedback in the management of hypertension. *Lancet*, **1**, 62–5.

Patel, C. H. (1984). Yogic therapy. In *Principles and practice of stress management* (eds. R. L. Woolfolk and P. M. Lehrer), pp. 70–107. Guilford Press, New York.

Patel, C. H. and North, W. R. S. (1975). Randomized controlled trial of yoga and biofeedback in the management of hypertension. *Lancet*, **2**, 93–5.

Paul, G. L. (1966). *Insight versus desensitization in psychotherapy*. Stanford University Press, Palo Alto, Calif.

Paul, G. L. (1967). Strategy of outcome research in psychotherapy. *Journal of Consulting Psychology*, **31**, 109–18.

Pekala, R. J. (1980). An empirical–phenomenological approach for mapping consciousness and its various 'states'. Doctoral dissertation, Microfilm No. 82–02, 489, Michigan State University.

Pekala, R. J. (1982). *The phenomenology of consciousness inventory (PCI)*. Psychophenomenological Concepts, Thorndale, Pa.

Pekala, R. J. (1985a). A psychophenomenological approach to mapping and diagramming states of consciousness. *The Journal of Religion and Psychical Research*, **8**, 199–214.

Pekala, R. J. (1985b). *Mapping the structures and patterns of consciousness: user's manual for the phenomenology of consciousness inventory*. Psychophenomenological Concepts, Thorndale, Pa.

Pekala, R. J. and Kumar, V. K. (1986). Hypnosis, psygrams, and patterns of consciousness. Unpublished manuscript, Jefferson Medical College, Pa.

Pekala, R. J. and Levine, R. L. (1981). Mapping states of consciousness via an empirical–phenomenological approach. *Imagination, Cognition, and Personality*, **1**, 29–47.

Pekala, R. J. and Levine, R. L. (1982). Quantifying states of consciousness via an empirical–phenomenological approach. *Imagination, Cognition, and Personality*, **2**, 51–71.

Pekala, R. J., Wenger, C. F. and Levine, R. L. (1985). Individual differences in phenomenological experience: States of consciousness as a function of absorption. *Journal of Personality and Social Psychology*, **48**, 125–32.

Pelletier, K. R. (1977). Effects of the transcendental meditation program on perceptual style: increased field independence. In *Scientific research on the transcendental meditation program* (eds. D. W. Orme-Johnson and J. T. Farrow), Vol. 1, pp. 337–45. Maharishi European Research University Press, Los Angeles.

Perls, F., Hefferline, R. and Goodman, P. (1973). *Gestalt therapy*. Penguin, Harmondsworth.

Persinger, M. A. (1984). Striking EEG profiles from single episodes of glossolalia and transcendental meditation. *Perceptual and Motor Skills*, **58**, 127–33.

Peters, R. K., Benson, H. and Porter, D. (1977a). Daily relaxation response breaks in a working population: I. Effects on self-reported measures of health, performance and well-being . *American Journal of Public Health*, **67**, 946–53.

Peters, R. K., Benson, H. and Peters, J. M. (1977b). Daily relaxation response breaks in a working population: II. Effects on blood pressure. *American Journal of Public Health*, **67**, 954–9.

Piggins, D. and Morgan, C. (1977). Note upon steady visual fixation and repeated auditory stimulation during meditation in the laboratory. *Perceptual and Motor Skills*, **44**, 357–8.

Pirot, M. (1977). The effects of the transcendental meditation technique upon auditory discrimination. In *Scientific research on the transcendental meditation program* (eds. D. W. Orme-Johnson and J. T. Farrow), Vol. 1, pp. 331–4. Maharishi European Research University Press, Los Angeles.

Popper, K. R. (1959). *The logic of scientific discovery*. Hutchinson, London.

Prince, R. (1978). Meditation: some psychological speculations. *Psychological Journal of the University of Ottawa*, **3**, 202–9.

Privette, G. (1983). Peak experience, peak performance and flow: a comparative analysis of positive human experiences. *Journal of Personality and Social Psychology*, **45**, 1361–8.

Progoff, I. (ed.) (1969). *The cloud of unknowing*. Julian Press, New York.

Puente, A. E. (1981). Psychophysiological investigations on transcendental meditation. *Biofeedback and self-regulation*, **6**, 327–42.

Puente, A. E. and Beiman, I. (1980). The effects of behavior therapy, self-relaxation, and transcendental meditation on cardiovascular stress response. *Journal of Clinical Psychology*, **36**, 291–5.

Puryear, H., Cayce, C. and Thurston, M. (1976). Anxiety reduction associated with meditation: home study. *Perceptual and Motor Skills*, **43**, 527–31.

Rachlin, H. (1974). Self-control. *Behaviorism*, **2**, 94–107.

Rachman, S. and Wilson, G. T. (1980). *The effects of psychological therapy*, 2nd edn. Pergamon Press, New York.

Rahula, W. (1959). *What the Buddha taught*, Grove Press, New York.

Raskin, M., Bali, L. R. and Van Peeke, H. (1980). Muscle biofeedback and transcendental meditation: a controlled evaluation of efficacy in the treatment of chronic anxiety. *Archives of General Psychiatry*, **37**, 93–7.

Rigby, B. P. (1977). Higher states of consciousness through the transcendental meditation programme: a literature review. *Journal of Chronic Disease and Therapeutics Research*, **1**, 35–55.

Rimol, A. G. P. (1977). The transcendental meditation technique and its effects on sensory-motor performance. In *Scientific research on the transcendental meditation program* (eds. D. W. Orme-Johnson and J. T. Farrow), Vol. 1, pp. 326–30. Maharishi European Research University Press, Los Angeles.

Rivers, S. and Spanos, N. P. (1981). Personal variables predicting voluntary participation in and attrition from a meditation program. *Psychological Reports*, **49**, 795–801.

Robinson, J. P. and Shaver, P. R. (1973). *Measures of social psychological attitudes*. Institute for Social Research, University of Michigan, Michigan.

Rogers, C. R. (1961). *On becoming a person*. Constable, London.

Rogers, C. and Livingston, D. (1977). Accumulative effects of periodic relaxation. *Perceptual and Motor Skills*, **44**, 690.

Rosenberg, M. (1965). *Society and the adolescent self-image*. Princeton University Press, Princeton, NJ.

Rosenberg, M. (1979). *Conceiving the self*. Basic Books, New York.

Rosenberg, M. and Turner, R. H. (eds.) (1981). *Social psychology: sociological perspectives*. Basic Books, New York.

Rosenthal, R. (1966). *Experimenter effects in behavioural research*. Appleton-Century-Crofts, New York.

Rosenthal, R. and Frank, J. D. (1956). Psychotherapy and the placebo effect. *Psychological Bulletin*, **53**, 294–302.

Rosenthal, R. and Rubin, D. B. (1978). Interpersonal expectancy effects: the first 345 studies. *Behavioral and Brain Sciences*, **3**, 377–415.

Ross, E. D. (1981). The aprosodias. *Archives of Neurology*, **38**, 561–9.

Ross, E. D. and Rush, J. (1981). Diagnosis and neuroanatomical correlates of depression in brain damaged patients. *Archives of General Psychiatry*, **38**, 1344–54.

Ross, J. (1972). The effects of transcendental meditation on anxiety. Unpublished MA thesis, University of Edinburgh, Scotland.

Ross, J. (1977). The effects of the transcendental meditation program on anxiety, neuroticism, and psychoticism. In *Scientific research on the transcendental meditation program* (eds. D. W. Orme-Johnson and J. T. Farrow), Vol. 1, pp. 594–6. Maharishi European Research University Press, Los Angeles.

Rotter, J. B. (1966). Generalised expectancies of internal versus external control of reinforcement. *Psychological Monographs*, **80**, 1–28, (Whole No. 609).

Routt, T. J. (1977). Low normal heart and respiration technique. In *Scientific research on the transcendental meditation program* (eds. D. W. Orme-Johnson and J. T. Farrow), Vol. 1, pp. 256–60. Maharishi European Research University Press, Los Angeles.

Sato, E. (1958). Psychotherapeutic implication of Zen. *Psychologia*, **1**, 213–18.

Schaffer, N. D. (1982). Multidimensional measures of therapist behavior as predictors of outcome. *Psychological Bulletin*, **92**, 670–81.

Schalling, D., Cronholm, B. and Asberg, M. (1975). Components of state and trait anxiety as related to personality and arousal. In *Emotions: their parameters and measurement* (ed. L. Levi), 603–17. Raven Press, New York.

Schuman, M. (1980). The psychophysiological model of meditation and altered states of consciousness: a critical review. In *The psychobiology of consciousness* (eds. J. M. Davidson and R. J. Davidson), pp. 337–78. Plenum, New York.

Schur, E. (1976). *The awareness trap: self-absorption instead of social change*. Quadrangle, New York.

Schwartz, G. (1974). The facts on transcendental meditation: TM relaxes some people and makes them feel better. *Psychology Today*, **7**, 39–44.

Schwartz, G., Davidson, R. and Goleman, D. (1978). Patterning of cognitive and somatic processes in the self-regulation of anxiety: effects of meditation versus exercise. *Psychosomatic Medicine*, **40**, 321–8.

Seeman, W., Nidich, S. and Banta, T. (1972). Influence of transcendental meditation on a measure of self-actualization. *Journal of Counseling Psychology*, **19**, 184–7.

Seer, P. (1979). Psychological control of essential hypertension: review of the literature and methodological critique. *Psychological Bulletin*, **86**, 1015–43.

Seligman, M. E. P. (1975). *Helplessness: on depression, development, and death*. Freeman, San Francisco.

Shafii, M. (1973). Silence in the service of the ego: psychoanalytic study of meditation. *International Journal of Psychoanalysis*, **54**(4), 431–43.

Shafii, M., Lavely, R. A. and Jaffe, R. D. (1974). Meditation and marijuana. *American Journal of Psychiatry*, **131**, 60–3.

Shafii, M., Lavely, R. A. and Jaffe, R. D. (1975). Meditation and the prevention of alcohol abuse. *American Journal of Psychiatry*, **132**, 942–5.

Shafii, M., Lavely, R. A. and Jaffe, R. D. (1976). Verminderung von zigaretten-rauchen also folgc tranzendentaler meditation (decrease of smoking following meditation). *Maharishi European Research University Journal*, **24**, 29.

Shapiro, A. K. and Morris, L. A. (1978). Placebo effects in medical and psychological therapies. In *Handbook of psychotherapy and behavior change* (eds. S. L. Garfield and A. E. Bergin), 2nd edn., pp. 369–410. John Wiley, New York.

Shapiro, D. A. (1975). Some implications of psychotherapy research for clinical psychology. *British Journal of Medical Psychology*, **48**, 199–206.

Shapiro, D. A. (1981). Comparative credibility of treatment rationales: three tests of expectancy theory. *British Journal of Clinical Psychology*, **20**, 111–22.

Shapiro, D. A. (1985). Recent applications of meta-analysis in clinical research. *Clinical Psychology Review*, **5**, 13–34.

Shapiro, D. A. and Firth, J. A. (in press). Prescriptive versus exploratory psychotherapy: outcomes of the Sheffield psychotherapy project. *British Journal of Psychiatry*.

Shapiro, D. A. and Shapiro, D. (1982a). Meta-analysis of comparative therapy outcome studies: a replication and refinement. *Psychological Bulletin*, **92**, 581–604.

Shapiro, D. A. and Shapiro, D. (1982b). Meta-analysis of comparative therapy outcome research: a critical appraisal. *Behavioural Psychotherapy*, **10**, 4–25.

Shapiro, D. A. and Shapiro, D. (1983). Comparative therapy outcome research: methodological implications of meta-analysis. *Journal of Consulting and Clinical Psychology*, **51**, 42–53.

Shapiro, D. H. (1976). Zen meditation and behavioral self-control strategies applied to a case of generalised anxiety. *Psychologia*, **19**, 134–8.

Shapiro, D. H. (1980). *Meditation*. Aldine Publishing, Chicago.

Shapiro, D. H. (1982). Overview: clinical and physiological comparisons of meditation with other self-control strategies. *American Journal of Psychiatry*, **139**(3), 267–74.

Shapiro, D. H. (1984). Classic perspectives of meditation: toward an empirical understanding of meditation as an altered state of consciousness. In *Meditation: classic and contemporary perspectives*, (eds. D. H. Shapiro and R. N. Walsh), pp. 13–23. Aldine Publishing, New York.

Shapiro, D. H. (1985). Clinical use of meditation as a self-regulation strategy: comments on Holmes's conclusion and implications. *American Psychologist*, **40**, 719–22.

Shapiro, D. H. and Walsh, R. N. (1982). *Beyond health and normality: explorations in exceptional psychological well-being*. Van Nostrand, New York.

Shapiro, D. H. and Walsh, R. N. (eds.) (1984). *Meditation: classic and contemporary perspectives*. Aldine, New York.

Shapiro, D. H. and Zifferblatt, S. M. (1976a). Zen meditation and behavioral self-control. *American Psychologist*, **31**(7), 519–32.

Shapiro, D. H. and Zifferblatt, S. M. (1976b). An applied clinical combination of Zen meditation and behavioral self-management techniques: reducing methadone dosage in drug addiction. *Behavior Therapy*, **7**, 694–5.

Shostrom, E. L. (1966). *Personal orientation inventory: an inventory for the measurement of self-actualisation.* EdITS, San Diego, California.

Siebert, J. R. (1985). Absorption and meditation. Unpublished Master's thesis, Roosevelt University.

Simon, D. B., Oparil, S. and Kimball, C. P. (1977). The transcendental meditation program and essential hypertension. In *Scientific research on the transcendental meditation program* (eds. D. W. Orme-Johnson and J. T. Farrow), Vol. 1, pp. 268–9. Maharishi European Research University Press, Los Angeles.

Skinner, B. F. (1974). *About behaviorism.* Knopf, New York.

Smith, E. and Miller, F. (1978). Limits on perception of cognitive processes: a reply to Nisbett and Wilson. *Psychological Review,* **85,** 355–62.

Smith, J. C. (1975). Meditation as psychotherapy: a review of the literature. *Psychological Bulletin,* **82,** 558–64.

Smith, J. C. (1976). Psychotherapeutic effects of transcendental meditation with controls for expectation of relief and daily sitting. *Journal of Consulting and Clinical Psychology,* **44,** 630–7.

Smith, J. C. (1978). Personality correlates of continuation and outcome in meditation and erect sitting control treatments. *Journal of Consulting and Clinical Psychology,* **46,** 272–9.

Smith, J. C. (1985). *Relaxation dynamics: nine world approaches to self-relaxation.* Research Press, Champaign, Illinois.

Smith, J. C. (1986). *Meditation: a sensible guide to a timeless discipline.* Research Press, Champaign, Illinois.

Smith, M. L., Glass, G. V. and Miller, T. I. (1980). The benefits of psychotherapy. Johns Hopkins University Press, Baltimore.

Spanos, N. P., Stam, H. J., Rivers, S. M. and Radtke, H. L. (1980). Meditation, expectation and performance on indices of nonanalytic attending. *International Journal of Clinical and Experimental Hypnosis,* **28,** 244–51.

Spanos, N. P., Steggles, S., Radtke-Bodorick, H. L. and Rivers, S. M. (1979). Nonanalytic attending, hypnotic susceptibility, and psychological well-being in trained meditators and nonmeditators. *Journal of Abnormal Psychology,* **88,** 85–7.

Spielberger, C. D., Gorsuch, R. L. and Lushene, R. E. (1970). *Manual for the state-trait anxiety inventory.* Consulting Psychologists Press, Palo Alto, Calif.

Spurgeon, C. (1970). *Mysticism in English literature.* Kenikat Press, Port Washington.

Sprung, M. (1979). *Lucid exposition of the middle way.* Routledge and Kegan Paul, London.

Srimad bhagavata (1969). Gita Press, Gorakhpur, India.

Stek, R. and Bass, B. (1973). Personal adjustment and perceived locus of control among students interested in meditation. *Psychological Reports,* **32,** 1019–22.

Stigsby, B., Rodenberg, J. C. and Moth, H. B. (1981). Electroencephalographic findings during mantra meditation (transcendental meditation). A controlled quantitative study of experienced meditators. *Electroencephalography and Clinical Neurophysiology,* **51,** 434–42.

Stiles, W. B. (1983). Normality, diversity and psychotherapy. *Psychotherapy: Theory, Research and Practice,* **20,** 183–9.

Stiles, W. B., Shapiro, D. A. and Elliott, R. K. (1986). Are all psychotherapies equivalent? *American Psychologist,* **41,** 165–80.

Stone, R. A. and DeLeo, J. (1976). Psychotherapeutic control of hypertension. *New England Journal of Medicine*, **294**, 80–4.

Strupp, H. H. and Hadley, S. W. (1977). A tripartite model of mental health and therapeutic outcomes: with special reference to negative effects in psychotherapy. *American Psychologist*, **32**, 196–7.

Stryker, S. (1968). Identity salience and role performance. *Journal of Marriage and the Family*, **30**, 558–64.

Stunkard, A. (1951). Interpersonal aspects of an Oriental religion. *Psychiatry*, **14**, 419–31.

Suler, J. R. (1985). Meditation and somatic arousal: a comment on Holmes's review. *American Psychologist*, **40**, 717.

Suzuki, D. T. (1960). Lectures on Zen Buddhism. In *Zen Buddhism and psychoanalysis* (ed. E. Fromm), pp. 8–29. Grove Press, New York.

Tart, C. T. (1971). A psychologist's experience with transcendental meditation. *Journal of Transpersonal Psychology*, **3**, 135–40.

Tart, C. T. (1975). *States of consciousness*. E. P. Dutton, New York.

Taylor, C. B., Farquhar, J. W., Nelson, E. and Agras, S. (1977). Relaxation therapy and high blood pressure. *Archives of General Psychiatry*, **34**, 339–42.

Tellegen, A. and Atkinson, G. (1974). Openness to absorbing and self-altering experiences ('absorption'), a trait related to hypnotic susceptibility. *Journal of Abnormal Psychology*, **83**, 268–77.

Thapa, K. and Murthy, V. H. (1985). Experiential characteristics of certain altered states of consciousness. *Journal of Transpersonal Psychology*, **17**, 77–86.

Titchener, E. B. (1898). The postulates of a structural psychology. *The Philosophic Review*, **7**, 449–65.

Tjoa, A. (1975). Meditation, neuroticism and intelligence: a follow-up. *Gedrag, Tijdschrift voor Psychologie*, **3**, 167–82.

Tjoa, A. (1977). Some evidence that the transcendental meditation program increases intelligence and reduces neuroticism as measured by psychological tests. In *Scientific research on the transcendental meditation program* (eds. D. W. Orme-Johnson and J. T. Farrow), Vol. 1, pp. 363–7. Maharishi European Research University Press, Los Angeles.

Travis, T., Kondo, C. and Knott, J. (1976). Heart rate, muscle tension, and alpha production of transcendental meditation and relaxation controls. *Biofeedback and Self-Regulation*, **1**, 387–94.

Truax, C. B. and Carkhuff, R. R. (1967). *Toward effective counseling and psychotherapy*. Aldine Publishing, Chicago.

Tucker, D. M., Watson, R. T. and Heilman, K. M. (1977). Discrimination and evocation of affectively intoned speech in patients with right parietal disease. *Neurology*, **27**, 947–50.

Tulpule, T. (1971). Yogic exercises in the management of ischemic heart disease. *Indian Heart Journal*, **23**, 259–64.

Turnbull, M. J. and Norris, H. (1982). Effects of transcendental meditation on self-identity indices and personality. *British Journal of Psychology*, **73**, 57–68.

Turner, R. H. (1976). The real self: from institution to impulse. *American Journal of Sociology*, **84**, 1–23.

Underwood, G. (ed.) (1982). Aspects of consciousness: *awareness and self-awareness*, Vol. 2. Academic Press, London.

Vahia, N. S., Doongaji, D. R., Jeste, D. V., Ravindranath, S., Kapoor, S. N. and Ardhapurkar, I. (1973). Psychophysiologic therapy based on the concepts of Patanjali. *American Journal of Psychotherapy*, **27**, 557–65.

Valle, R. S. and King, M. (1978). An introduction to existential–phenomenological thought in psychology. In *Existential–phenomenological alternatives for psychology* (eds. R. S. Valle and M. King), pp. 3–17. Oxford University Press, New York.

Van den Berg, W. and Mulder, B. (1976). Psychological research on the effects of the transcendental meditation technique on a number of personality variables. *Gedrag, Tijdschrift voor Psychologie*, **4**, 206–18.

Van den Bos, G. R. (1986). Psychotherapy research: a special issue. *American Psychologist*, **41**, 111–12.

Van den Bos, G. R. and Pine, C. D. (1980). Research on the outcome of psycho-therapy. In *Psychotherapy: practice, research, policy* (ed. G. R. Van den Bos), pp. 23–69. Sage Publications, Beverly Hills, Calif.

Van Nuys, D. (1973). Meditation, attention, and hypnotic susceptibility: a correlational study. *International Journal of Clinical and Experimental Hypnosis*, **21**, 59–69.

Wallace, R. K. (1970). Physiological effects of transcendental meditation. *Science*, **167**, 1751–4.

Wallace, R. K. and Benson, H. (1972). The physiology of meditation. *Scientific American*, **226**(2), 84–90.

Wallace, R. K., Benson, H. and Wilson, A. (1971). A wakeful hypometabolic physiologic state. *American Journal of Physiology*, **221**, 795–9.

Walrath, L. C. and Hamilton, D. W. (1975). Autonomic correlates of meditation and hypnosis. *American Journal of Clinical Hypnosis*, **17**, 190–7.

Walsh, R. (1977). Initial meditative experiences: part I. *Journal of Transpersonal Psychology*, **9**, 151–92.

Walsh, R. (1978). Initial meditative experiences: part II. *Journal of Transpersonal Psychology*, **10**, 1–28.

Walsh, R. (1983). Things are not as they seemed. In *Awakening the heart* (ed. J. Welwood), pp. 103–119. Shambhala, Boulder, Colorado.

Walsh, R. (1984). Initial meditative experiences. In *Meditation: classic and contemporary perspectives* (eds. D. H. Shapiro and R. Walsh), pp. 265–70. Aldine, New York.

Walsh, R. and Roche, L. (1979). Precipitation of acute psychotic episodes by intensive meditation in patients with a history of schizophrenia. *American Journal of Psychiatry*, **136**, 1085–6.

Walter, D. O. (1963). Spectral analysis for electroencephalograms: mathematical determination of neurophysiological relationships from records of limited duration. *Experimental Neurology*, **8**, 155.

Walter, D. O, and Brazier, M. A. B. (eds.) (1969). Advances in EEG analysis. *Electroencephalography and Clinical Neurophysiology*, Supplement 27.

Walter, D. O., Rhodes, J. M., Brown, D. and Adey, W. R. (1966). Comprehensive spectral analysis of human EEG generators in posterior cerebral regions. *Electro-encephalography and Clinical Neurophysiology*, **20**, 224.

Warrenburg, S. and Pagano, R. R. (1982/3). Meditation and hemispheric specialization: Absorbed attention in long-term adherents. *Imagination, Cognition and Personality*, **2**(3), 211–29.

Warrenburg, S., Pagano, R., Woods, M. and Halstala, M. (1980). A comparison of somatic relaxation and EEG activity in classical progressive relaxation and transcendental meditation. *Journal of Behavioral Medicine*, **3**, 73–9.

Washburn, M. C. (1978). Observations relevant to a unified theory of meditation. *Journal of Transpersonal Psychology*, **10**, 45–65.

Watson, J. B. (1913). Psychology as the behaviorist views it. *Psychological Review*, **20**, 158–77.

Watts, A. W. (1957). *The way of Zen*. Penguin, Harmondsworth, Middlesex.

Watts, A. W. (1961). *Psychotherapy East and West*. Pantheon, New York.

Watts, F. N. (1979). Psychological theory and the religious mind: meditation and perception. *Theoria to Theory*, **13**, 115–25.

Waxman, S. and Geschwind, N. (1975). The interictal behaviour syndrome of temporal lobe epilepsy. *Archives of General Psychiatry*, **32**, 1580–6.

Wechsler, A. F. (1973). The effect of organic brain disease on recall of emotionally charged versus neutral narrative texts. *Neurology*, **23**, 130.

Weldon, J. T. and Aron, A. (1977). The transcendental meditation program and normalization of weight. In *Scientific research on the transcendental meditation program* (eds. D. W. Orme-Johnson and J. T. Farrow), Vol. 1, pp. 301–6. Maharishi European Research University Press, Los Angeles.

Welwood, J. (1982). The unfolding experience: psychotherapy and beyond. *Journal of Humanistic Psychology*, **22**, 91–104.

Welwood, J. (ed.) (1983). *Awakening the heart: East/West approaches to psychotherapy and the healing relationship*. Shambhala, Boulder, Colorado.

West, M. A. (1977). Changes in skin resistances in subjects resting, reading, listening to music, or practicing the transcendental meditation technique. In *Scientific research on the transcendental meditation program* (eds. D. W. Orme-Johnson and J. T. Farrow), Vol. 1, pp. 224–9. Maharishi European Research University Press, Los Angeles.

West, M. A. (1979a). Physiological effects of meditation: a longitudinal study. *British Journal of Social and Clinical Psychology*, **18**, 219–26.

West, M. A. (1979b). Meditation: a review. *British Journal of Psychiatry*, **135**, 457–67.

West, M. A. (1980a). Meditation, personality and arousal. *Personality and Individual Differences*, **1**, 135–42.

West, M. A. (1980b). Meditation and the EEG. *Psychological Medicine*, **10**, 369–75.

West, M. A. (1982). Meditation and self awareness: physiological and phenomenological approaches. In *Aspects of consciousness: Vol. 2, awareness and self awareness* (ed. G. Underwood), pp. 199–234. Academic Press, London.

West, M. A. (1985). Meditation and somatic arousal reduction. *American Psychologist*, **40**, 717–19.

West, M. A. (1986). Meditation: psychology and human experience. In *Beyond therapy: the impact of Eastern religions on psychological theory and practice* (ed. G. Claxton), pp. 243–67. Wisdom, London.

Westcott, M. (1974). Hemisphere asymmetry of the EEG during altered states of consciousness. BA dissertation, Durham University.

White, J. (ed.) 1974. *What is meditation?* Anchor, New York.

Wicklund, R. A. (1975). Objective self awareness. In *Advances in experimental social psychology* (ed. L. Berkowitz), pp. 233–75. Academic Press, New York.

Wieser, H. G. and Mazzola, G. (1985). Do the right and left hippocampi independently distinguish musical consonances and differences? *Electroencephalography and Clinical Neurophysiology*, **61–3**, S153.

Wilder, J. (1962). Basimetric approach (law of initial values) to biological rhythms. *Annals of New York Academy of Science*, **98**, 1211–20.

Wilkins, W. (1984). Psychotherapy: the powerful placebo. *Journal of Consulting and Clinical Psychology*, **52**, 570–3.

Williams, P. and West, M. (1975). EEG responses to photic stimulation in persons experienced in meditation. *Electroencephalography and Clinical Neurophysiology*, **39**, 519–22.

Williams, P., Francis, A. and Durham, R. (1976). Personality and meditation. *Perceptual and Motor Skills*, **43**, 787–92.

Wilson, A. F. (1986). The social context of yogic practices: personal growth in a yoga Ashram. Paper presented at the International Conference on Eastern approaches to Self and Mind. University College Cardiff, Cardiff, Wales, 11–14 July, 1986.

Wilson, A. F., Honsberger, R., Chiu, J. T. and Novey, H. S. (1975). Transcendental meditation and asthma. *Respiration*, **32**, 74–80.

Woolfolk, R. L. (1975). Psychophysiological correlates of meditation. *Archives of General Psychiatry*, **32**, 1326–33.

Woolfolk, R. L. and Lehrer, P. M. (eds.) (1984). *Principles and practice of stress management*. Guilford Press, New York.

Woolfolk, R. L., Carr-Kaffashan, L., McNulty, T. F. and Lehrer, P. M. (1976). Meditation training as a treatment for insomnia. *Behavior Therapy*, **7**, 359–65.

Wundt, W. (1897). *Outlines of psychology*. Gustav Stechart, New York.

Yeaton, W. H. and Sechrest, L. (1981). Critical dimensions in the choice and maintenance of successful treatments: strength, integrity, and effectiveness. *Journal of Consulting and Clinical Psychology*, **49**, 156–67;

Younger, J., Adriance, W. and Berger, R. (1975). Sleep during transcendental meditation. *Perceptual and Motor Skills*, **40**, 953–4.

Zaichkowsky, L. D. and Kamen, R. (1978). Biofeedback and meditation: effects on muscle tension and locus of control. *Perceptual and Motor Skills*, **46**, 955–8.

Zamarra, J. W., Besseghini, I. and Wittenberg, S. (1977). The effects of the transcendental meditation program on the exercise performance of patients with angina pectoris. In *Scientific research on the transcendental meditation program* (eds. D. W. Orme-Johnson and J. T. Farrow), Vol. 1, pp. 270–8. Maharishi European Research University Press, Los Angeles.

Zurcher, L. A. (1977). *The mutable self: a self-concept for social change*. Sage Publications, Beverly Hills, Calif.

Zurcher, L. A. (1984). The self concept of agents for social change. Paper presented at the International Interdisciplinary Conference on Self and Identity. University College Cardiff, Cardiff.

Zurcher, L. A. and Snow, D. A. (1981). Collective behavior: social movements. In *Social psychology: sociological perspectives* (eds. M. Rosenberg and R. H. Turner), pp. 447–82. Basic Books, New York.

Zuroff, D. C. and Schwarz, J. C. (1978). Effects of transcendental meditation and muscle relaxation on trait anxiety, maladjustment, locus of control, and drug use. *Journal of Consulting and Clinical Psychology*, **46**, 264–71.

AUTHOR INDEX

SUBJECT INDEX